Lisa Hendey is the sister friend of Catholic motherhood! We know her so well through her work for families, her website, and her engaging podcasts. Lisa now brings us her book in which she openly discusses the essential elements of a Catholic mom's life in an exceptionally delightful, engaging, dynamic, and practical manner. You'll be turning pages and feeling as if Lisa is there by your side lovingly offering her insight and warm encouragement. You're going to love this book!

Donna-Marie Cooper O'Boyle
Host of EWTN's *Everyday Blessings for Catholic Moms*

Every mom needs a few good tools in her belt, to help her handle life's challenges and *The Handbook for Catholic Moms* belongs on your short list of indispensable resources. Does your marriage need a tune-up? Does your friendship garden need cultivating? Could your parenting skills use a little remedial attention? This book offers sound advice to help you meet these and other challenges with confidence and grace.

Heidi Hess Saxton
Author of *My Big Book of Catholic Bible Stories*

Lisa Hendey's passion for Catholic motherhood is born of many influences and I am proud to know that her experience as a Notre Dame student ranks among the most significant. This book is overflowing with Lisa's generous spirit, deep compassion, and infectious enthusiasm for her family, her Church, and the vocation of Catholic motherhood. She makes a wonderful and most welcome contribution to our faith community.

Rev. Theodore M. Hesburgh, C.S.C.
President Emeritus
University of Notre Dame

Warm, wise, funny, compassionate, faith-filled, and, above all experienced in the joys and struggles of family life, Lisa Hendey's new book will be a lifesaver to Catholic women who try, hope, and pray to be good moms.

Rev. James Martin, S.J.
Author of *My Life with the Saints*

CatholicMom.com has long been a treasured Internet gathering spot. *The Handbook for Catholic Moms* is a welcome extension of Lisa's wisdom and energy, enriched by the experiences of the community of women who have found community, support, and strength through CatholicMom.com.

Amy Welborn
Author of *A Catholic Woman's Book of Days*

Kudos to fellow blogger Lisa Hendey for such a comprehensive, holistic companion for women who can use their faith as a tool to empower themselves as mothers, as wives, and as individuals on the pilgrimage of life.

Therese Borchard
Author of *Beyond Blue*

There is a saying: "A candle loses nothing by lighting another candle." For years, Lisa has been the candle that lights so many others. This book is wonderful for Catholic moms (and others) to experience the Light burning inside as well as around Lisa Hendey. She is a gift to people of faith and journey.

Deacon Tom Fox
Columnist and Podcaster at Deacontomonline.com

The Handbook for Catholic **Moms**

Nurturing Your Heart, Mind, Body, and Soul

Lisa M. Hendey

Creator of  CatholicMom.com

NEW PROVIDENCE MEMORIAL LIBRARY
377 ELKWOOD AVENUE
NEW PROVIDENCE, NJ 07974

ave maria press AmP notre dame, indiana

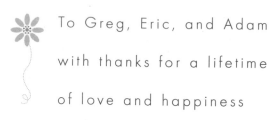

To Greg, Eric, and Adam

with thanks for a lifetime

of love and happiness

Scripture texts used in this work are taken from *The New American Bible* copyright ©
1991, 1986, and 1970 by the Confraternity of Christian Doctrine, Washington, DC, and
are used by permission of the copyright owner. All rights reserved. No part of *The New American Bible* may be reproduced in any form or by any means without permission in writing from the publisher.

© 2010 by Lisa M. Hendey

All rights reserved. No part of this book may be used or reproduced in any manner whatsoever, except in the case of reprints in the context of reviews, without written permission from Ave Maria Press®, Inc., P.O. Box 428, Notre Dame, IN 46556.

Founded in 1865, Ave Maria Press is a ministry of the Indiana Province of Holy Cross.

www.avemariapress.com

ISBN-10 1-59471-228-X ISBN-13 978-1-59471-228-9

Cover image © Jupiter Images.

Cover and text design by Katherine Robinson Coleman.

Printed and bound in the United States of America.

Library of Congress Cataloging-in-Publication Data

Hendey, Lisa M.
  The handbook for Catholic moms : nurturing your heart, mind, body, and soul /
Lisa M. Hendey.
        p. cm.
  ISBN-13: 978-1-59471-228-9 (pbk.)
  ISBN-10: 1-59471-228-X (pbk.)
  1. Mothers—Religious life. 2. Motherhood—Religious aspects—Catholic Church.
I. Title.
  BX2353.H44 2010
  248.8'431—dc22

                                2009049529

Contents

Preface

Writing a book is a daunting task. At many times during this project I was tempted to lay aside my laptop and simply go shopping instead. After all, who am I to be giving you advice on anything, and particularly on a topic as important as motherhood? Like most of you reading this book, my training has been on the job—a series of dramatic trial and error opportunities, with ten steps back for every one step forward. So let me say up front that I don't come to this work considering myself an expert. In truth, with this project—as with so many others I've undertaken in my life—I have hoped to learn as I go. Learning with you, first crawling, and then with the most unstable of baby steps, I want to continue along my own path of trying my very best to become a better Catholic mom, a healthier woman, and ultimately a better person.

First, let me explain to you that I am not setting out to write a typical parenting book. You will not find here the mysterious key to unlocking the mind of a two-year-old or the heart of a petulant teenager. I don't have solutions for getting a baby to sleep through the night or for dealing with a sarcastic adolescent. Rather, I am writing this book to try to support and encourage *you* in your role as a Catholic mom and to encourage all of us to nurture ourselves as mothers, so that we have the energy, spirit, and peaceful souls to help take care of those who fill our homes and our lives.

When I'm asked in a social setting that ubiquitous question, "What do you do?" I invariably respond with the same reply: "I'm a mom." This, my vocation, began in a dramatic and quite definite way nearly nineteen years ago in partnership with my husband Greg with the arrival of our son Eric. But in a more subtle way, it began long before that blessed event.

I'd fallen in love with Greg at first sight as he strolled across the quad at our *alma mater*, the University of Notre Dame. Mutual friends introduced us, and I still remember the moment a few months later when Greg finally asked me on a date. We entered into the sacrament of matrimony together, in the breathtaking Basilica of the Sacred Heart at Notre Dame, the year after our graduation.

After five years of marriage, three during Greg's medical school and two in his emergency medicine residency, we took the giant leap of faith into parenthood. I was so career oriented at that time that Eric could likely have been born on my desk at work. My definite plans to return as soon as possible to my career were laid aside the moment I began to explore day care options. For us, the choice was clear—I "retired" and set myself to the full-time task of learning to become a mom. With Adam's birth three years later, my apprenticeship continued and took on new challenges.

Greg, although incredibly supportive of my faith life and of raising our sons in the faith, had not yet joined the Church himself. I felt a huge responsibility to be the primary faith educator of my sons and realized how short I fell in my own preparation for this role. I was looking for support and companionship from other moms struggling with the same things I was.

Just over ten years ago now, I was learning web design in a volunteer position at my boys' Catholic school when I came up with the crazy idea to start a little website that would celebrate Catholic motherhood. In creating the site, I hoped to explore and learn about faith and family topics and to build a community of like-minded mothers with whom I could share support and encouragement. And so, CatholicMom.com, was born. In those early days, the site was a tiny endeavor and the "hit counter" marked visits to our little domain in the dozens each day. But from the very beginning, it was apparent to me that there was a tremendous need for this type of place—a safe, loving environment where we women could gather together to learn, to discuss, and, most importantly, to pray for one another in our vocation as mothers.

From those very seminal moments of the site through today, one mainstay in my life has been the daily e-mails I receive from moms around the world who are struggling in their vocation as "Mom." These e-mails often carry a tone of quiet desperation and pain that tears at my heart. They come from women who feel burned out, overwhelmed, and often very alone in their own little corners of the world. This is an easy thing to have happen when you're a mom. Overnight, with the incredible miracle of birth, your life is transformed. We go from creatures of independence to women who can't even find five minutes to use the bathroom alone. Along with the countless blessings of becoming "Mom" are the occasions of sacrificial service we provide on an hourly basis. Many of us are ill-equipped to cope with these transitions, and we run the risk of becoming bitter and resentful in the care of our families.

Blessedly, we belong to a larger family, our Catholic Church. It's my firm belief that within our Catholic traditions we have many of the tools necessary to refresh and renew our souls and spirits. In my writing and in my personal life, I am vitally interested in looking daily at my own private journey toward being a better person. The journey is multifaceted, so it's necessary to work, a bit at a time, on each of those facets. Focusing on any one of them uniquely and ignoring the others throws off the balance necessary to keep life's wheels rolling along smoothly. My own personal experience with non-invasive breast cancer during the writing of this book has left me even more convinced of every mom's need to care for herself in every way possible.

In this book, we'll take a look at four areas of focus, endeavoring to take those first "baby steps" in each, toward the ultimate goal of caring for ourselves better as moms, as women, and as Catholics.

Heart: developing nurturing relationships with our family, our friends, and ourselves

Mind: becoming life-long learners, seeking creative outlets, exploring career and work issues, and employing time management and personal productivity tactics

Body: examining nutrition, fitness, sleep, stress reduction, and preventative care matters

Soul: coming to know and love the many resources, devotions, and concepts in the fullness of the Catholic Church that can help us care for ourselves and for the most important people in our lives

The Pew Forum on Religion and Public Life issues an annual report in its attempt to promote a "deeper understanding of issues at the intersection of religion and public affairs." In its 2008 report titled "U.S. Religious Landscape Survey," Pew looked at the percentage of Americans switching religious affiliations and found that in the United States the Roman Catholic Church "has experienced the greatest net losses as a result of affiliation change." About a third of Catholic survey respondents indicated that they no longer identify themselves with the Catholic Church. "This means that roughly 10 percent of all Americans are former Catholics."

In my heart, this sad news was a rallying cry for us Catholic moms and dads, who are truly on the frontlines in the battle for our families' souls. If we, as parents and as individuals, do not truly embrace the many graces and blessings offered to us in the Church, how can we possibly expect to pass them along to our children? I hope that some-day I'll experience the same joy my parents do when they attend the baptism or first communion of one of their grandchildren—the joy in knowing that they have done their most important job of sharing a love of Christ and his Church with their children. If we moms don't embrace and truly love our faith traditions, then we may be adding to the next generations of former Catholics. On the other hand, if our children look to us and find happy, productive, and selfless models of Christ's love incarnate, as I did in my own mom, their desire to be a loving part of the Body of Christ will be all the greater.

In his April 2008 apostolic journey to the United States, Pope Benedict XVI stressed the theme "Christ Our Hope." Everywhere he turned, the Holy Father was embraced and greeted with infectious enthusiasm. Speaking to a huge youth rally at St. Joseph Seminary in Yonkers, New York, Benedict XVI said,

> Let us pray for mothers and fathers throughout the world, particu-larly those who may be struggling in any way—socially, material-ly, spiritually. Let us honor the vocation of matrimony and the dignity of family life. Let us always appreciate that it is in families that vocations are given life.

Acknowledging those struggles that each of us face every day and buoyed by our prayers for one another, I invite you, my fellow Catholic moms, to join me on a journey of love—loving and caring for ourselves more so that we can better love and care for our families, our neighbors, our Church, and the world it is sent to serve.

PART I: Heart

NURTURING OURSELVES
THROUGH THE CREATION AND SUSTENANCE
OF EMOTIONALLY HEALTHY RELATIONSHIPS

A Match Made in heaven

An Overview of Catholic Marriage Commitments

"This one, at last, is bone of my bones and flesh of my flesh; This one shall be called 'woman,' for out of 'her man' this one has been taken." That is why a man leaves his father and mother and clings to his wife, and the two of them become one body.

—Genesis 2:23-24

This year, Greg and I will celebrate a monumental wedding anniversary, our twenty-third year of marriage together. You won't find the twenty-third anniversary on most lists of milestones, nor are there many personalized greeting cards wishing couples congratulations upon twenty-three years of wedded bliss. Those are reserved for the big numbers like ten, twenty-five, or fifty.

In fact, your "monumental" anniversary year likely differs from mine, because you and your husband have walked your own path to sacramental marriage. Let me explain to you why I plan to celebrate in a big way on number twenty-three. It has little to do with traditions, and a lot to do with the fact that I was nearly twenty-three years old the year that I joined my husband in lifelong partnership. In my mind, there is significance in the fact that this will be the year my marriage exceeds my single life—meaning of course that I've spent more time being one with Greg than living on my own. Certainly, as I age, my memories of our life together far exceed those that existed before our wedding.

When we married, the notion of "I" and "me" was set to the side in favor of "we" and "us." We are a team. Although my humanity sometimes keeps me from thinking as much, my marital vows oblige me to think of Greg as an extension of myself, and thus selfish decisions need to be set aside.

And so you'll find me celebrating number twenty-three this year, rejoicing in the fact that I've been Mrs. Hendey for longer than I was ever Miss Bartholomy, and that my husband's love, companionship, and continual support have given me a life more beautiful than any I ever imagined.

Lessons I've Learned

1. Serve one another.

We have our husbands to thank for helping us to earn the most important job title most of us will ever hold—mom. So it feels fitting to begin a book about nurturing ourselves as Catholic moms by looking at the human relationship that is most central to our happiness and success at being mothers.

For most of us, the march toward motherhood began with an exchange of vows and the grace of a sacrament. Whether you married a fellow Catholic, or someone who is of another faith (like my husband at the time of our wedding), as a Catholic, you promised to lovingly accept children from God and to raise them in the Catholic Church.

Love is never something ready made, something merely "given" to a man and woman, it is always at the same time a "task," which they are set. Love should be seen as something which in a sense never "is" but is always only "becoming," and what it becomes depends upon the contribution of both persons and the depth of their commitment.

—Pope John Paul II

Before I jump into my thoughts on how we, as Catholic moms, can nurture ourselves though our vocation to marriage, I want to share a few words with those moms who may be reading this book and are not married. I want you to know that I respect the tremendous work you do every day to serve your family. I want to applaud your courage for standing up to your responsibilities in countless ways. I want to give you affirmation for your decision to choose life for your children and to take the challenging steps of raising them in our faith, on your own. I try to share some further thoughts for you (from my admittedly limited view) in chapter 6, You're Never Alone.

When we marry, notions of self are set by the wayside as we begin our families. Whether parenthood is years away or just around the corner, life as a wife prepares us for the total giving of self that will occur once our babies are born.

In my early married life, I remember chafing a bit at having to bend my agenda, goals, and desires to meet the needs of a husband who, as a medical student, led a crazy lifestyle. I regret to say that it took me years to recognize that I should alter my schedule to better lovingly serve my spouse. In an age where we are taught to be strong, independent women, that phrase, "serving my spouse," may sound old-fashioned. But through the years, I've found great joy in accepting the fact that the little things I do out of love for my husband can be signs of my love not only for him, but for my God who gave me a vocation to marriage and to motherhood. I have also grown to more readily recognize the countless ways that Greg bends his desires and will to serve me. Truly marriage is about serving one another day in and day out.

2. *Keep Christ at the center.*

Watching my parents through a partnership that has lasted nearly fifty years has taught me many things about marriage. The first, and always the foremost, is to keep Christ at the center of my marriage.

For many years, I struggled with this concept. Greg was not Catholic when we married, and although he was incredibly supportive of my faith life and the raising of our children in the Church, I fell short in the lofty goal of making our marriage a triune partnership between Greg, God, and me. I was confounded by the fact that we weren't one of those seemingly perfect couples I saw seated around me every Sunday at Mass. Although Greg regularly came with us to church, my disappointment that he didn't share my Catholic faith traditions hurt my heart deeply.

"Look at Mrs. ____ (fill in your own blank)," I'd think to myself each Sunday in Mass. "There's her husband, Mr. ____, all dressed up in his suit and tie. He's even a Knight of Columbus! She's really lucky. Why can't Greg be the kind of husband who gathers our family for the rosary each night like Mr. _____ does?!"

It wasn't until I came to peace with Greg's own spiritual journey and began to pray deeply for my husband that I would say I really put Christ at the center of our relationship. Prior to that, I let disappointment, envy, and shortsightedness stand in Christ's spot in our relationship.

Maybe you're fortunate, and you are "equally yoked" in your faith life with your spouse. But for many of the Catholic moms I've spoken with, this is not the case. We may be much more traditional, regular, or communicative in our practice of our Catholicism than our spouses, or in some cases much less. And we, as wives and as mothers, lay a lot of blame and judgment on our spouses and ultimately on ourselves for the fact that our husbands don't compare spiritually with men we know. "If only I were a better person, a better Catholic," I would think to myself for many years, "then Greg would want to be a part of the Church."

How very selfish of me to insert myself and my needs into the spiritual life of my husband, rather than seeing the situation for what it was—Greg's unique journey toward a God who loves him unconditionally. By the time Greg joined the Catholic Church through the Rite of Christian Initiation of Adults (RCIA), we had been married seventeen years. I wish I had spent the first fifteen years of that initiation

For many people and in much of our cultural environment, love is about how two people make each other feel. In the seven years I've been married, I've found that concentrating solely on feelings is like eating frosting without the cake: you can enjoy it for a while, but eventually you're going to realize there's something missing underneath.

Romantic gestures are all about feelings, but it turns out that true love has to do with so much more than feelings. Ultimately, true love is sacrifice and self-gift and being willing to die for the ones you love, as Christ did. In our daily lives, where we can only hope for faint echoes of that love, true love is every single thing we do that brings us closer to perfection and to Christ—the one who loves best.

A happy side effect of that kind of loving is that it brings us closer to the ones for whom we are giving of ourselves, in a way that all the romantic gestures in the world could never do. In my years of marriage, the moments when I've loved my husband best have had nothing to do with gifts or poems or romantic dinners. I've nurtured our marriage most when I've found the grace to make sacrifices for him. Even the tiny ones he never knew about brought us closer together.

As for him, he never loves me better than he does when he takes the baby so that I can sleep in. Forget flowers; I'll take an extra hour of sleep any day! That's real romance.

Arwen Mosher is a happily married mother of two. She blogs at www.ennorath.typepad.com.

process praying more fervently for my husband, *just as he was,* than judging myself and not truly appreciating the depth of his quiet, unassuming spirituality.

So yes, "keeping Christ at the center of our marriage" should include the raising of our children in the faith, the attendance of Mass, the familial celebration of sacraments together, and the nurturing of one another's spirituality. But equally as important, I believe this means treating our spouses as we would treat Christ should we have the occasion to find him physically sitting in our own homes. In Catholic marriage, through our loving service to our husbands, we have the unique opportunity to truly shower the love we hold in our hearts upon others just as Jesus called us to do. We have the gift every day of praying for our husbands, our partners in parenthood—not praying to fill in the gaps or shortcomings we think we see in them, but praying for them in their vocations and lifting them spiritually via our prayers.

Every day, as I live my life with Greg, I try to look to his example of Christian living through the many things he does to support Eric, Adam, and me. I pray for his soul, for our walk together toward the potential of an eternal life in God's presence, and in thanksgiving for my life partner—just as he is—and Christ's very obvious presence in our marriage. I've learned that sometimes that presence, that "keeping Christ at the center," looks different in my marriage than it does in anyone else's, and that acceptance is a true and deeply rooted grace to me.

3. *Nurture your marriage above extended family.*

In Genesis 2:24 we hear "That is why a man leaves his father and mother and clings to his wife, and the two of them become one body." Many of us heard these words proclaimed during the Liturgy of the Word at our weddings. I've always felt that they are a prophetic reminder to us that our wedding vows and our marital relationship should come first in our hearts.

Struggles with extended family are so prevalent that they have become a cliché in our society. Even after over twenty years of marriage, I still do little things to seek the approval of my mother-in-law, hoping that she will see me as a worthy mate for her son. My approval-seeking ways are fine if kept in moderation, but should really never become a roadblock between the woman who loves my husband as much as I do and me.

Keeping family relationships in their proper perspective is one of the most important ways we as Catholic moms can nurture our marriages, and ultimately ourselves. Many things that happen within a marriage are best kept within the confines of our homes, rather than being aired in public, even within our families of origin. As close as I am to my mother and my sisters, my relationship with Greg should always come first and foremost.

This is also an important thing to remember when extended family "situations" arise that may place a strain on our marriages, and ultimately upon us as women. When in doubt, cling to your husband and become one with him. If this means having to take a pass on a nephew's Little League game or Thanksgiving dinner rounds to three houses (none of which are your own), do so for the sake of your spirit and for your relationship with your soul mate and life partner.

One of the best presents our parents ever gave Greg and me as we launched our lives together was their permission to begin our own independent family life. We love spending time with both sides of our family, but have never succumbed to doing so out of guilt. Early on, speak with one another and with your families about your desire to create your own family traditions and work together to make these your greatest priority. If family commitments call you to attend functions outside your home, communicate with one another and lift up one another rather than heading into attack mode or bearing resentment. Be lovingly honest with your extended families about your goal to live your marriage as your top priority. Extended family members, who love you, should respect your efforts as long as you include them graciously in your married and family life with love and open communication.

4. Play together.

One of the things that struck me with force when we had Eric was that my "fun" time with my husband greatly decreased, and I know this happens almost universally for other moms. We get so wrapped up in the care, feeding, and education of our kids that we are likely to neglect spending time with our husbands. Our communication runs the risk of falling into staff-meeting mode with quick exchanges about who's going to handle everything that needs to happen in our busy lives. But having fun with our spouses is one of the greatest gifts we can give our children, as it models for them the true joy of a vocation to the married life.

I'm not saying that you need to plan elaborate date nights every week with your spouse—those are great, but life's realities mean that a "date" may be more likely to happen only once a year. Rather, what I'm saying is that we should aim to turn the times that we *do* have together into moments of fun and happiness. Some of my fondest memories of my parents from my childhood involve them just "goofing around" together while my mom worked in the kitchen. Kisses were stolen, tickles were traded, and a dance even broke out some evenings, all played out before five sets of watchful eyes. My parents taught me that marriage was fun, not by taking extravagant trips or heading to huge social occasions, but simply by their genuine love of one another's company.

Look for occasions to laugh and to smile with your husband. Learn to love a few of his passions and share yours with him as well. Suck it up and watch a football game on a Sunday afternoon, just to be together. Attack household duties with an eye toward making them fun—even if that means dancing in the kitchen while you load the dishes.

Date nights can be a great way to nurture yourself and your marriage, but don't think you have to spend a lot of money to have a wonderful evening. Set the table at home, prepare a special feast for the two of you complete with candlelight. Hold hands and talk, or just rest comfortably in each other's company. Remember why you fell in love with your husband and the things about you that drew him to you.

> The matrimonial covenant, by which a man and a woman establish between themselves a partnership of the whole of life, is by its nature ordered toward the good of the spouses and the procreation and education of offspring; this covenant between baptized persons has been raised by Christ the Lord to the dignity of a sacrament.
>
> —Code of Canon Law, 1055

5. Be generous with unspoken signs of love.

I've learned in my marriage to look for nonverbal signs of love from my husband. The truth is that sometimes, if I'm being truly attentive, these unspoken signs of love can touch me even more deeply than the regular "I love you" phrase we share with one another. When I rush out to my car to find a freshly filled gas tank, I never cease to smile because my husband knows that filling up my car is one of the biggest ways he can show his love for me.

Another nonverbal sign of love is the vacuum cleaner I hear running upstairs most Saturday mornings. Since I hate to vacuum, Greg's attention to this particular weekly chore is a constant reminder of how blessed I am to be married to this man. The truth is, we never sat down and had a division of labor conversation where we decided he would vacuum and I would sweep—he just started doing it one week because he knew how much I dislike it.

Because Greg is so generous with his love for me in so many little ways, I try to look for ways of my own to show my commitment to him. I am by nature a messy person. It's not really that I'm a slob—I just get so busy with so many different things at once that I tend to leave things scattered a bit. But because I married a neat freak, I make special efforts to keep things organized in the areas where my husband would be driven crazy by my stacks of "stuff." I guess you can't really call a clean kitchen counter a renewal of wedding vows, but in our case it is definitely an unspoken sign of how much I love my husband that I often try to rush to clear things up a bit when I know that he is on his way home. Call me old-fashioned, but I want his return at the end of the day to be as warm and welcoming as I can make it—I'm not donning pearls and fresh mascara or laying out his slippers, but the least I can do is try to help him arrive home to a welcoming environment.

Your nonverbal signs of love for your spouse will be completely different than mine, as they should be. Perhaps what I am trying to say here is that I believe in the importance of both spoken and unspoken love affirmations. I believe in hugs goodbye and "I love you!" at the end of every phone call. But I also believe in a fresh cup of coffee sweetly delivered with a smile or a trash can taken to the curb so that he gets a week off from doing that particular chore.

Study your spouse and look for your own special ways of showing your love for him, both in spoken words and in small acts of love. In lovingly serving one another in large and little ways, we nurture our marriages and our souls.

6. Get help when you're "broken."

Marriages come in all shapes and sizes. Many of them encounter rough patches that feel like spiritual and emotional droughts. In the same way that we may sometimes feel a void in our relationship with God, we can encounter moments of physical and emotional separation from our spouses. When these moments occur, it is important for our families and ourselves as women and moms that we reach out for needed support and counseling. If you face difficulty in your marriage, there are many resources that can support and encourage you in finding help.

The Church: Call your parish and make an appointment to speak with your pastor or other trusted member of the pastoral staff. Do not try to have this conversation randomly after Mass on Sunday, but rather schedule a time to receive his or her pastoral counsel. He or she will likely have local resources to recommend that will help you to receive the services you need. Your pastor or another member of his staff should be able to minister to you spiritually and can help you remain close to the sacraments.

Retrouvaille: *Retrouvaille* is a French word meaning "rediscovery," and the Retrouvaille program is designed to assist couples with marital problems, including those who are considering marriage separation or those who are already separated or divorced and want help. Catholic in origin, Retrouvaille operates around the country in local communities. To learn more about the Retrouvaille program in your area, call 800-470-2230 or visit www.retrouvaille.org.

Catholic Charities: Across the United States, local Catholic Charities agencies are at work providing counseling and support services to strengthen and encourage families. Their counselors are available to assist with a variety of issues that may be affecting your marriage, including, but not limited to, addiction services, mental health services, and pregnancy and adoption services. To find your local Catholic Charities agency, visit www.catholiccharitiesusa.org.

Mom's Homework

- -

✓ Recall your celebration of the Rite of Marriage in a special way by watching the video of your wedding or viewing pictures of that special day with your husband and children. Recall the readings and songs you selected for your liturgy and consider compiling a CD of these to share with your husband and to enjoy yourself.

✓ Make a pilgrimage to the church where you were married or "adopt" a special church and attend Mass there together annually to celebrate your anniversary.

✓ Look for three ways you might enjoy some play time with your husband. Take a walk together, watch his favorite sport together, tackle a small home project as a team, or simply sit quietly in one another's company once a week.

✓ Look for a few nonverbal ways you can show your love for your spouse. Do these lovingly and without expecting his comment or appreciation. Offer them as a prayer for your marriage.

✓ Speak with your parents or find an older couple whose marriage you admire and invite them to dinner. Ask for their wisdom on what has worked and sustained them in marriage.

✓ Smile at your husband, hug him, enjoy his company, and let your children see your happiness with one another. Holy Cross Father Theodore M. Hesburgh, president emeritus of the University of Notre Dame, is credited with having once said, "The most important thing a father can do for his children is to love their mother." I think Fr. Hesburgh's words of wisdom apply to us moms as well!

Web Resources

For Your Marriage (USCCB): www.foryourmarriage.org
An initiative of the United States Conference of Catholic Bishops that includes marriage preparation information and a wealth of resources and encouragement for married couples

Worldwide Marriage Encounter: www.wwme.org
Turn a good marriage into a great marriage by learning realistic and well-established techniques of loving communication

Retrouvaille: www.retrouvaille.org
Help for struggling marriages

Pastoral Solutions Institute: www.exceptionalmarriages.com
Licensed Catholic pastoral counselors who provide telephone counseling services with solid Catholic theological principles

CHAPTER TWO

Somebody's mom

A Mother's Relationship
with Her Children

Train a boy in the way he should go; even when he is old, he will not swerve from it.

—Proverbs 22:6

My Story

A knock at my window roused my attention as I sat crying in the school parking lot on Eric's fifth day of first grade. Eric's sobs matched mine. Three-year-old Adam added his own high-pitched wails to the mix, empathizing with the distress of his older brother.

"What's wrong?" my good friend Martha inquired as the window lowered and the plaintive sobs were released. My distress led her to assume that we must have just received the news of a death or disaster.

"Eric just got his name on the board AGAIN!" I whimpered. "This is the fifth day in a row he's been in trouble for talking. What am I doing wrong? How come he keeps getting in trouble? I just have the feeling he's destined for juvenile hall, or worse . . ."

"Did the name on the board say 'Mrs. Hendey'?" Martha astutely queried. When my response confirmed that the name in question was indeed Eric's, Martha told me to stop my crying—his name, written on the board by an old-school teacher, was not an indictment of me nor of my parenting skills. She rightly guessed that I'd never been the kind of first grader who'd had my name on the board and taught me an important lesson in separating my own identity from those of my children.

Life Lessons

It's so tempting for us moms to let our own egos get wrapped up precariously in the lives of our children. We glow inside when they achieve, and we berate or blame ourselves when they fall short. We come by these feelings honestly—having given our hearts over to our children, we can't help but celebrate and suffer with them. The problem occurs when we begin to tie our own sense of self and purpose so closely to theirs that we impose upon them the persons we want them to become.

Having been raised by the world's best parents, I aspire to have the same relationship some day with my own children that I have with my mom and dad. My parents welcomed me, the oldest of five, to the family ten months after their big, Catholic wedding. When I look back now at old family photos, I realize just how young my parents were when I came along. When I was only a few months old, they hitched a trailer to the back of their 1960 Chevrolet convertible and set off from Fort Wayne, Indiana, to a new life in California. My mom recounts a bit of the journey, underscoring the huge leap of faith they were taking with this exodus.

I really don't remember a whole lot except the night we crossed the Little Bighorn Mountains. We had visited Mount Rushmore in the afternoon and saw many people on the side of the road whose cars had overheated. Keep in mind, we were almost twenty-three years old with a two-month-old baby that I knew not at all how to care for, we had never been to California or in the mountains, and we knew NOTHING about cars. In our wisdom, we thought it would be better to cross the mountains at night since we were pulling a travel trailer with everything we owned. We drove for six hours, on a very dark night—on very curvy roads—two lanes in those days with hairpin curves. We did not see another car! We just said one rosary after the other!

Throughout my childhood, I felt closely bonded to both of my parents. I'll admit to being a daddy's girl, and nothing meant more to me than having love and approval from my parents. Being a compliant kid, I had relatively little need for rules and curfews. The worst possible penalty in my book was to *disappoint* my parents—to make a choice that let them down or lessened myself in their eyes. Erin, who came next in line, and I spoiled my parents as two girls who rarely caused them trouble. Patrick was next in line, the much-anticipated eldest boy in the family, and he made up for the girls' compliant natures and did so in style! Brady and Michael, their babies, benefited from their years of parenting expertise.

While we were closely bonded as a family, Mom and Dad took great care to clearly delineate their roles as parents. They led full lives of their own, both professionally and socially. While our home was always the chosen hangout with our teenage friends, my parents were constantly present as a fun, yet supervisory, presence. In adulthood, the bonds we formed with them as children have blossomed into more mature relationships. If you ask any of the five of their children with whom they'd most like to spend social time, we would all readily ask for an evening in the company of our parents. They have walked the tightrope of parenting—they raised and nurtured five of us and now bask in the love and friendship that come as the fruits of those many years of dedication and care.

I share my frame of reference here because it forms the basis for what I believe is the most nurturing relationship a mother can have with her children—for both the kids and the mom. Our children don't need us to be their best friends. In my life, my husband, my parents, siblings, and a few trusted girlfriends fill those roles. In fact, I shuddered recently when I heard a woman gush, "My daughter is my BFF!"

Along with love, the things our children most need from us are faith, structure, and adult feedback.

Mom, the Prayer Warrior

Parents are called to be the primary educators of our children. Foremost, this compels us to the duty of their faith formation. It's our role to nurture in them a relationship with God that will shepherd them through life's many challenges. From their earliest days, the images we implant and cultivate within them will blossom into lifelong convictions. As moms, we have the opportunity to embody for them firsthand the beauty of unconditional love.

But when families are strong and united, children can see God's special love in the love of their father and mother and can grow to make their country a loving and prayerful place. The child is God's best gift to the family and needs both mother and father because each one shows God's love in a special way. The family that prays together stays together, and if they stay together they will love one another as God has loved each one of them. And works of love are always works of peace.

—Blessed Mother Teresa

Our children need to know that we pray for them unceasingly—and we need to live up to our end of that bargain. My friend Pat once shared with me that every morning, as she drove her daughter to school, she would pray the rosary. Pat's daughter often spent the morning commute studying. Every morning, Pat would ask her daughter, "What would you like for me to pray for today?" This prompting often led to discussions of situations her daughter faced in a way that transcended the normal limited flow of teen-to-mom communication. So Pat would pray for her daughters' requested intentions, in her presence and outside of it, and her daughter always had the assurance of her mother's constant spiritual support.

In our family, we too share morning car prayers. It's a tradition passed down from my own mother. At the outset of every family road trip, we prayed a rosary for a safe and fun journey. Prayers were recited on the way to school, and family grace, with hands joined around the table, preceded every meal. Spiritual bouquets, hand-crafted construction paper cards filled with promised Masses and rosaries, were treasured gifts.

With my boys, car prayers as we depart the garage for school each morning are reflexive. What better way to start our days than to give God praise for our many blessings and to invite his strength and guidance throughout our days? My boys know that praying for them is one of my most important roles as a mother. I also invite them regularly to remember one another in prayer. Hopefully, by modeling an implicit trust in God's loving intervention in our lives, I can help them build rich prayer lives and a close relationship with Jesus, who is ultimately the best friend any of us could ever want.

Faith must be at the core of our relationship with our children. Faith must be lived out in our own lives and passed along to them with love and compassion. When we are troubled by situations with our children, it's helpful to share these burdens with not only a loving Father, but also with a Blessed Mother who can lovingly intercede on our behalf. We can also invite our children to pray for us, their mothers—to let them know that we need their support and God's intervention in our vocation as parents. In turn, when we celebrate moments of "mom victory" in our homes, it's also right and good to pause and offer thanks for blessings small and great.

Mom, the "Bad Guy"

I've never been afraid to be the "bad guy" in my home. When Eric was born, Greg was a third-year resident in an intense emergency medicine program at UCLA. In order for me to stay home with Eric, Greg picked up moonlighting shifts to take the place of my lost income. He worked long, hard hours and endured crazy commutes on the Los Angeles freeways. When he came home from work, the last thing he wanted to do was discipline an errant toddler. I remember particularly well one night when he came home late and I was ready to blow a gasket over some minor parenting trauma. Eric's transgression of the day eludes memory now, but I do remember that it was one of those "Wait until your father gets home" moments. When Greg entered our small apartment, sleep-deprived after a long shift, I tried to explain to him what "his" son had done and how he needed to back me up on my disciplining of Eric. Looking back now, I realize that it was pretty ludicrous to expect that a time-out several hours after the transgression would have done Eric any good. Greg looked at me and explained sweetly that his time with Eric those days was so limited that he didn't want to walk in the door and instantly reprimand his baby. He wanted to get down on the floor and wrestle, play cars, and do anything that would light up the eyes and smile of that precious little boy. "I don't want to be the bad guy," he confided. "I want to be the one who says 'Yes'!"

Well, there are times when somebody's got to be the bad guy, especially when it comes to parenting. Greg has had his share of playing bad cop over the years, but the fact that I'm typically the one on hand when disciplinary moments arise has made me the primary rule setter and arbitrator in our home. My parents' role modeling of a united front was a great example for Greg and me. As parents and partners, we regularly discuss rules, structure, and norms within our family. We try our very best to be fair, consistent, and reasonable parents and to reinforce one another. But I've learned over the years that my parenting decisions are not always going to be popular . . . and I'm OK with that.

When I was growing up, one of the few rules that I had was a prohibition against seeing "R" rated movies. In the days before the advent of "PG-13" my mom and dad laid down an embargo on films that were too advanced for us. I remember feeling a great sense of relief at being able to say, "Sorry, but my mom would kill me!" when everyone was heading off to see the midnight showing of *The Rocky Horror Picture Show*. Another of my striking memories occurred during my freshman year in high school. A senior boy invited me to see the group America in concert. Petrified by the thought of not only a "date," but also my first real rock concert, I asked my mother to forbid me to attend. I didn't want to lie to the senior, making up an excuse, but I also knew I wasn't ready. My mother's willingness to be the bad guy in this situation took the pressure off of me. The guy in question deemed my mom "totally uncool" and found another date, leaving me to mature a bit before entering the dating scene a few years later

For whatever reason, I've grown up to be a stricter parent than my own mother ever was. Perhaps it's because today's parenting climate is fraught with so many more perils than my parents faced in their day. My mom never had to deal with Internet predators or Amber

Once, when my daughter Eileen was not quite three years old, I walked into my bathroom and found her washing her hands. She had pushed a stepstool up to the sink, but still she was too small to reach the faucet. Somehow she had managed to hoist herself onto the lip of the sink and was balanced there precariously on her stomach, her hands busy with a cloud of bubbles and a rapidly diminishing bar of soap.

When she saw me, her eyes grew wide with alarm, and she cried out, "Don't a-rupt me! I doing my 'portant work!" The words of scolding I'd been about to utter died on my lips as I took in her 'portant work.

Handwashing is such an ordinary, mundane activity, but to this tiny, tousle-haired girl, it was a task imbued with immense weight and significance. I stood there watching her in a kind of awe. Round and round went the slippery bar of soap in her hands, her fingers opening and closing around the iridescent froth. She was frowning a little in concentration, or maybe from the cold edge of the sink pushing into her belly, but by her utter absorption in the task she radiated a deep satisfaction. She was washing her hands with all her might and main.

How often, I wondered, did I give myself to a task that completely? How often did I slow down and find the wonder in the ordinary—the shimmer of light in the curve of a soap bubble? There was grace in that moment, and I knew it was a gift, as if God had stopped time for me, for one small second, so that I might see and remember what this little girl of mine had not yet grown too busy to forget. It's all "portant work": every diaper change, every load of laundry, every scrubbed sink. The most tedious chore hides some kind of magic, like the cloud of rainbow bubbles hidden inside a dull and chunky bar of soap.

Melissa Wiley is the homeschooling mother of six children and the author of The Martha Years *and* The Charlotte Years, *two series of books about the ancestors of Laura Ingalls Wilder. Visit her at www.melissawiley.com/blog.*

Alerts. She didn't have to verify that our soccer coaches weren't registered sex offenders. My siblings and I never would have fallen prey to cyber bullying or having our reputations smeared on a social networking site.

I happily play the role of bad guy. I am the mom whose kids didn't have toy guns except for the ones they made out of blocks or Legos. We have "bedtime" and "family time" in our home. My kids are the ones who weren't simply dropped off at the movie megaplex and picked up a few hours later in their early elementary school years. Now that we've hit the teenage years, I'm even meaner. I set time limits for phone calls. I screen questionable movies in advance. I prohibit outings to homes where a parent will not be present. "Totally uncool," I know. I guess I've grown up to be a bit like my mom, which I consider to be a very good thing!

Our children have plenty of friends, but only a couple of dedicated parents. One of the best things we can do for them, and for ourselves as moms, is to fashion a loving relationship based upon trust and respect. We need to be less concerned with our popularity rating than with raising decent citizens. But we also can't become dictatorial in our approach. Our kids need to understand the reasons behind the boundaries we set. We also need to exercise flexibility when these boundaries need to be revised or expanded. I tease my boys that they would both make first-class attorneys—they've always been great at negotiating their boundaries and limitations. At times, they have convinced me that increased privileges are in order based upon their record of good choices. Ultimately, through prayerful discernment, we moms need to be unafraid to make choices and decisions that we feel are ultimately in the best interest of our still-maturing children.

Mom, the Builder

In his epistle to the Colossians, St. Paul exhorted parents with the words "do not provoke your children, so they may not become discouraged" (Col 3:21). Just as we seek to build and nurture our own self-esteem, we have perhaps the biggest role in shaping the self-confidence and level of contentment in our children during their formative years.

Again, I find myself looking to my parents as great role models in the building up of happy and well-adjusted kids. My mom sat through countless "shows," listening to Erin and me sing, dance, and play really bad guitar versions of our favorite songs. She hand-sewed Barbie clothes and served as the Camp Fire leader. She was "pizza mom," the perennial hot lunch volunteer at the Catholic school. She nurtured our interests, but also held us to the highest of standards. If a report card was presented containing six As and one B+, you can bet she always asked first about the one class where we fell short. But the trick was the tone with which she inquired. Rather than a tone of nagging or discouragement, it was one of inspiration that always encouraged us to strive to be our very best in all things.

That's the tone I think we moms should be taking with our children, and it's the one I think St. Paul had in mind when he instructed early Christian families. As moms, we have the ability to both build up and tear down with the messages we send to our children. How many people find themselves in therapy today rehashing horror stories of "mommy dearest"? As Catholic moms, we are the face of God in our children's lives. Sometimes this unconditional love calls us to the task of course correction. But this must always be done gently, lovingly, and with an eye toward building up the dignity of our children as persons.

Our children have minds and hearts of their own. One of my greatest challenges as a mom has been accepting my boys for the people they are becoming. Outside of faith and family issues, our children emerge gradually and follow their own paths. They find passions and discover dislikes. We must always be careful to encourage and support their interests, even when these don't line up perfectly with what we envision and hope for them.

My boys attended a wonderful Catholic elementary school where one of the cultural trends was to play soccer. Our Saturday mornings soon began to revolve around standing next to the fields, with their friends' parents who quickly became our friends, cheering our kids on to victory. Eric played until middle school, before ultimately taking up football. Adam, on the other hand, struggled with soccer. A fair-skinned blond, he was very susceptible to our Fresno heat and would develop migraine headaches at practice. On top of his physical suffering, he was suffering inside from a real dislike of the sport of soccer. I unwisely forced the issue for a few years—everyone else was doing it, so why didn't Adam like it? I thought he would grow into a love of the game. But after a few seasons, it became apparent that soccer was really not for him. We shopped around for alternative sports that could be done inside, out of the heat, and ultimately settled on fencing, which has become Adam's sport of choice.

As a mom, it can be disappointing sometimes when our children choose paths that stray from what "everybody else" is doing. We may need to subjugate our own egos a bit when our daughters decide against cheerleading or our sons would rather play chess than baseball. I hope that it's some motherly maturity that has brought me to the realization that I am most happy when I'm watching my boys pursue something that they truly love, regardless of whether it's a passion I share. What a wonderful gift to watch those we love most develop their own God-given talents and abilities in ways that bring him glory and praise and bring them great joy!

Blending In

While Mike and Carol Brady made it look so easy to pack six children into two bedrooms with one shared bathroom and start a fresh, new brood, the reality faced by many Catholic families today is not so simple. With an increasing number of blended families being reported in U.S. Census data across the United States, it's important to pause here for a small discussion on the special situations faced by moms living as a part of a blended family.

Stepfamilies may come together as a result of many different paths, including divorce, annulment, death of a spouse, or marriage to a spouse with children from a previous relationship. Each of these equations will bring differing factors into the mix and many will merit family and individual counseling to help children and their parents cope with loss, grief, or difficult family dynamics.

"The hardest challenge I have had with my second marriage has been keeping my spouse first (after God, of course!)," confides Christine.

> When my first husband left me, I did the best I could to be a good mom to my three young children. The challenge of being a single mom for five years really brought the kids and me together. We bonded in a way similar to survivors of a war, or a horrible tragedy. Then I was blessed to meet and marry a wonderful man who also had three children.

> It was so difficult to meld our very different parenting styles together. But the hardest thing was keeping all our children from resenting their new stepparents. We had to honor each other above the children. It was (and still is) sometimes difficult for me to not take the kids' sides during arguments or discussions, because we were a team of sorts.

> My husband and I have both have really learned to rely on God's grace and mercy to guide us as parents of our children, stepchildren, and the two additional babies with which we've been blessed!

If you, as a stepmother or as part of a blended family, find yourself or the children of your family in need of counseling, please reach out immediately to your healthcare provider as well as your pastor or his delegate.

"I'll be honest; it's a struggle," shares Diana, a mother of four with one teenage child from a previously annulled marriage.

> Hindsight being 20/20, I should have put my daughter in therapy as soon as I got divorced. I think some pro-active behavior then would have saved me (as well as my daughter) some trouble now. It's all about grief. She's still dealing with the fact that her parents are not together, and adjusting to life with me being married to someone else, as well as adding more children into the family. All this after she was an only child for eleven years. She's got a lot to deal with, as a fourteen-year-old young woman. I have her in therapy now twice monthly, and go myself as well, to help me figure out how to parent a teenager with my ex-husband.

> Stepparents begin in a hole, as far as I can tell—it's a very confusing role for everyone involved. You're NOT a mother or father replacement, but yet, no one really knows what the role is. Does that make sense?? My daughter will often say, "He's not my father." And, she's right, he's not. But he's my husband, and part of the adult parenting team in my household, and I expect her to treat him with the same level of respect given to me.

Many parishes and dioceses provide services for blended families. If such support groups and services do not exist in your diocese, maybe you can work with your pastor or bishop to help begin greatly needed initiatives in your community.

In my conversations with many moms on the topic of blended families, a few recurrent themes emerged. The two most consistent were the relationship between a stepparent and the children in her life and the role of faith in a blended family. As you can imagine, the responses were varied, yet enlightening.

Commenting on the unique relationship between a woman and her stepchildren, respondents to my queries seemed to fall into two camps. Approximately half felt strongly that stepmothers should treat children as their own. That is to say they should assume a role with them that is nearly, if not exactly, the same as the one they assume with their biological children. In other words, as AGM advises, "Treat the kids as your own." They are, after all, a very real part of your life now.

> The kids may not be your biological kids, but they are a part of you now. Good men can be father figures and good women can be mother figures; even without the official title of "mom." If you adopted an orphaned child, would you treat them as an "adopted child" or as your own? You are in a way adopting this stepchild, too. Don't make them feel unconnected to you. And yes it is going to be very hard, but don't take it personally—biological motherhood is very hard, too.

On the other side of the equation, many stepmothers take the "friend" approach, concerned about appearing to be trying to supplant or replace the children's biological mother. These women see their role as more of a supportive, consultative role in the child's life. Often the age of the children involved and the dynamics between your husband and his former wife (or the children's mother) will provide sensible clues as to the most helpful roles for a stepmom to assume. Most of all,

When they become parents, spouses receive from God the gift of a new responsibility. Their parental love is called to become for the children the visible sign of the very love of God, "from whom every family in heaven and on earth is named."

—Pope John Paul II

keep in mind that just like no one else will be a biological mother just like you will, no one else can be the stepmother you will be.

Many experts on the topic of blended family relationships recommend that, at least initially, the biological parent of the child take the primary role in disciplinary situations. This will, of course, vary depending upon your family's makeup and the presence and involvement of a biological mother or father. Stepmother Lisa shares the following wise counsel:

> My advice for a stepparent comes from my mom. "Love does not take offense." In my experience a stepparent/child relationship is a sensitive one, but one that can bring so much healing and forgiveness to all families and individuals. It helps when I remind myself to think the best and not take offense. Love them first.

In speaking with moms who are part of blended families, many of them emphasized the importance of their Catholic faith in nurturing their marital and parental relationships. Several of them strongly recommended frequent reception of the sacrament of penance as well as building strong faith traditions in the new family. In an article encouraging and supporting Catholic stepfamilies, Bill Boomer, director for the department of Marriage and Family Ministries in the Diocese of Cleveland (www.clevelandcatholiccharities.org/mfm/stepfamilies.htm), recommends the following:

> Seek God's grace and guidance when considering marriage and in the responsibilities of parenting. Couples that share faith, prayer and worship together deepen their loving bond and commitment. Grieving the loss of a previous marriage that ended through death or divorce requires forgiving: letting go of past hurts and disappointments, exonerating a previous spouse from blame and taking responsibility for one's own failures. Only then will a new marriage have a chance to succeed. The hurts, misunderstandings, loyalty conflicts, angers and resentments that accompany stepfamily life need the healing medicine of prayer and forgiveness. Regularly receive the Sacrament of Reconciliation or seek the spiritual counsel of a priest to heal and strengthen your spirit.

Difficulties may arise when a blended family brings together children and parents from varying faith traditions. "I was grateful that my stepsons' mom didn't object when my husband and I took them to Mass when they were with us," shares NRN. As with so many other aspects of living successfully in a blended family, communication and mutual respect are the keys to blending varying faith traditions in a new home. Keep the lines of discussion open between yourself, your spouse, and the other adults in your children's lives and continue to remember all the members of your beautiful, blended family in your prayers. Consider turning to one of the patron saints of stepfamilies, St. Adelaide, St. Leopold the Good, or St. Thomas More, for their special intercession on your family's behalf.

A Prayer for Stepfamilies

> Blessed are you, God of creation! It is difficult to parent two batches of kids and love them into one family. Look on stepfamilies, Lord.

Give them courage to build new relationships, the willingness to adjust to one another's habits, likes, and dislikes, and an ability to laugh over small things. Bless all the grandparents, aunts, uncles, and cousins who are coming on board as family. Bless this widening embrace of family with patience, joy and love.

Amen.

—Faith and Fest 1996
Archdiocese of Omaha

Somebody's Mom

When our children are born, we take on new layers of identity. Along with being "Lisa" and "Greg's wife," when my eldest came along I assumed the role of "Eric's mom" and subsequently the added identity of "Adam's mom."

In nurturing and developing my relationship with my boys, I want them to remember that along with being their mom, I am also still "Lisa." I want them to look at their mom and find a woman who is happy, fulfilled, and living each day to the fullest. I want them to realize that in becoming the very best I can be for myself, I blossom in my role as mother as well.

What a blessing, at every stage of our children's lives, to be present to them in the nurturing role of "mom." Let's remind ourselves that giving them our best also means caring for and nurturing ourselves. Doing so helps in every part of our mom jobs, whether as teacher, as "bad guy," or as cheerleader.

Mom's Homework

✓ Pray for and with your children every day. Establish regular prayer rituals as a family. Listen to your children's struggles and challenges and let them know you will be praying for them. Ask them to pray for you in your role as mom, too!

✓ Talk with your husband about family standards in your home. Set aside time to anticipate needed guidelines for your children's developmental stages. Don't be afraid to be the "bad guy."

✓ Listen to how you give feedback to your children. Are you hypercritical or overly permissive? Remember how your words impact the self-esteem and dignity of your children.

✓ Plan fun outings with your children regularly and spend time listening to what they are really trying to tell you.

✓ Let your children know the real you. Discuss your passions with them. Let them see you reading books, engaging in hobbies, and most importantly nurturing your own faith life with prayer and spiritual development.

Web Resources

Teaching Catholic Kids: www.osv.com/OSV4MeNav/
   TeachingCatholic Kids/tabid/220/Default.aspx
   Featured articles and family activities from Our Sunday Visitor

CatholicMom.com Parenting Columns: new.catholicmom.com/
   category/columnists
   *Wisdom, wit, and insight from a broad cross-section of Catholic
   parents*

CHAPTER THREE

Soul sisters

Friendship and Companionship Among Women

This is my commandment: love one another as I love you. No one has greater love than this, to lay down one's life for one's friends.

—John 15:12-13

My Story

From Fresno, California, to New York City and back that's the distance my closest friend Mara and I have walked together in the past eighteen years. Granted, our walks have largely been side by side on adjoining treadmills at the gym three mornings per week. And truthfully, since Mara is three years younger than I am and in much better shape, she's likely done twice my distance.

I can't remember the day I met Mara, but I thank God daily for the moment he brought this "soul sister" into my life. In truth, we're polar opposites in many ways. Mara's creativity, unsurpassed thoughtfulness, and flexibility challenge my type A, introverted nature. Since we both have two sons and husbands who work crazy, nontraditional hours in medicine, we found ourselves calling one another on those lonely Sunday afternoons when "normal" dads were home watching the NFL but ours were at the hospital. When many families were sitting down to traditional meals, Mara and I could be found pushing toddlers on playground swings, talking about everything under the sun.

We've worked our way through potty training and the terrible twos to dealing with teenagers and their marvels and mishaps. We've faced pregnancies, health scares, and aging bodies together. We've taken a few "girls' weekend" escape trips and completed two marathons together. But mostly, we've just talked, side by side on those treadmills a few mornings a week.

I've often told my husband Greg that he owes Mara a tidy sum for the money she's saved him in providing my free therapy for nearly two decades. Mara likely knows the inside of my head more than just about anyone with the exception of my own mother and sisters. Since my family is spread around the country, Mara is my local "soul sister"—the one who is always here for me when I most need a friend—I'm likely unworthy of all she's shared with me, but never unappreciative of her gifts. She's one of my life's greatest blessings.

The Essential Gift

Volumes have been written about the difference in communication styles between men and women. Knowing that my husband Greg will always be my very best friend, reading some of these books and articles has me also knowing that there are some topics better talked out with a good girlfriend rather than the main man in my life.

Put any group of women together and watch how long it takes us to start swapping labor and delivery stories, even if we're just newly acquainted. God wired us, uniquely equipped to nurture and care for not only our families, but for one another as well.

The friend who can be silent with us in a moment of despair or confusion, who can stay with us in an hour of grief and bereavement, who can tolerate not knowing . . . not healing, not curing . . . that is a friend who cares.

—Henri Nouwen

I'm mature enough to recognize the incredible gift of womanly friendship in my life and to see its essential place in my caring for myself emotionally. But I haven't always been blessed with this gift. For long periods in my life, I was without close woman friends. Perhaps having sisters made me more particular about opening myself up to just anyone—I was spoiled growing up with two best friends living in my own home. It took me a long time to recognize and to learn to nurture the gift of good friendships—I owe some friends big apologies for having been self-interested and a bad communicator.

From where I sit now, I firmly believe that each of us needs to seek out and nurture supportive female friends in our lives. Finding those friendships, helping them to blossom and grow, and keeping them in their proper perspective in the overall scheme of life can be a big challenge.

Making New Friends

Maybe you're one of the lucky moms I meet in my kids' school parking lot. You're busy arranging lunch dates with girlfriends you've known since childhood. But if you're like me, you may find yourself in a new city, feeling lonely and wondering how to find female companionship and support in your life.

On my thirtieth birthday, Eric and I kissed Greg goodbye, jumped in the car and drove the four hours north to our new apartment in Fresno. Greg, finishing off his residency, remained at home to help the movers and finish off some last minute details.

I remember arriving at our new apartment with two sleeping bags, a small television and VCR, some clothes, and a toddler with a raging case of chicken pox. Empty white walls greeted us and I lapsed into a major pity party. Here I was in a new city, an old woman (yes, thirty felt old then!), not knowing a soul in my new world. No career, no parish, no friends, and no one to wish me a happy birthday but an itchy toddler and a large purple dinosaur on videotape.

I let myself cry out loud for an hour while Eric soaked in the bath tub. Then I broke out the yellow pages and starting making phone calls. I called the local church, the library, the YWCA, and even the maternity ward at the local hospital. I was desperate for friends. Within a few hours, I had something on my calendar for each day of the following week—a mom's group at church, storytime at the library, even a "newcomers" playgroup for moms just like me trying to cope with being a new mom in a new land!

We moms are blessed that our children and their activities frequently provide us avenues for meeting new friends. Most of my best friends now are women I met at playgrounds, standing next to soccer fields, or at church. No matter your employment status, it's a safe bet there are other moms in similar situations with similar schedules who want to connect mom-to-mom. Here are a few ideas for meeting new friends.

Church: These days, many of our parishes have wonderful women's ministries. Contact the parishes in your area, or your diocesan office of family life, to inquire about women's Bible studies, parish guilds, cooperative childcare, and marriage enrichment groups in your area. If your parish does not have any of these types of ministries available, or doesn't have them at times that work for you, schedule an appointment with your pastor and volunteer to start something. It's likely that there are others like you who would love to gather at church for fellowship, prayer, fun, and support. Rather than joining existing groups at neighborhood churches from other denominations, please consider being the brave soul who starts something new and special in your own parish.

Your Community: Whether you've lived in your neighborhood your whole life or are new to the area, treat yourself like a newcomer to make new friends. Break out the phonebook and find out what's going on in your neck of the woods. Places to try include:

* library
* zoo
* city hall
* visitor's bureau
* civic groups
* YWCA or other women's organizations
* local hospitals' maternity and women's health departments

Your Child's School: Whether your child is a preschooler or a sopho-more in high school, it's likely that his school would welcome your participation and input. Take an active role in your child's education by meeting the families in her classroom. It's always a comfort to know the homes where your children will be invited to play, and later to hang out, and to know the parents of your children's friends. Volunteer in your child's class if you can, drive on field trips, or speak to the teacher about other ways you can help out if your work sched-ule keeps you from volunteering during school hours. Host a get-together for school families in your home so everyone can get to know one another, or arrange a family picnic after school or on a weekend.

My one word of caution about school-related friendships is to avoid the sometimes-caustic atmosphere of gossip that sometimes crops up in such venues. School parking lots can be filled with groups of moms who stand around spreading mean-spirited talk about teach-ers, school staff, and other students. Be the ray of light at your child's school who works to build a sense of community rather than the one who spends time and negative energy building up walls.

Volunteer Venues: When children are older and require less "hands on" attention, it can sometimes be difficult to foster new friendships. Take advantage of extra time in your day or week to volunteer for a cause you believe in. Giving of yourself and helping others in need may help you to focus less on your own loneliness and more on life's blessings. You will likely meet special new friends in the process.

Know Your Neighborhood: My nephews Evan and Tyler attend pre-school in an inner-city high-rise in Chicago. Every afternoon as they leave school, they pause to say hello to the florist whose business adjoins their classroom. Whenever I am with them and witness this ritual, I'm reminded of the PBS television series, *Mr. Rogers' Neighborhood*. Befriending the people in your neighborhood—wherev-er it is and whatever it looks like—by being kind and friendly can lead to blossoming friendships. Pause to ask the grocery clerk about her day and learn to greet her by name. Frequent a hairdresser, even if it is at a discount stylist. Invite your next-door neighbor for coffee on a winter's evening. In today's world where we've become very imper-sonal in our communication, take time to smile and genuinely listen to people. You never know who you'll meet in the process.

Virtual Friends—The "Real" Thing: In earlier times, women nur-tured their friendships through letters and the written word. Families

The blessing of a sister can never be properly articulated. What could possibly be better than a sister who loves and understands you? A special someone you can talk to about sisterly things; who you can love unconditionally. I am blessed with two sisters: Alice Jean and Barbara. I cherish our sisterly love.

As a mother, I have often stopped to observe the sisterly interactions of my own three daughters. The special relationships among them have continuously warmed my heart. They are blessed to have one another for sure, through both their differences of opinion and the wonderful sharing of their hearts and souls.

And then there's the blessing of the other *sisters* that God puts into our lives—those special women that you connect minds with and join hearts to. Those extraordinary sister-friends whom you may have never even met in person, but that come to your rescue through e-mail or the telephone with prayers and love. And the ones you've been blessed to meet who commiserate with you over a cup of tea and who jump for joy with you over your happiness. How can we ever describe the blessings of sisters? We can't, we just know.

Donna-Marie Cooper O'Boyle is a wife, mother, catechist, journalist, and the author of several books including the best-selling Catholic Prayer Book for Mothers, The Heart of Motherhood, Prayerfully Expecting, Grace Cafe: Serving up Recipes for Faithful Mothering, The Domestic Church: Room by Room, Mother Teresa and Me: Ten Years of Friendship *and* The Heart of Catholicism. *Visit her website at www.donnacooperoboyle.com.*

spread apart by great distances communicated their family histories in missives sent and received over long spans of time. Today, the Internet provides women with great opportunities for companionship and support that harkens back to those old Pony Express days.

When I started CatholicMom.com in 1999, little did I imagine that it would one day lead me to a family of soul sisters spread around the country and even in distant parts of the world. I count as true friends many women I will likely never meet in person. In online venues, we share stories about our families, ask for advice and support, and lift one another in prayer. I daydream about one day hitching our trailer to the back of my SUV and taking off on a "Catholic Mom Victory

NEW PROVIDENCE MEMORIAL LIBRARY
377 ELKWOOD AVENUE
NEW PROVIDENCE, NJ 07974

The virtue of chastity blossoms in friendship. . . . Chastity is expressed notably in friendship with one's neighbor. Whether it develops between persons of the same or opposite sex, friendship represents a great good for all. It leads to spiritual communion.

—Catechism of the Catholic Church, 2347

Tour." It's likely that I'd have a place to stay in just about every state of the Union based on online friendships that have been nurtured over these last ten years.

Seek out and take advantage of the various social networking and interactive sites that enable you to find fellowship with like-minded women. But be cautious in such interactions: always keep your own personal security and privacy first and foremost. Also, avoid letting online relationships hamper your real relationships with your spouse, your children, and your family. If you find yourself avoiding responsibilities in your home or at work or falling into inappropriate communication online, log off, and seek help.

Mom's Homework

✓ Take inventory of women in your life who provide you support and companionship, your "soul sisters." Make time this week to call them or write them a brief note of love and thanks.

✓ If you don't have any close friendships in your life, take one simple step today to start cultivating new relationships. Make one phone call this week to your church or to one of the organizations I've suggested above and find an activity to place on your calendar for next week. At this event, introduce yourself to at least one new person. Do not become discouraged if your efforts don't immediately result in new friendships, but rather begin to cultivate a new attitude of openness to new friends in your life.

✓ Spend ten minutes in silent prayer for the blessing of friendship in your life and for the intentions of your friends.

✓ Invite a friend or acquaintance to join you for a cup of coffee or a walk this week.

✓ At the playground, in the school parking lot, or at Mass on Sunday, go out of your way to say hello or introduce yourself to someone you don't know.

Web Resources

Catholic Mom Community: www.cmomc.org
A community of Catholic moms called to live out the vocation of marriage and motherhood in simplicity and love

Faith and Family Live!: www.faithandfamilylive.com
Everyday moms offer one another inspiration, support, and encouragement in Catholic living

4Marks: www.4marks.com
Catholic social networking

CHAPTER FOUR

Faith family

Finding a Parish and Nurturing your Faith Community

Be filled with the Spirit, addressing one another (in) psalms and hymns and spiritual songs, singing and playing to the Lord in your hearts, giving thanks always and for everything in the name of our Lord Jesus Christ to God the Father. Be subordinate to one another out of reverence for Christ.

—Ephesians 5:18-21

My Story

In my family growing up, Sunday was the highlight of our week. The 12:15 Mass at St. Barbara's found us in attendance as a family, although frequently scattered around the church in various serving roles, with my dad lectoring, me playing guitar, or one of my brothers serving on the altar. After Mass, we would spend at least thirty minutes in the parking lot, chatting with friends prior to heading out to a late family lunch at our favorite Mexican restaurant. The routine so rarely varied that we could typically count on our favorite waitress to hold our family table for us. Savoring the Lord's Day was something my parents taught me from the earliest of ages. Perhaps their job was made easier by the fact that we lived in a parish with a vibrant school, active ministries, and clergy who truly felt like part of our family. We considered church a home away from home, not some place we just went for an hour on Sunday.

When I left home to attend college at the University of Notre Dame, my sense of church as a faith family continued, as my practice of Catholicism became even more integrally woven into the fabric of my day-to-day life. I became a daily communicant, attending Mass in my own dorm, at a nearby male dorm, or in the basilica crypt, depending upon the day's activities. I could stroll to the grotto for a rosary or pause in one of the scores of chapels across campus for quiet prayer time at any hour of the day or night. Being a part of a faith family was not something I had to work at on the Notre Dame campus. We worshipped alongside our friends almost as regularly as we dined or partied together and with the same sense of joy and fellowship.

After graduating from college, part of learning to deal with the "real world" was finding a parish home. I expected to instantly replicate that sense of faith family I'd known as a child and a student, and was devastated when, for many years, I fell into the trap of just showing up at church on Sunday and feeling lonely and disconnected. I blamed the priests, the "cliques" within the parishes we attended, the out-of-touch liturgy planners and music ministers—in truth, just about everyone but myself, for my not feeling a part of the Body of Christ in my community.

It took a brand new Catholic, a friend who asked me to do her "a favor" by sponsoring her through the process of the Rite of Christian Initiation of Adults, to open my eyes and lead me to the truth about finding a faith family. When, as an adult, I learned to ask how I could serve my parish rather than be served by it, I felt my life change for the first time in years as we began to put down roots in a parish community that would blossom into that spiritual home I had sought for years.

Selecting a Parish

Perhaps you are blessed to have already joined or to have always lived in a parish that feeds your family spiritually and emotionally. If that's the case, jump ahead to the next chapter, but not before pausing to write your parish priest a letter of thanks and appreciation and stopping to count your blessings in prayer.

You cannot pray at home as at church, where there is a great multitude, where exclamations are cried out to God as from one great heart, and where there is something more: the union of minds, the accord of souls, the bond of charity, the prayers of the priests.

—St. John Chrysostom

Most of us, at some point in our lives, will find ourselves "church shopping." Either through relocation or changing life circumstances, we may have the necessity to find and become a part of a new parish. We should take the selection of and moving into a parish every bit as seriously as we would the purchase of a home or the selection of a school for our children. In today's world of priest shortages, choices may not abound and you may find yourself with only one option when it comes to joining a parish. If that is the case, or if you are indeed already a longstanding member of a parish community, take time to establish a true family relationship within your parish.

"Bless Me, Father"

As a part-time employee of my parish and a longtime volunteer, I've learned that many of our parishioners attend Mass on Sunday without ever taking time to register in the parish until they need something—a sacrament, an education in our parish school, or a priest to visit a sick relative, or even—sadly—a funeral. Don't be one of those statistics. Take the time to register in your parish this week and get to know more about your church.

Schedule an appointment with your pastor and introduce your family during the week rather than grumbling when the poor man doesn't recognize you or know your name when folks surround him after Mass on Sunday. The priests I've known and worked with have so many responsibilities on their plates these days. But universally, the care of their flock is among their highest priorities. In today's world of scandal and safe-environment regulations, our relationships with our priests are forever changed. But your priest, as the head of your new faith family, deserves to know you and your family and to be assured of your support and service.

The same holds true of course for those in parishes with parish administrators. Introduce yourself to him or her and try also to make time to get to know the pastor when he is available. Also try doing the same with other members of your parish's pastoral staff such as the director of religious education, the pastoral associates, parochial vicars (associate pastors), or deacons. While they, too, have a huge amount of work and responsibility on their plates, they will likely appreciate and sincerely welcome your initiative.

Seek to Serve

I am convinced that the only way to truly make your parish community feel like your faith family is to actively seek out opportunities to serve that family. Just as we moms show our love to our husbands and children by sharing our gifts with them, so can we share our skills, abilities, and time with our fellow parishioners.

When our children are very young, our primary obligation is to be physically and emotionally present to them, and this may limit our ability to actively volunteer at church. If you find yourself unable to commit to parish volunteer time, adopt the tremendous role model of St. Thérèse of Lisieux, who became a prayer warrior for missionaries even though she was cloistered in her convent. Speak with your pastor and let him know that you would like to participate in your parish through an active prayer ministry. Many parishes have prayer lines— telephone or e-mail chains that advise members of prayer intentions. Commit to a few moments of prayer time each day for the intentions of your parish community. Another wonderful ministry for moms of young ones is to be a part of the team at your parish that cares for the church building and altar. At our parish, I joined the altar guild when my children were young and spent time every week straightening the pews, dusting, and laundering items. Being in the church with the sisters who led this silent team of angels taught my children a reverence

One of the most persistent issues many of us have experienced is that of finding a church that is a good fit—a worship place that is comfortable, inviting, and uplifting; a truly welcoming parish that has good music, good homilies, and good fellowship. That's what I looked for; that's what many say they are looking for. And so I say, "I understand. I completely relate."

These expressed desires are stronger in me the further back in time I look—and I'd like to explain that. There was a time when church was about me. I don't mean that I wasn't trying to feel and experience God. But it was about what I got out of it. That was my understanding of church.

However, as I went through four years of deacon formation and as I began to understand what was really happening in the Mass, I began to understand that Jesus is offering himself to the Father at every Mass—good homily or not, music of an angelic choir, or an off-key soloist.

I heard Fr. Larry Richards say something like this: On those Sundays when everything—*everything*—works for you and the music lifts your heart and the readings are meaningful and the homily speaks directly to where you are on your journey—that day—that Sunday—is God's gift to you. And on a Sunday when none of it works—when you feel like you have wasted an hour—that day—that Sunday, is your gift to God! I do admit that I still have to keep re-learning this. But not so much anymore.

Wherever you are in your walk, I pray that you will (mostly) come to the point that you recognize that we come for the celebration of the liturgy—the "summit" and "fount" of our Christian life (*Constitution on the Sacred Liturgy,* 10). The rest is either a gift or reason for surrender.

Reverend Mr. Tom Fox is a deacon in the Diocese of Tucson. Visit him online at www.deacontomonline.com.

for the sanctity of the church building and opened my heart to other ways to serve my parish.

One of the best ways to immediately meet and connect with your fellow parish families is to volunteer in ministries that involve your children. Moms of very young children might consider forming a babysitting co-op or a mother's playgroup to support their fellow moms. At CatholicMom.com, we've assembled a variety of resources to help you found a moms' group. If no such group exists at your parish, meet with your pastor or parish administrator and ask his or her permission to begin meeting. Start simply with weekly gatherings that last an hour to ninety minutes and focus on getting to know one another. These "baby steps" may eventually lead to more formal meetings where you and your fellow moms gather to pray the Rosary or study the Bible together.

If your children are school aged or older, consider volunteering in your parish religious education program or school. Both will put you in touch with other families with like-aged children. You may fear that you are not adequately qualified to teach in the religious education or catechetical programs of your parish, but you will likely find that your parish has the tools and training necessary to make sharing your faith with young parishioners into a true joy. In addition, at CatholicMom.com we do our best to support teachers with free religious education resources, games, coloring pages, and lesson plans related to the Sunday Liturgy of the Word.

When my children became old enough, I was fortunate to be commissioned as an extraordinary minister of Holy Communion in my parish. I cannot express to you what a tremendous privilege it is to serve my parish in this capacity once per month. When I am sharing the Eucharist with my fellow parishioners, I truly feel a closeness and connection to the Body of Christ in our parish. Another wonderful way to serve your parish is as a greeter, usher, lector, or music minister. Most parishes desperately need adults to serve in these volunteer ministerial roles and will welcome your involvement.

If teaching or liturgical ministry does not fit into your lifestyle or skill set, speak with your pastor, school principal, or director of religious education/formation and ask how you might support your parish with your time and talents. This might be as simple as assisting with clerical work or as wonderful as sharing your professional abilities as an accountant, computer analyst, or attorney. Be clear as to the parameters of your availability, but also try to open your heart to the potential of truly sharing yourself with your faith family.

Knights in Shining Armor

Many parishes have Knights of Columbus ministries that are the backbone of the parish. Although membership in the Knights is limited to men, the services they provide exist to support and encourage families in the faith. Prior to Greg's joining the Church, I had several

A parish is a definite community of the Christian faithful established on a stable basis within a particular church. . . . It is the place where all the faithful can be gathered together for the Sunday celebration of the Eucharist. The parish initiates the Christian people into the ordinary expression of the liturgical life: it gathers them together in this celebration; it teaches Christ's saving doctrine; it practices the charity of the Lord in good works and brotherly love.

—Catechism of the Catholic Church, 2179

friends in the Knights of Columbus who watched out for and supported our family. These men prayed unceasingly for my husband and engaged my sons when Greg was not able to join us at Mass. Older Knights are frequently stand-in grandpas for those of us whose families are spread around the country. Encouraging your spouse to join the Knights of Columbus in your parish will provide an instant gateway to spiritual support and true fellowship with other parish families.

Scout It Out

If you are fortunate enough to have a parish Boy Scout or Girl Scout program or other service club for school-aged parishioners, encourage your children to get involved and you will find an instant connection to other families. Parish-based scouting programs teach young people important life skills. Your son or daughter will meet and begin to develop relationships with other scouts. You and your husband will make friends in the process as well.

Don't let those uniforms dissuade you—a commitment to scouting can be flexible for any family. If your child is a real "go getter," he will love the advancement system of the programs. But if your child wants to be involved for mostly social reasons, there is a home for her in scouting as well. Scouts advance at their own pace and are supported and encouraged according to their own unique set of abilities. Another wonderful feature of parish-based scouting programs are the various religious awards that can be earned. These supervised programs will vastly enhance your child's knowledge of and commitment to his or her personal faith life. Finally, scouting is fun! Through our parish scout troop, our boys camped, slept overnight on submarines, hiked, learned crafts like leatherworking, and had many great hours of fun with friends. A chaplain always supported our parish troop, and we were united as a scouting community by a mutual commitment to our Catholic faith.

Regardless of whether you are new to your parish or have been a member of the community for years, make an effort to see your fellow parishioners as members of your "faith family" and look for opportunities to love, serve, and support these special people in your life.

Mom's Homework

✓ If you are not already registered in your parish, formally register this week. If you are already a registered parishioner, contact the parish office to update your family's data.

✓ Schedule an appointment with your pastor this month to introduce your family or write your pastor a note of support and encouragement.

✓ Consider taking on some type of volunteer ministry in your parish: baby-sit, clean the church, teach a religious education class, volunteer to fold bulletins, or serve in a liturgical ministry. By serving your fellow parishioners, you will meet people, form relationships, and begin to truly feel a part of your faith family.

✓ Consider your family's stewardship potential and make a family commitment to regular financial support of your parish. The amount of your support matters less than your attitude in giving and your consistent financial support.

✓ If a mom's ministry or mother's group does not already exist in your parish, meet with a friend or two and enlist them to help you begin a simple ministry. Meet with your pastor or other parish leader and seek his support and guidance.

Web Resources

Mass Times: www.masstimes.org/txt
Offers Mass times for the United States and other countries from information provided by diocese and individual parishes

Busted Halo Church Search: www.bustedhalo.org
Church recommendations and reviews from young adults around the country

U.S. Catholic Parishes Online Directory: www.parishesonline.com/scripts/default.asp
Online U.S. directory of the Catholic Church. Find Catholic churches, Mass times, pastors, bulletins, maps, dioceses, schools, and more

CHAPTER FIVE

Special circumstances

Mothering Adoptive, Foster, or Special Needs Children

It is the LORD who marches before you; he will be with you and will never fail you or forsake you. So do not fear or be dismayed.

—Deuteronomy 31:8

My Story

She first caught my attention one Sunday night after Mass several years ago, walking around the parish grounds and holding hands with a young woman who appeared to be about twenty years old and to have some developmental disability. I have deduced over the years that this particular mom is likely close to sixty, a devoted single mother living in the apartment building across the street from church with her now-adult daughter.

I don't know her name (in my mind, she is "Anna"), but she figures prominently in my prayers many Sundays at Mass as I watch her continually minister to her daughter's needs. As a young mother who struggled with very overactive young boys at Mass, I remember looking at Anna and her daughter and thinking about a life spent truly living out the most physically and emotionally demanding aspects of our mothering vocation.

The most remarkable thing about Anna is that in years of occasionally observing her and her lovely daughter at Mass or around our parish, I have never once seen this devoted mom look upset or frustrated. She goes about her mothering with a quiet sense of serenity that has edified and inspired me over the years. Sometimes, when I am fatigued with the more mundane aspects of my life as a mom—yet another load of laundry or stomachs that never seem to be filled—I think of Anna and the service she has rendered to and will continue to shower upon a very special daughter for a lifetime. I send up a silent prayer for the two of them and thank Anna for her loving example.

Every Family Is Unique

In all honesty, I struggled greatly with how to approach writing this particular chapter and the one immediately following it on single parenting, because I have not yet faced the challenges that many moms will address in life. I've learned to "never say never," so I won't close my heart to the possibility that perhaps someday God will call our family to adoption, to foster care, or to the care of a child with special needs. But I didn't want to let my limited experience in these arenas keep me from addressing some very real issues that face moms who live out their mothering vocations in these special and unique ways.

Blessedly, several experienced moms have agreed to step in and share their expertise and perspectives on how we, as mothers, can nurture and care for ourselves when life takes an unexpected turn. In

Mothers of children, even if they have a thousand, carry each and every one fixed in their hearts, and because of the strength of their love they do not forget any of them. In fact, it seems that the more children they have the more their love and care for each one is increased.

—St. Angela Merici
(Patron Saint of Disabled Persons)

corresponding with many of these special moms, a common denominator comes to mind—no two families are exactly alike. God calls some moms to care for ten children. In some instances, like mine, he may think we have our hands full with two! Some families may be blessed through adoption or the foster care system; others may welcome children who face medical or emotional challenges.

Many of the moms I spoke with for this chapter resented being singled out as anything more than just a "mom," eschewing the adjectives "adoptive," "foster," or "special needs." Others felt each of these three categories deserved a chapter of its own, as they surely present unique sets of opportunities and obstacles for moms. In the end, I decided to take a brief look at how the "experts" in these types of families manage to care for and nurture themselves. The reality is that many of their suggestions are universal to any mom. Since these topics deserve much greater space and attention than I can give them in one chapter, I've provided additional resources at the conclusion of the chapter for adoptive, foster care, and special needs moms seeking additional support and information.

Open Hearts, Open Arms

I think adoptive mom Sue hit the nail on the head with this statement. "My first thought is that all children are a blessing and individuals. Regardless of the circumstances of their birth, a mother will love them equally. Not the same, as *they are not the same*, but equally." While adoptive mothers and those who open their hearts and homes to children through the foster care system may love their children equally, it's also critical that they nurture and care for themselves in the process.

Being "Mom" to three wonderful children who joined our family through adoption is an incredible blessing and joy in my life, but also brings challenges other mothers may not face. All three of my children have different birth parents and different cultural, social, and medical histories. Those differences bring diversity and opportunity along with challenges. Many adoptive mothers lack support or understanding when our children have unique behavioral or medical issues, or a different ethnic background. Assumptions or misconceptions can bring well-intentioned but hurtful comments.

As adoptive mothers we find ourselves in the role of mother to our child, student of a new culture or ethnicity, educator to family and friends, sleuth to discover the child's history, researcher to uncover medical or behavioral help, and activist to ensure our child's needs are met. And then we have to multiply that for each new child joining the family. Some days I find that overwhelming and question my ability to succeed and be what my children need.

Prayer reassures me that this is my calling from God, and he sustains me through those times giving me strength, courage, and understanding. Mother Teresa said, "Do not think that love, in order to be genuine, has to be extraordinary." I know God called me to be the mother of these specific children and that we were meant to be together. He is by my side daily helping me to be the mother they need, and that is all I need.

Mary Birks is a Catholic wife and adoptive mom of three wonderful children living in Michigan.

It's important not to look too far ahead with traumatized children. The wild little monster who smears the walls and hides food under his bed may well turn out to be a happy, affectionate child. Adoption and foster care changes YOU as well—almost always for the better, helping us to grow in virtue and root out selfishness and other sinful habits. Your family's journey may get bumpy, with highs and lows all along the way. Be gentle with yourself as well as your children, and keep them as close to you as you can. You stand the best chance of forming the solid, healthy attachments you will need to raise your children to adulthood if you concentrate on forming those attachments from the very beginning. That means putting everything else on hold for that first year in order to bond with your children. The younger the child, the more critical this is—especially if the child is preverbal. Time is critical—your child must experience the fact that he or she can trust you to care for him or her, no matter what. Words are not enough.

If you feel overwhelmed, do whatever is necessary to get the support you need from friends and family. Pay them, if necessary. Floors and dishes can wait (or be delegated) while you bond, both individually and as a family. But your personal needs (sleep, nutrition, exercise, prayer) cannot be neglected if you want to attend to your child's needs. This is a marathon, not a sprint!

Sleep is especially important. You may not get much in the beginning, even if you foster or adopt older children. Hire a sitter for a few hours. Nap when they nap. Consider the advantages of co-sleeping (perhaps on a mattress beside your bed) to give your child an extra sense of security.

Be aware of your own stress levels: clenched fists, tightness in the chest, tension headaches, increase in alcohol or unhealthy eating habits or television viewing habits. Find ways to lower your stress levels: Go on a brisk walk (run around the playground while the kids play, if necessary), or take a warm shower or bath. Have a cup of tea and play some soft music or scripture tapes. Take the kids to a weekday holy hour (Jesus doesn't mind the noise!), and tell the Lord about the things that worry you most. If you just feel like screaming, go out to the car, turn on the radio, and sing along, loud and strong and in a different key!

Above all, remember to find the joy, to capture the happy moments of parenting that made you want to do this in the first place. Take a few minutes to jot down the little stories before they get away from you. Make some cookies, and go wild with sprinkles. Teach them a silly song (buy a few children's tapes, if you don't know any silly songs). Play with your child in a bubble bath. Have Mickey Mouse pancakes for dinner. If they're acting out, it's probably a sign that they need a little extra attention. The same is true for you!

Remember: you are an extraordinary mom. You are facing extraordinary challenges and may make a few mistakes along the way. Don't worry. Love covers a multitude of sins! Receive the sacraments—especially Eucharist and confession—as often as you can. The Lord never gives us a task to do without giving us the grace to get the job done. Day by day, moment by moment, the grace is there for the asking.

Heidi Hess Saxton is an author and speaker, and founder of the Extraordinary Moms Network (EMN), an online resource for mothers of adoptive, foster, and special needs families. She and her husband Craig foster-adopted their two children in 2002, and live in southern Michigan. Heidi's books include My Big Book of Catholic Bible Stories *and* Raising Up Mommy: Virtues for Difficult Mothering Moments, *both available at http://extraordinary momsnetwork.wordpress.com.*

Tara, her husband, and four sons recently welcomed a beautiful baby girl into their home through the foster care system after she was born prematurely and exposed to drugs. Tara shares a bit of their story here.

> We knew that there are more than half a million foster children in this country and that so many are needing loving families to care for them. We knew that God asks us to use our gifts, and give what we can to others. The love of a family is something we had to give. It certainly is not always easy, but loving this girl has been one of the most important journeys our family has taken on so far. Falling in love with her was the easy part. The hard part is being so attached to her and not knowing if she will stay another week or forever. I feel that even though she may leave, we have all been so blessed to learn a real, tangible lesson about loving someone in the moment, because truthfully we never know how much time we will have with those whom are so precious to us. This has been a true opportunity for my husband and I to teach our boys about sacrificial love, the kind God has for us. I have constantly asked Our Lady to please stay with us every step of the way, and of course, she has. I would encourage anyone who thinks God is whispering to them about these children, to please look into it. Blessings await!

Sassy, a mom who has adopted seven children with special needs, offers the following words of wisdom:

> Remember that you are human and you can't do it all by yourself. Spend at least twenty minutes each and every day with your spouse, without children. If it means that you go to your room and shut the door on the world for twenty minutes, do it. Baby monitors are wonderful tools—use them.

> Smile. Start with your lips, let it spread to your eyes and then to your heart. Once it reaches your heart nothing is so bad you can't deal with it.

> Use respite care and all medical and mental care available to you. It's okay to cry. It's okay to say, "I don't know, I just don't know."

> Love them—if you do, you've given them everything. Be consistent, be firm, be flexible when needed. Have a routine and delegate. Have fun. Feel the joy.

Often families are not prepared for the birth of a child with a disability or the development of impairments. Our pastoral response is to become informed about disabilities and to offer ongoing support to the family and welcome to the child.

—Welcome and Justice
for Persons with Disabilities, 9

Many adoptive moms I have spoken with struggled with others' use of the term "real mom" when it came to identifying or explaining their relationship with their children's birth mother. The truth is, you are your child's "real mom" the moment you open your heart and your home to that child. As an adoptive mom, you may find yourself having to do a bit of community service in educating others in your life to the realities of your family. Your joy in welcoming a new soul into your family and your light and love as a mother will shine forth and help others to know that you were destined to be this child's mom, that God called you to this particular vocation and has spent a lifetime preparing you to take on this role.

The Person, the Soul, Not the Disability

Kathy is the mother of an adorable daughter who grows, plays, communicates, laughs, and gets into stuff just like any other child. Kathy's daughter also happens to have been diagnosed as having the chromosomal disorder Down Syndrome, which may impact upon the way she lives her life. But Kathy is quick to point out that "Rosemary is not Down Syndrome. She's my baby *who happens to have DS.* Focus on the person, the child, the baby—not on the 'problem'."

Ann Marie, raising a child who has been diagnosed with learning disabilities, shares, "I hate the phrase, *'God sends special children to special parents.'* The truth is that we become capable of raising a child with special needs because our kids encourage and inspire us to grow as needed."

Jennifer, mom to a school-aged son with a disability, counsels families to be a light to others in their communities and parishes. "Go places as a family—what a way to be a witness to the faith when all of the children are together. You'd also be surprised how many people are patient and willing to wait for my son to speak." Jennifer also recommends sharing with the priests, deacons, and liturgical ministers at your parish about your child's special circumstances. Seek out support and resources from your parish community. If you find your parish ill-equipped to respond to your needs, turn to your diocese or work with your parish to establish programs. This may mean that you need to volunteer some of your time to educate your pastor and fellow parishioners and to help them in their service of your family and others facing exceptional parenting circumstances.

Lisa Barker, noted author, is a mother of five children, one of whom is facing a protracted battle with a terminal illness. With humor and grace, Lisa exemplifies for me our true call to service as mothers. Lisa shares this.

> LAUGH. Listen to comedy, read humor. Laughter can shed so much stress in a matter of seconds.
>
> Cry when you feel like crying. Don't worry or feel bad if you don't feel like crying.
>
> Accept hugs. They are as important as prayer.
>
> Tell people what you do need. And don't fear telling people "no thanks." So many have offered counseling to help us grieve that we were overwhelmed with offers! It's okay to say no, too.
>
> Offer this up for other souls, the souls in purgatory, the souls in danger of going to hell.
>
> Savor this opportunity to care for Jesus in the disguise of your very sick little one . . . and give the other kids plenty of opportunity to help or hang out with their sibling, but don't mandate it. Most kids want to be a part of care or comfort. It empowers them and keeps grief at a healthy level because they can DO something for their sibling—like getting pillows, or making cards, or bringing a favorite toy, or watching a movie together . . . Don't isolate them from each other. They all need each other. And this helps them prepare for the end and store up many good memories.

When I first heard the words, "Your son has autism," my immediate thought was, "I can't do this." That was also my second, third, and fourth thought. After calming down a bit and speaking to my husband, we both knew that since God had provided us this extraordinary child he would also provide us the means to care for him. We just had to trust his plan. That is not always easy but it is always worthwhile. Part of God's plan for us to care for Ryan was to take care of ourselves and our family, too. You need to be at your peak to undertake the work of providing for any child, but a special needs child presents unique challenges, and like the difference between an Olympic athlete and an amateur, you need to gear up. For David and I this means monthly date nights to reconnect as a couple, frequent confessions to reconnect with God, and the occasional time out on our own. He might go hit a bucket of balls or have a beer with a friend. I might wander about a bookstore or have a mani/pedi.

It is really important to realize you can't do everything. Focus on what is really important for you to accomplish each day and only do that; if more is done pat yourself on the back. Another piece of advice I always give is, "ask for help." Having a child that is very different from other people's children can make you feel cut off from the community. The truth is that people are generally very kind and willing to be helpful if only they know what is needed. Ask a friend to babysit while you run errands. If someone offers to make a meal or take over a chore, let them. It's a kindness to allow others to practice charity and no shame to admit you need help.

We lost Ryan in a tragic accident in August 2009. He remains with us always in deepest love and in our enduring memories.

Mary Ellen Barrett, home-educating mother of seven, blogs at Tales from the Bonny Blue House, http://maryellenb.typepad.com.

It wasn't long after the adoption of our first special needs child that I realized "I can't do this!" Even with the help of my husband John, who is a "we're-in-this-together" kind of guy, I knew I was in over my head!

That was when I turned to the best mother I know—Mary, the Mother of God. When you think of it, all children are God's children and are merely "on loan" to us. Ultimately, he wants them back with him for all eternity, and if there is anyone who will pray and guide us in this parenting adventure, it is his own Blessed Mother. Prayer then, became the key to my parenting. My routine included daily Mass when possible, and the rosary.

Yes, there were days so hectic that all I could do was "offer up" the interruptions and little sacrifices (laundry, sick kids, emergency errands, trips to the doctor, etc.), but that counts as a prayer too—if we intend it to be. The Morning Offering is a great way to begin the day!

That took care of the soul. For the body—an occasional lunch with a good friend is always uplifting!

Mary Ann Kuharski is a homemaker, wife, and mother of thirteen children, six of whom were adopted and of mixed-races with special needs. She is the author of four books: Raising Catholic Children, Parenting with Prayer, Building a Legacy of Love, *and* Outnumbered: Raising Thirteen Kids with Humor and Prayer. *Mary Ann and her husband John are founding members of PROLIFE Across AMERICA, "The Billboard People," a national educational organization broadcasting pro-life messages through the media. Mary Ann serves as its director.*

Calling All Moms

Regardless of the makeup of your family, mothering can be a stressful business. When you face even more stress as the primary caretaker of a child with a disability, emotional issues, or an illness, it is even more critical than ever that you take time to nurture yourself emotionally, mentally, physically, and spiritually.

Heart: Nurture your relationship with your spouse. Make one-on-one time with each of your children and involve them in the care of their siblings as appropriate. Call on extended family for their support and assistance. Make time for yourself and spend at least a few hours every month with a special friend.

Mind: Eliminate sources of stress that will add to your load, whether they are career oriented, volunteer duties, or simply self-imposed expectations. Pamper yourself by pursuing a hobby or personal interest. Educate yourself about your child's diagnosis. If your child is adopted or you are in the foster care system, or if your child has been diagnosed with a particular disability or illness, investigate resources and support groups that may help you to cope with difficulties as they arise.

Body: Make time daily to go outside for at least twenty minutes. Engage in some form of physical activity. Feed yourself and your family with simple, healthy foods. Get adequate sleep every day.

Soul: Pray for yourself and your family on a daily basis, seeking the intercession of the communion of saints. Attend Mass weekly and let your parish community support you in your vocation. Welcome the prayers of others knowing that this will benefit both your family and theirs.

Mom's Homework

✓ Find a mother's group or support group in your area where you can meet with other families facing special circumstances, if this will provide you encouragement for your parenting journey. If no such group exists, consider gathering weekly with a few like-minded friends for fellowship and conversation.

✓ Compile a "support system" list. Document the names, telephone numbers, and e-mail addresses of friends and relatives who have offered to help you in any way. Be willing to accept offers of transport, shopping, meals, and babysitting.

✓ Inform your pastor if your family is facing difficult circumstances. Request his support and keep him informed of what you are facing as a family.

✓ Treat yourself to "me time" at least once per week—take a long bath, browse in a bookstore, or take a walk outside.

✓ Journal about what you are facing and about your feelings. This will be a valuable treasure to you and your children in future years, when memories of these moments in your life have faded and dimmed.

Web Resources

Disability Resources

Welcome and Justice for Persons with Disabilities USCCB: www.usccb.org/doctrine/disabilities.shtml

Pastoral Statement of United States Catholic Bishops on People with Disabilities: www.ncpd.org/views-news-policy/policy/church/bishops/pastoral

National Catholic Partnership on Disability: www.ncpd.org

Prenatal Partners for Life: www.prenatalpartnersforlife.com

Adoption Resources

Extraordinary Moms Network: http://extraordinarymomsnetwork.wordpress.com

Little Flowers Foundation: www.littleflowers.org

Catholic Charities USA: www.catholiccharitiesusa.org

National Council for Adoption: www.adoptioncouncil.org

Priests for Life Alternatives to Abortion Resource Page: www.priestsforlife.org/crisis.html

U.S. Department of Health and Human Services: www.hhs.gov/children/index.shtml#adoption

CHAPTER SIX

You're Never alone

Parenting on Your Own

For I know well the plans I have in mind for you, says the LORD, plans for your welfare, not for woe! Plans to give you a future full of hope. When you call me, when you go to pray to me, I will listen to you. When you look for me, you will find me.

—Jeremiah 29:11-13

My Story

When I think of the bravery and fortitude of mothers who parent on their own, the first person who comes to my mind is my friend Michelle. A few years ago, Michelle lived out every wife and mother's nightmare when her young husband Dan was killed instantly in a tragic automobile accident.

Left on her own so suddenly to raise two young children, Michelle rose to the challenge heroically. Ironically, this meant learning not to carry the tremendous burden of being a single mother by herself. Buoyed by a supportive faith community, Michelle let herself be open to the possibility of asking for and accepting life-affirming support from family and friends. For those of us who grieved Dan's death with Michelle and her children, simple tasks such as making and delivering a warm meal or chauffeuring Jacob and Ellie ministered to our sense of loss perhaps as much as they aided Michelle.

My friend wisely sought the expertise of her personal physician to help soothe her insomnia and depression following Dan's death. She turned to trusted friends for financial and legal counsel. She was wise enough to let us know when she needed to be left alone with her children, and courageous enough to ask for help and a break when times became overwhelming. Her personal faith has seen her through good times and bad and she has become a bedrock for her family.

Five years after Dan's death, Michelle's attitude and strength continue to inspire me. As I watch my dear friend strive for balance and personal happiness for her family, I learn that like my friend Michelle, all mothers are truly never alone in our vocation if we open our hearts and lives to a loving God and to friends and family who walk life's path with us.

Surround Yourself with Support

Although I may have sometimes felt like a single mother in the early years of my marriage when Greg was a resident physician working long hours and erratic schedules, I have never faced half of what most single moms have to deal with on a day-to-day basis. For this reason, I'm thrilled that several mothers responded to my plea and shared the following wisdom on how they care for themselves and their families.

Many women parent alone, and do so for a variety of reasons. Like my friend Michelle, they may have lost a spouse in a too-early death. Some may never have married, or may have had a marriage end in annulment or divorce. Some mothers may find themselves temporarily single-parenting when their husband is relocated professionally or due to service in the military. No matter what the circumstances,

What was the first rule of our dear Savior's life? You know it was to do his Father's will. Well, then, the first purpose of our daily work is to do the will of God; secondly, to do it in the manner he wills; and thirdly, to do it because it is his will. We know certainly that our God calls us to a holy life. We know that he gives us every grace, every abundant grace; and though we are so weak of ourselves, this grace is able to carry us through every obstacle and difficulty.

—St. Elizabeth Ann Seton

moms who parent alone need to be especially cognizant of their own needs and self-care.

Regardless of their reason for being single, the moms I spoke with underscored the importance of turning to family and friends for support. For some women, this support may come in the form of extended family living nearby who can support you both physically and emotionally in child rearing. For those not living near family, it seems especially crucial that a mom develop a support system of friends, fellow parishioners, or others facing like circumstances. Perhaps there is opportunity for participation in a local or online support group.

Mothers of sons commonly expressed the need for single mothers to seek out healthy relationships with adult male role models for their growing sons. This support might be a formal "Big Brother" type of arrangement, or be a relationship developed with another family with like-aged sons. Scouting, sports teams, or parish communities are wonderful environments to seek supportive relationships with caring gentlemen who can support you in nurturing your sons.

As I spoke earlier of the importance of nurturing our friendships, single moms who are supported by female companions testify to the importance of surrounding yourself with women who care about you and your well-being. Even if you only see friends once a month or less, make an effort to keep in touch with those who care about you by e-mail and telephone. Sharing your needs, concerns, and triumphs with a trusted "soul sister" can help lighten your burden.

Single mothers are often in a position to help build strong, and perhaps more-resilient-than-most, relationships with their children.

These moms pull their families together as teams to face life's increased hurdles. It is especially important that moms recognize up front the special emotional needs that children facing death, divorce, or any type of parental separation will have. One widowed mom shared with me, "My daughter attends a Catholic school where 'family' is defined as a mother, a father, and a child. I remember my daughter coming home from school one day and announcing, 'We aren't a family any more because there aren't enough of us.' The loss of her father is an attribute my daughter will always have. It is my job to help her develop a healthy understanding of that attribute as she grows to adulthood." As in this mother's case, seeking professional counseling for yourself and your children can be a critical component of your healing process.

Additionally, please look to your child's teacher and to your pastor as caring co-partners in the raising of your child. It is their vocation to join with you in the nurturing of your precious treasures. If they are people you feel comfortable approaching, share with them on a regular basis the challenges you face and know that they can serve as an important component of your support system. Divorced mother Sue shared, "My children are extremely close even as adults and that is because they 'survived' the divorce and stuck together to get through it. Family can come together and be a strong unit. Healing can happen and issues can be dealt with. It is really up to the parent and to the children to make it happen."

It is important that as a single parent, you apply the same diligent, consistent discipline for your children that you would if you had a parenting partner. Try not to make parenting decisions from a position of guilt or anger about your situation. Lerin, whose young marriage to her high school sweetheart was annulled, hopes other single moms can avoid a parenting mistake she committed in raising her daughter:

> I think I parented too much out of guilt. Part of it was that she was my first baby, I was alone, and I had no idea what I was doing, but the other part was I felt so awful about the choice I had made in her father that I actually *never* wanted to say no! I always tried to make her "happy" and it led to a lot of stress. This was complicated by the fact that I was still in college, studying Early Childhood Education, and reading way too many psychology experts on parenting who did not share my faith! I recommend reading Dr. Raymond Guarendi's books on common-sense parenting to avoid those guilt traps I was firmly in!

It's not supposed to happen! You're a young mom, your children are not even school age, and you're thinking about where the family might go on a summer vacation when—a knock at the door, a sympathetic face, and your world is upended forever. You learn your husband has died! I was twenty-nine with three small children at home when my husband John was killed in a plane crash. I remember saying, "But John wouldn't want to be dead. He has plans. We have plans . . ."

Spiritually, my comfortable Catholic faith was severely tested. You see, I had simply assumed that if I did my best to be a reasonably good person, then God would ensure me a comfortable life. And that didn't include losing my much-loved husband! It was as if I had struck a bargain with God and God had let me down.

My journey forward was painful. On a practical basis, I had to process my grief—and my children's—and learn how to be a single parent, 24/7. So many tasks. Such a weight pressing down on my shoulders. I made mistakes. For a while I stopped going to church. But as I look back I see how God's grace guided me even when I didn't want to acknowledge God.

One powerful moment was this: about six months after John died, I reached for a juice glass in the kitchen. It slipped and shattered into little pieces on the floor. Immediately, I thought, "That's just how my life is. Shattered!" And then—a surprising image appeared in my mind: the stained glass window of a nearby church.

It was a beautiful window—and it was made of pieces of broken glass. In that moment, for the first time, I thought, "Maybe the shattered pieces of my life can still become beautiful. Different, but still beautiful." That image was a powerful indication of God's grace acting in my life.

Losing a husband when you're a young wife and mother is so terribly hard. Yet no matter how deep your grief or your anger, I assure you, from my own experience, that God will be there to give you courage, strength, and at some point, hope. Hope for the beautiful picture of what your life can still be.

Barbara Bartocci is a speaker and author of the Grace on the Go book series—prayers for caregivers, for dieters, for new moms, and for busy people. Visit her at www.BarbaraBartocci.com.

Being a single mother is not easy. It is difficult and overwhelming trying to suc-cessfully play both parental roles. Despite the surmounting negativity of divorce, you can bring peace into your life by spending time in adoration before the Blessed Sacrament. No matter what stage of divorce I was at, adoration was the key to balance and healing. I encourage others going through divorce to spend one hour each week with Christ, before the Blessed Sacrament. Whether you read a book, pray the rosary, journal, or just sit and look at the reserved Eucharist, you will find this one hour of your week to be your life preserver. In adoration, you will find:

The luxury of true peace and quiet
The time for yourself that is essential for good parenting
Consolation
Grace and strength for difficult tasks
Healing

Your family will be more complete and your children will experience more healing and stability if you focus on your own healing. Christ will show you the way if you stay close to him.

Lisa Duffy is coauthor of Divorced. Catholic. Now What?, *director/pro-ducer of* Voices of Hope *DVD, and founder of DivorcedCatholic.com. Happily married, Lisa lives in Georgia with her husband and three children.*

Along with seeking emotional support, it's very important that single mothers make special arrangements to ensure the physical safe-ty of their families. Temporarily "single" military spouse Rose advis-es having someone check in on you on a regular basis. "As a stay-at-home mom, when my husband is gone I can go for days with-out contact with another adult. Sometimes as I stumble on the stairs I wonder, 'What would happen if I fell and hurt myself?' Having some-one call me every day could prevent a lot of this worry and provide some much-needed adult contact."

A common denominator in the advice I was given by nearly every mom was that it's absolutely essential that single mothers ask for the support they need. "Ask, ask, ask," counsels Mary. "People can't read minds and don't want to intrude." Rose reminds us that help need not only come from family and friends.

Swallow your pride and ask for help. Military wives have a stereo-type to live up to of being "the rock." We are supposed to handle whatever comes our way on our own and do it with a smile. Our husbands repeatedly tell us how strong we are. The truth is, how-ever, there are times when that just isn't true. If you feel like you can't handle the housework, ask for help. If you feel you can't handle your emotions, ask for help. If your child is behaving errat-ically and nothing you have done is helping him or her cope, ask for help. Sometimes God doesn't want you to handle it alone.

Embrace the kindness of strangers. Remember, God not only puts friends in our lives to help us, he likes to use strangers, too. From the usher in the back of the church who held my son (who could not sit still) every Sunday so I didn't have to chase him when I was in my third trimester, to the mother in the crying room who offered to watch my kids while I went to communion so I didn't have to drag a screaming, kicking toddler up the aisle, to the man who held my son's hand while we were walking to the chapel just because "Sometimes they miss their Daddies," I never would have been able to get through all of those Masses alone.

Always remember that allowing others to support you and your family in ways small and large renders grace to the helper as much as to the one who is helped.

Listen to Your Body

In later chapters of this book, I will expound upon the need for all moms to nurture ourselves physically. However, I felt it especially important here to share some of the insights of self-care shared by our mom experts that may be unique to single mothers. Nearly every woman who contributed to this material recommended that single mothers need to seek consultation with a trusted physician. Some women may face serious depression or other maladies that can affect them both physically and emotionally. Understand that broken or suddenly interrupted relationships may have left you with deep emo-tional scars that will take time and professional expertise to heal.

The stress of single parenting may lead some women to habits that can cause deteriorating health. Use of drugs and alcohol, smoking, and overeating may be by-products of the stressful life led by a single mom.

If you face any of these issues, it is imperative that you have an honest conversation with your doctor. Your children rely on you now more than ever, and self-destructive habits can have devastating results on your entire family. Mary, a divorced mother of nine, advises that "walks with kids and dogs help" and shares that, "I am going to Weight Watchers to stay healthy, and I give back by helping others to quit smoking as I was helped." Make time several times per week for exercise activity that can strengthen you both physically and mentally.

Chrysa, a mother of six who went through divorce and the healing process of annulment, understands the importance of having a regular routine for yourself and your family. "Set a regular bedtime routine. Make sure that bedtime is appropriate for the age and don't let your children stay up late. You need that quiet time at the end of the day as well." Indeed, quiet time at the beginning or ending of every day is important for all of us and may be especially so for the single mom.

Supporting Yourself Intellectually, Financially, and Emotionally

Just as you must care for yourself through your relationships and good physical habits, as a single mom it is important that you support yourself intellectually and financially. We will address professional and career issues again in chapter 8, but it's important in this discussion of single parenting to look at the unique challenges faced by single mothers. Working outside the home will likely become a financial necessity for you. Make career-related decisions that not only financially but also emotionally contribute to your family's well-being. Some mothers may choose to work from home or follow the advice of one mother who shares, "I worked as a nanny and brought my daughter with me, as I wanted to offer her the most stability possible. The finances were tight, but I wouldn't have had it any other way." If you do find yourself working outside the home, seek a work environment that upholds family values and be honest with your supervisor about your circumstances and the level of commitment you can honestly give.

Most single moms who are hurting from loss of a spouse agree that it can be very helpful to the healing process to take part in support groups specifically targeted to your situation—either for those facing divorce or annulment, or for widows. Many Catholic parishes now provide specific ministries for families facing such loss. Contact your diocesan office of family life to learn about specific support groups in your area.

Sieglinde, a divorced mom raising three children on her own, points to a few lifestyle choices that have helped her to nurture herself. In addition to being active in her parish, she enjoys being a part of secular women's groups and coming together with friends who enjoy her hobbies of knitting and crocheting. She has also used her skills to begin her own tailoring business, which she runs from her home.

Sue, whose divorce left her parenting five children on her own, found that "keeping a journal also helps because after a while when you think you haven't gone very far in the healing, you can look back at your journals and see how far you really have come."

Despite a mom's best efforts to be all things to all people in her life, simplifying your life can be another key to happiness for you and your family. This may even involve lowering your expectations for some things, like the perfect house! "I have a messy house," confesses Mary. "I am not a bad mom because my house is messy. I have limits and so do the kids." Chrysa advises teaching children basic responsibilities and giving them simple daily chores, but also wisely helps keep things in perspective by saying, "Simplify things as much as possible. Learn what can be set aside and what can't. Your children will be with you for such a short time, but dishes and laundry will never go away."

You Are Not Alone

The greatest single gift any mother can embrace is the gift of her faith and the abundant grace showered upon us by a God who loves us unconditionally. In Part IV of this book, we will take a closer look at the gift of our Catholic faith, but here let us look at some specific ways in which single Catholic moms can nurture themselves spiritually.

Regardless of the size or makeup of your family, I hope you will embrace the concept that you never walk this journey alone. With a loving God guiding our steps, a compassionate Jesus with whom to share our innermost thoughts, and a loving Spirit to embolden us in our daily challenges, we carry out our vocation under a mantle of protection. Additionally, we are lifted and supported by our Blessed Mother, a mother who has constantly known in her heart the depth of our mothering vocation and to whom we can turn at any time for intercessory guidance and strength.

Embrace the sacraments and treasures of our faith that help you in your healing and parenting. If you are divorced and have not had your marriage annulled, you may find great solace in exploring the annulment process. Please meet with your pastor or his delegate to discuss the specifics of your situation and seek his guidance. If you are unable to speak with your own pastor for any reason, please contact your diocese for support or visit another priest in your area. Do your best to learn about and to truly

They should be encouraged to listen to the Word of God, to attend the Sacrifice of the Mass, to persevere in prayer, to contribute to works of charity and to community efforts for justice, to bring up their children in the Christian faith, to cultivate the spirit and practice of penance and thus implore, day by day, God's grace.

—Pope John Paul II

understand Church teachings when it comes to the topic of annulment, rather than rely upon what others may tell you or what you may have believed to be true in the past. Our Catholic Church wants to aid you and your family in your parenting vocation.

Tracy, a mom who is temporarily raising four young children on her own, recognized the hand of God in helping her get through the first year of her physical separation from her husband. "Looking back, I would say that the entire year was a 'single footprint' year, as I surely would have suffered a nervous breakdown without Our Lord carrying us each step of the way!"

Another young single mother shared with me that her conversion to the Catholic faith helped her survive the pervasive sense of loneliness she faced.

I was encouraged by some reading I was doing to offer my suffering to Christ, which I had never heard before in any other faith. Finding meaning in my suffering gave me a real sense of purpose, and I began to pray for Mary's intercession to make me a better and stronger mother. I would encourage other single parents to offer up their own sufferings and unite them with Christ, to prayerfully bear their pain with him. The suffering can be so intense, and the only way to get through the sickness in the middle of the night when you have to work in the morning, to get through a tantrum alone, to figure out what your child needs from you as the only parent—the *only* way to get through all that and to *still* have peace is to pray without ceasing!

Look for opportunities to become more a part of your parish family by actively serving your parish as you would your family. Become a lector, teach in your children's religious education class, or sing with your children in the family choir. Embrace regular healing through the sacrament of reconciliation and nurture your soul by receiving the Eucharist as frequently as possible. Seek out opportunities that may be offered in your parish to attend retreats or other support meetings for single parents.

When you feel you are running on empty or falling short of the standards you set for yourself as a mom, when loneliness and pain feel overwhelming, or when you just can't take another day, please turn to God for his never-ending love and support. Just as St. Thérèse of Lisieux turned her life into a prayer in her own "little way," know that you can offer each and every day as your own unique prayer. God hears and knows those quiet thoughts that lie deep within our hearts, and his grace and love are always draped around you and your family. You are never alone!

Mom's Homework

✓ Schedule an appointment with your pastor, another parish priest, deacon, or lay pastoral minister at your parish or in your diocese for spiritual and pastoral counseling. If he or she is unaware of your family circumstances, discuss these and seek support in your motherly vocation. Make an effort to receive the sacrament of reconciliation at least once per liturgical season.

✓ Create a list of "must do" household responsibilities and a master schedule of who will complete each task and when they need to be completed. Include your children in this process and explain to them that their contribution to their family is needed and valued.

✓ Make a "go to" list of family and friends who can aid and support you in both emergency and everyday situations that arise. Post this list in a prominent place in your home and be certain that your children know whom to contact in the event of an emergency.

✓ Ensure that your Last Will and Testament are updated and that a family member or friend knows of their whereabouts and your intentions for the care of your children.

✓ Research local area support groups, retreats, and other women's groups that meet regularly to share one of your interests or hobbies. Begin to cultivate a support network and friends by regularly attending these activities.

Web Resources

National Catholic Ministry to the Bereaved: www.griefwork.org
   Offering support and healing to the bereaved and their ministers

Widows of Prayer: www.widowsofprayer.org
   Prayer ministry for Catholic widows

North American Conference of Separated and Divorced Catholics:
   www.nacsdc.org
   Bringing healing, reconciliation, and new life to the divorced and separated

DivorcedCatholic.com: www.divorcedcatholic.com
   Providing answers and insights for divorced Catholics

A Widow's Walk with Christ: www.ewtn.com/series/2008/2/
   widows_walk.htm
   Widowhood from a Catholic perspective

PART II: Mind

BUILDING SELF-ESTEEM, COMPETENCE,
AND A JOY FOR LIFE BY
NURTURING OUR INTELLECTUAL ABILITIES

School's Never OUt

The Joy of Becoming a Lifelong Learner

Hear, my son, and receive my words, and the years of your life shall be many. On the way of wisdom I direct you, I lead you on straightforward paths. When you walk, your step will not be impeded, and should you run, you will not stumble. Hold fast to instruction, never let her go; keep her, for she is your life.

—Proverbs 4:11-13

My Story

Throughout my life, I've been fascinated by learning new things. As a child, I was one of those girls who loved school and the feel of a freshly sharpened number two pencil. That love continued through my attainment of my undergraduate and graduate degrees, leading me to pursue my double majors in French and government at Notre Dame, and a master's degree in adult education at Vanderbilt when Greg and I were newlyweds.

I've long since forgotten most of the outlines I memorized to cram my way through college and graduate school. I'll admit to being a procrastinator who spent too many late nights typing out a paper that was due within hours or memorizing French vocabulary words in the wee hours of the morning. I frequently wish I had those student days to live over again—I would have approached my studies much differently and with a greater sense of appreciation for the pure joy of learning than I had "back in the day."

But blessedly, the world God created for us and the life he's blessed me with afford me opportunities every day to learn new things. Some days, those life lessons have to do with a point of faith or of child psychology. Other days, my personal schooling may involve untangling a computer problem or learning alongside my children about an artist or historian. Every day, I give thanks for a mind that is eager to be filled and for a treasure trove of discoveries just waiting to be made.

Home as a Classroom

Motherhood puts an entirely refreshing spin on the concept of attaining "lifelong learner" status. We've all read the manuals that offer a theoretical take on parenting but reveal little about the peculiarities of raising the unique individuals who inhabit our homes.

I figured out early on in my mothering career that I was better off putting away *What to Expect When You're Expecting* and turning to my own mother for real-world wisdom. I continue to call her almost reflexively when "mom emergencies" arise. I have learned to carefully listen to this grand master of parenting who successfully guided five children through the minefields of early childhood and teenage years and into well-adjusted adulthood. Every day, my mom carries a well-charged cell phone to respond to the numerous teaching moments that will inevitably come up. We call on her for everything from the secret family recipe for "Impossible Pie" to the proper handling of a disciplinary situation. She continues to be one of my most important teachers, showing me that our vocation of motherhood is a lifelong commitment of love and that my job as mother will not be over when I send my sons off to college.

My two favorite "school of life" professors have never earned a dime for the education they've given me on a daily basis. My sons, Eric and Adam, have taught me new and amazing lessons every day since even before they left the womb. Some of those instructions have been value-oriented in nature, like patience or gratitude, but equally as many have been pearls of truly "bookish" knowledge. From their earliest years, both loved to be read to and favored nonfiction. As we worked our way from board books to bestsellers, I learned about everything under the sun, from the unpronounceable names of dinosaurs to the accomplishments of presidents. With the boys, I had my eyes opened to concepts of history, natural science, and geography that had never before interested me. Their zest for learning has always been infectious. Exposing them to museums or historic sites opened my own eyes to a world waiting to be discovered. The most important thing Eric and Adam have taught me is to look at our world as a classroom and to approach life as a scholar, questing for knowledge for the pure joy of learning something new.

Most moms would probably agree that our children are our greatest teachers and that our homes are life's most fruitful classrooms. It is up to us, as women, to see those teachable moments that present themselves every day and to open our hearts and our minds to the learning that can happen. Today, as you go through your daily routine, approach life with an open mind and a heart disposed toward learning something new. Ask yourself the "why, what, where, when, and how" questions that unlock some of the world's greatest mysteries. Mentally document at least one new thing you've learned each day and rejoice in the blessings of curiosity and wisdom.

Faith Focus

Responding to our vocational calling as Catholic moms, we must also look to continually educate ourselves on matters of faith. Our Holy Father, Pope John Paul II, often referred to our living out of family life as the "domestic church." Indeed, it is our primary job as parents and parishioners in our domestic churches to pass along the teachings and traditions of our Catholic Church to our children.

To meet that responsibility, it is our duty to continually learn about our Church and to teach our children the basic precepts of

Catholicism. While, according to the book of Hebrews, "Faith is the realization of what is hoped for and evidence of things not seen," there is still much about our Church that can be concretely taught and studied. One of my favorite ways of learning about our faith is to thoroughly prepare for each Sunday Mass by studying the Liturgy of the Word. I also consistently read about the lives of the saints, studying these holy men and women both in the historical context of our Church and also simply in the lives and times in which they lived. On most Sundays, now that my children are older, I take notes during our priests' homilies and try to follow up on points of learning offered during these sermons. For moms of young children, meditating upon the Sunday readings in advance of or immediately following Mass can make up for the fact that you may entirely miss what's happening in the heat of the moment as you care for your little ones.

Grant me, O Lord my God, a mind to know you, a heart to seek you, wisdom to find you, conduct pleasing to you, faithful perseverance in waiting for you, and a hope of finally embracing you.

—St. Thomas Aquinas

Our parishes and dioceses can be fonts of wisdom in learning about our faith. Take advantage of Bible study courses, adult learning events, and parenting and family life seminars offered within your diocese. Many dioceses around the country also offer religious education or eucharistic congresses where you can listen to renowned faith leaders or apologists. The Internet is another wonderful source for educating ourselves on the faith, but we need to remember to seek out reputable sources online and turn to the Vatican and the U.S. Conference of Catholic Bishops when seeking to check for orthodoxy.

Learning about our own Catholic faith is a joy but also a duty for Catholic moms. The day is coming, sooner or later, when your child will come to you with questions of faith. Are you prepared to witness to your child about the fullness of Catholicism? I've learned that rather than trying to have all of the answers when it comes to my children's questions, it is my job to go to the source *with them* and to learn alongside them. For example, when Adam recently questioned the Church's teaching on married priests, we spent time together studying the catechism and papal encyclicals on the topic.

Three Principles of Learning

My seasons of learning have been as varied as my seasons in mothering. Looking back at twenty-one-plus years of being a mother, three learning principles come to light.

1. Stay close to God through daily prayer and his Word.

   Mary, the Blessed Mother, said: "Do whatever he tells you" (Jn 2:5). First learn what God wants, then, learn by doing it. "Seek first his kingdom and his righteousness, and all these things shall be yours" (Mt 6:33).

   Use helps like the *Magnificat*, or a page-a-day bible, or attend Mass. Even ten minutes a day before your children wake, or at the playground, or waiting for a carpool . . .

2. Learn together.

   My learning often paralleled my children's! It was like a second childhood learning how to read the *Catechism*, make bread, watercolor, use a computer, read historical fiction, visit a desert, grow a crystal, and snorkel, to name a few.

   I also found new mentors by taking classes, or just asking someone to teach me what they knew.

3. Dream.

   This question stirs creativity: what would you do if you knew you could not fail? Put another way: what would you learn, if you gave yourself the permission to learn it? This, coupled with the first principle, got me through graduate school in my forties.

   If something is worth doing, be willing to do it badly at first. Give yourself the luxury of time to learn to do it well. You would do as much for your children.

   "For everything there is a season, and a time for every matter under heaven" (Eccl 3:1).

Pat Gohn is married to Bob and together they have raised three young adults. Pat holds a master's degree in theology and when she is not writing or active in lay ministry, she is reading her way through the pile of books on her nightstand! Visit her at www.PatGohn.com.

We moms are not compelled to have all of the answers to our children's (or our own) questions about the Catholic Church. What we do need to have is an attitude of openness to our children's inevitable queries and a sense of responsibility and of happiness in helping them to find the answers. As my children mature intellectually, it has been a source of pride and humility for me to learn alongside them about the treasures of our faith.

Everyday Learning

If "all the world's a stage," then surely there is a classroom on that stage! Wherever we turn these days, learning opportunities abound. It is crucial that our children look to us as role models of lifelong learning, as people who believe that learning is a blessing, not a chore to be crossed off the list. Let our children see us reading, and they learn that a book can be a friend and a source of adventure. Take our children to a museum, zoo, or historical site, and we send them the message that history and biology are living entities that can be great sources of enjoyment and enlightenment.

Our communities are filled with learning resources. One of my favorite places in the world has always been the public library—we make regular visits to check out books, movies, and music. Many communities also offer town hall lectures, orchestral concerts, and clubs that cater to everything from hobbyists to historians. Travel through time at a local Renaissance faire or see history come alive in a Civil War reenactment. Many local museums offer memberships that are honored by establishments across the country. For example, with our $25 membership at our local art museum, we have reciprocal access to hundreds of galleries all over the nation.

Even the television in your home can be a partner in your ongoing education. With today's multiple programming outlets, documentaries and mini-series can provide educational viewing that both entertains and explores our world, with no additional cost. Use your family's viewing hours as a teaching tool by pre-screening programs and watching listings for worthwhile films and series.

Now more than ever, the Internet has turned our homes and communities into true classrooms. Many universities now participate in the OpenCourseWare project that enables us to become "cyberstudents." With access to a computer and an Internet connection, you can attend a lecture at Yale or audit a course at countless other prestigious institutions of higher learning. I regularly turn to the "University of YouTube" when I have a specific need for information—online videos have helped me with everything from debugging computer messes to teaching my teenage son to tie a double Windsor knot. At iTunes U, colleges and institutions around the country offer free educational audio and video content you can take anywhere with you on your MP3 listening device or computer.

Mom, the Scholar

Since there are no educational prerequisites for taking on the job of mom, we all come to our positions with varying degrees of formal education. When I "retired" from my full-time job after Eric's birth, some of my friends and colleagues insinuated that my years spent pursuing a graduate degree were a wasted effort. But the truth is, no formal education is ever a waste. Every minute I spent in a classroom or studying languages or education has come together to make me the person I am today. I may not use my college Russian studies on a daily basis, but those years spent memorizing the declension of verbs helped form the communicator I am today. I constantly thank my parents for the gift of my formal education and see it as one of my life's greatest blessings.

Many moms have sacrificed their own formal education in pursuit of their motherly vocation. Whether it's finishing high school or pursuing a law degree, at some point, you may feel yourself called to seek a formal degree. A few years ago, my dear friend TJ felt called to complete the bachelor's degree she had abandoned when her young family needed her at home full time. As her children reached school age, she decided to return to school herself to fulfill her lifelong dream of earning a degree. TJ did her schoolwork alongside her children, giving them a real-life role model of diligent study skills. Her family worked together as a cohesive unit to make her dream come true, and her children became stronger and more responsible as a result. TJ so enjoyed her studies that she went on to enroll in a graduate program that enabled her to attend school on weekends and earn her master's degree. At TJ's graduation party, it was obvious to see her children's pride in her accomplishment. Yes, her family made sacrifices and had to pitch in more than ever before to make things work, but the entire family learned and grew together in pursuit of TJ's educational goals.

Perhaps you too dream of someday returning to school to pursue an educational dream. I would love to return to university some day to study theology. Right now, that goal does not jive with my primary responsibilities to my husband and children. But one day, God willing, I will find myself in a classroom again formally studying this Church I love so dearly.

Closely examine your family's situation and finances and speak honestly about your goals with your husband if you are married. Come up with a realistic plan of attack that will work with your current circumstances without you neglecting your family. Right now may not be the perfect time for you to go back to school, but do not set aside your educational dreams and goals. Speak with counselors at your local educational institutions and determine what will be involved in seeking your degree. Many colleges and universities offer transitional programs for adults looking to return to school. Other schools offer "distance learning" degrees that enable students to take courses on the Internet with only a small investment of time spent in actual classrooms. Earning a degree as a mom will likely take more planning and a longer time to achieve, but the results will impact not only you, but also your entire family.

In the meantime, learn to love learning and embrace education, whether formal or informal, as an everyday gift from God and a treat to share with your children.

> The family is, so to speak, the domestic church. In it parents should, by their word and example, be the first preachers of the faith to their children; they should encourage them in the vocation which is proper to each of them, fostering with special care vocation to a sacred state.
>
> —Lumen Gentium, 11

Mom's Homework

✓ Look for an opportunity each day to learn something new. Document your discoveries in a journal or begin your own blog online and write about what you learn.

✓ Talk with your children about the joy of learning and together, as a family, come up with a learning project. Visit an area museum, zoo, or historical site and spend time after your visit talking about what you learned.

✓ Join a book club in your community or online. Strive to read at least one book per month and to speak with someone who has also read that book. Many libraries offer community book clubs, and Catholic book clubs abound on the Internet.

✓ This month, research and attend one faith formation event in your diocese. Attend a mother's Bible study, a parish mission, or even sit in on one of your children's religious education classes.

✓ Investigate resources offered by your local library system. Obtain a calendar of events and take your children to a story hour, concert, or book discussion at your library. Obtain a library card and begin visiting the library on a weekly basis.

✓ Assess your own long- and short-term educational goals. Document your dreams, plan realistic steps to achieve them, and converse regularly about your goals with your spouse and children.

Web Resources

Catechism of the Catholic Church: www.usccb.org/catechism/text
  Online, searchable version of the Catechism

OpenCourseWare Consortium: www.ocwconsortium.org
  Institutions working together to advance education and empower people worldwide through opencourseware

iTunes U: www.apple.com/education/mobile-learning
  Collection of free educational media available to students, teachers, and lifelong learners

Church Documents on Catholic Education: www.soe.usfca.edu/institutes/icel/catholic_Eddocs.html
  Vatican and USCCB documents from the University of San Francisco

John Henry Cardinal Newman, *The Idea of a University:* www.newmanreader.org/works/idea
  An eloquent defense of liberal education

Working Things **Out**

A Balanced Look at Career Issues and Mothering

She obtains wool and flax and makes cloth with skillful hands. Like merchant ships, she secures her provisions from afar. She rises while it is still night, and distributes food to her household. She picks out a field to purchase; out of her earnings she plants a vineyard.

—Proverbs 31:13-16

My Story

These days, I have no problem with that "cocktail party" question, "What do you do?" that so many mothers have come to dread. For years, I felt the necessity to explain my circumstances, offering my previous professional credentials and the fact that I had chosen full-time "at home" status due to my husband's crazy work schedule. In an almost apologetic manner, I would try to liven up my mom resume by expounding on community volunteer work or other activities that might lead the question poser to believe that I did something more than sit home, watch soaps, change diapers, and eat bon bons.

These days, without hesitation, my automatic response to this question is, "I am a mom!" I leave it at that, answering with the natural enthusiasm for the vocation that fills my heart. If the conversation continues, the person I'm speaking with may also learn that I write, design websites, and run my own home business. But if it doesn't, they've learned the one aspect of my life that most defines me—they've learned my life's work and the calling that brings me the greatest joy.

Answering God's Call

The word "vocation" is derived from the Latin *vocare*, meaning "to call." In becoming moms, each of us has responded in our own way to God's unique calling in our lives. Our paths to this vocation and the circumstances in which we live out our lives' work are as many and varied as our individual personalities and family makeup. We have each emulated Mary's affirmation, "Behold, I am the handmaid of the Lord. May it be done to me according to your word" (Luke 1:38).

First and foremost, our work is a mother's work. In partnership with our husbands and according to God's plan, we welcome life into this world. Whether through our own conceiving or by adoption, or joining together in a blended family, we nurture and care for the day-to-day needs of God's most precious gifts, our children, and are help-mates to our spouses. We pass along the treasures of our faith to our families and ensure their formal education. Our daily work consists of the tasks of running our homes, feeding our families, and doing our very best to stay sane in the process.

Blessed Mother Teresa once said, "It is not the magnitude of our actions but the amount of love that is put into them that matters." I try to remind myself of this attitude when I am washing yet another load of laundry, mopping a floor, or cooking for boys who never seem to be full. By beginning each day with the following prayers, I do my best to mentally summon the intercession of St. Thérèse of Lisieux who once said, "Without love, deeds, even the most brilliant, count as nothing." I try diligently to live out my own version of her "Little Way," recognizing each task of every day as a unique expression of my love for the God who has so abundantly blessed me.

Morning Offering

O Jesus, through the immaculate heart of Mary, I offer you the prayers, works, joys, and sufferings of this day for all the intentions of your sacred heart, in union with the holy sacrifice of the Mass throughout the world, in reparation for my sins, and for the intentions of the Holy Father. Amen.

Allegiance Prayer

Dear God in Heaven, I pledge my allegiance to you. I give you my life, my work, and my heart. In turn, give me the grace of obeying your every direction to the fullest extent.

We each have our own unique vocational calling. In saying "yes" to your role as mother, you have opened your heart to your life's greatest work.

Giving Our Best

I am greatly saddened by the "mommy wars" that have emerged over the past several years, pitting mothers against one another over the issues related to career and employment. The truth is, every mother is a "full-time mom" whether her family circumstances lead her to work outside the home or within the home.

My own mother, who held a variety of employment statuses during my upbringing, formed my personal view of this situation. By profession, my mom was a teacher who worked on and off at various schools during my childhood. For many years, she did not work and devoted herself to the insanity of raising five busy children. During one particularly difficult time when finances were very tight in our home for a few years, my mother worked the graveyard shift at the telephone company and came home to care for a toddler and four school-aged children, catching catnaps throughout the day.

My parents worked as a cohesive unit to ensure that we were cared for and kept a firm faith life as the foundation of our family and of their marriage. If I was asked at any point in my childhood what my mother's job was, regard-less of whether she was work-ing outside the home or not, I said, "She's a mom." That response came easily for me, and still does, because my mother always gave the very best of herself to her mother-ing vocation.

It is more important to teach by a life of doing good than to preach in eloquent terms.

—St. Isidore

In my life these days, I am surrounded by terrific mothers who carry on their work in an amaz-ingly diverse number of ways. Some work full time in their homes devoting themselves exclusively to their domestic responsibilities. Others work part time or full time in careers as lawyers, business-women, teachers, and healthcare professionals. I have many friends who are employed at home full time in the homeschooling of their children. Some of my friends operate home businesses and manage their nonfamilial work around the naptimes and bedtimes of little ones. Some are married to husbands who have made the decision and commitment to be in the home full time caring for little ones.

Every family has a unique and special set of life circumstances. Our job, as mothers, is to place our children and their upbringing at the center of our lives. What that will look like and how it will play out in each of our homes will be different. You know in your heart whether you are giving God the "first fruits" of your labor on a daily basis. Whether within or outside of our homes, we need to take pride in our work and offer it as our daily prayer.

As workers in our own little corners of God's vineyard, let us ask ourselves the following questions when it comes to our employment:

* Am I listening for and responding "yes" to God's unique calling in my life?

* Do I place the needs of my husband and children at the top of my priorities in life?

* Am I offering the performance of each day's tasks and responsibil-ities as a prayer?

* Am I performing my vocation to the best of my ability, with pride in my work, regardless of how insignificant or unimportant the world at large may deem that work to be?

* Do I perform my work with a joyful heart? Am I resentful, judgmental, overbearing, or uncaring in my service to others?

* Do I carry out my work for self-serving purposes, for public recognition, or in pursuit of material possessions?

* Have I given thanks to God today through my actions and glorified him through the fruit of my labors?

Life's Balancing Act

As I read through this inventory of questions I've posed to you and to myself, I recognize that many days I fall short of answering them affirmatively. When my sons were infants and toddlers, I frequently fell into the bad habits of frustration, impatience, and envy. In particularly bad moments, I asked myself selfishly, "I walked away from my career for this? Was I nuts?" I spent too many years comparing my sons to other children and subsequently judging them, and myself, too harshly in the process.

We all want to know that we are doing a good job. In a mother's work, however, there are no performance appraisals or merit pay increases. We're in it for the long haul, and it's likely that we will not see for many years the end result of all of our efforts. While we may be able to cross tasks such as "fold laundry" or "wash dishes" off our to-do lists, our work is truly never complete. During my radiation treatments for breast cancer, I met an eighty-two-year-old mother named Rose who drove her daughter to daily treatments at the Cancer Center. "It's my job as a mom to care for my daughter," Rose once told me. Those words helped underscore for me the incredibly long-term "job security" that comes with a mom's career.

If you are working outside of or inside your home, homeschooling, or engaged in volunteer duties, you deal every day with the "balancing act" of managing multiple demands on your time. Let's take a look at a few factors that can help you make the most of your vocational calling and your day-to-day work.

Purpose: Take time to consider the purpose of your work on a regular basis. If you have a career on top of your mothering vocation, examine your motivation in doing your work. Does your work support and serve others? Have you overextended yourself in a way that shortchanges your family?

Communication: Whether or not we work outside our homes, we are part of a team. All of us blessed to have spouses with us need to work in partnership with our husbands and our children, when they are old enough, to get the job done. Stay-at-home moms especially can sometimes slip into thinking all the work of homemaking falls to them. On a regular basis, take time with your spouse to discuss your work. Engage his support for your work in the home and share your needs and concerns with your husband. Our husbands are not mind readers. Too frequently, we may bear resentment toward them for being insensitive to our needs. Just as a team of professionals might carry on monthly staff meetings, we need to come together regularly on the home front to develop game plans, long-term goals, and short-term survival strategies.

If you are employed outside of the home or running a home business, communicate regularly with your supervisor and colleagues about the realities of your life as a mother and an employee. Keep them informed of life circumstances that may have an impact upon the performance of your work. Offer positive suggestions such as alternative schedules that will help you meet obligations both at home and to your employer.

Support: Regardless of the nature of your work, surround yourself with a solid support team. Let the first member of that team be God by carrying on daily prayer conversations with him and letting him know your needs and intentions. Seek support from family and friends who can help you in your work and reciprocate by helping them when you can do so. If you have the assistance of childcare professionals or teachers in the raising of your children, meet with them regularly to engage their assistance. See "Finding Help" for additional ideas on seeking support.

Coffee Break: Whether you work in or out of the home, take regular breaks throughout the course of your day to refresh yourself spiritually, mentally, and physically. A mother's work can be emotionally draining and physically demanding. Allow yourself regular intervals of rest throughout the day where you pause for prayer, quiet time, a bubble bath, a walk, a cup of coffee, or a chat with a friend.

Work Environment: If you are employed outside the home, do your best to choose a position with an employer who will share your family values and support your family commitment as your greatest priority. In today's troubled economic times, we may be unable to come

Avodah is the Hebrew word that means both "work" and "worship." The way in which *avodah* is used interchangeably throughout Genesis and Exodus reflects the very real understanding that God can be honored with our work. John Paul II understood this innate way in which work and worship were tied together when he wrote his encyclical, *Laborem Exercens.*

> Work is a good thing for man—a good thing for his humanity—because through work man not only transforms nature, adapting it to his own needs, but he also achieves fulfillment as a human being and indeed, in a sense, becomes "more a human being."

As Catholic women, we are often called to embrace ways in which our talents can benefit our family and our community. In doing this, we are practicing *avodah* in that our work is also a way in which we worship our Creator by using the gifts he has given us and by showing our obedience to his word.

We often believe, mistakenly, that witnessing refers only to the act by which we subtly, or not so subtly, bring our faith into our conversations. But *avodah* implies that working diligently, honestly, and with integrity, wherever that may be, is a way to worship—and witness as well.

Cheryl Dickow is the author of Renewing Your Christian Self in a Secular World *and* Elizabeth: A Holy Land Pilgrimage. *She is the associate editor of "Today's Catholic Woman,"* http://woman.catholicexchange.com.

A Word for the Working Girls

In *On the Dignity of Women,* John Paul II recalls these words from the Closing Statement of the Second Vatican Council:

> The hour is coming, in fact has come, when the vocation of women is being acknowledged in its fullness, the hour in which women acquire in the world an influence, an effect, and a power never hitherto achieved. That is why, at this moment when the human race is undergoing so deep a transformation, women imbued with a spirit of the Gospel can do so much to aid humanity in not falling.

The pope taught that in an increasingly technological—or "virtual"—age, women would be essential to safeguarding the meaning and dignity of the human person. The "feminine genius" for receiving God's love and revealing to others their true dignity is a spiritual motherhood to be exercised not only in the convent or in the home, but in the workplace as well, for those whose unique talents or concrete circumstances place them there. From the earliest days of the Church, wherever there have been souls who need Christ, there have been Christian women to witness to him. He calls us where he needs us, and where is there more need of witness than in the workplace today?

Rebecca Ryskind Teti is a wife, mother of four, and a contributing editor to Faith & Family *magazine.*

up with the dream position that enables us to "have it all." If required overtime, a difficult commute, or unreasonable work expectations have an impact on your ability to carry out your primary duty as mother, it may be time to reassess your employment situation. You might be surprised by the creative ways your family can change lifestyle habits like consuming, entertainment, and eating. There is a wealth of information available on how to simplify and spend less, sometimes making employment issues easier to tackle.

If you are employed full time within your own home, take pride in your work environment. Realizing that little ones may make house-keeping a challenge, living and working in a relatively clean home environment will help you ward off depression and frustration. Wake up every day with a plan, realizing that life's events may take you down a different path. Dress every day for your work. Leave the tele-vision and other distractions put away until your day's work has been faithfully executed. Take pride in your mothering profession as you would in any other career and give each day your fullest effort.

Living Our Dreams

Edith Stein, a Catholic convert and martyr who would later go on to be canonized St. Teresa Benedicta of the Cross by Pope John Paul II, firm-ly believed in the vocational calling of women to relationships, mother-hood, and professional lives, and once said, "One could say that in case of need, every normal and healthy woman is able to hold a position. And there is no profession which cannot be practiced by a woman."

In today's society, no woman should feel as though she cannot go on to live the life of her dreams. Our commitment to our lives as moth-ers may mean that for several years, we place our own personal goals and aspirations to the side as we care for our families. We may decline promotions, cut back on our hours, or leave the workforce altogether. These transitions can feel painful.

As a young mother, I often yearned for the corporate environment I had grown to love and for the professional friends I left behind. My little ones never said, "Wow Mom, you changed that diaper really well!" But today, as I watch them grow into young men all too quickly, I wouldn't trade a moment of the time I've spent working as a mom.

I also could never imagine when I left behind the world of busi-ness suits and briefcases that my life would take me along the path to such complete fulfillment. Offering each of my days as a prayer to God and opening my heart to his plans for my vocation have blessed me beyond my wildest imagination. When my children no longer live in my home or need my day-to-day hands-on care, my job as their mother will continue in new and exciting ways. There will also be time then for new dreams and aspirations, new goals and careers. I hope that each one of you will find the same joy and satisfaction in offering your life's work for a greater purpose and answering God's unique call for your life.

Finding Help

The following are possible sources for finding occasional babysitting support and assistance:

* Try a professional agency like SitterCity.com, which will help you in finding and interviewing suitable sitters.

* Network with friends to create a babysitting co-op where you swap services with one another.

* Locate local homeschooling families with responsible teenage students who may be available for daytime assignments.

* Post a notice in your parish bulletin or seek out members of your parish's youth group or young adult ministry who may be available to babysit.

* Hire a "mother's helper," an adolescent or early teenager who will assist you around the home under your supervision.

* Consider the possibility of bringing your children with you if the situation permits this, but always call in advance to discuss the logistics and to inform your host of the fact that you will be bringing your children. This will allow them to make baby-proofing arrangements if necessary.

Mom's Homework

✓ Meet on a monthly basis with your spouse, including your older children if appropriate, to create your family's mission statement and to assess your progress toward meeting your mission.

✓ Build a strong support system that will enable you time for needed breaks, self-care, and personal development.

✓ Take time every day to enjoy the little moments that make up our lives as mothers. Rock babies, read to toddlers, play Legos, and swing on the swing set as frequently as possible. Do not wish away the early years of childhood and the physical demands of parenting little ones. Believe it or not, some day you will miss these moments! Make the most of them now.

✓ Speak with your older children about your vocation. Let them know that you are doing your very best to raise them and that you expect their best in contributing to their own spirituality, family, and educational goals.

✓ Define your short- and long-term career goals, documenting them and creating a long-term strategy for achieving your goals.

Thank you, women who work! You are present and active in every area of life—social, economic, cultural, artistic and political. In this way you make an indispensable contribution to the growth of a culture which unites reason and feeling, to a model of life ever open to the sense of "mystery," to the establishment of economic and political structures ever more worthy of humanity.

Pope John Paul II

Web Resources

The Dignity of Women: http://dignityofwomen.com
Celebrating the 20th anniversary of Mulieris Dignitatem

Women for Faith and Family: www.wf-f.org
Affirmation for Catholic women

Catholic Professional and Business Clubs: www.cpbclubs.org
A national non-profit organization that allows Catholics in business to meet and network with other Catholics to enrich their business and spiritual lives

CHAPTER NINE

Beating the clock

Personal Productivity and Time Management

There is an appointed time for everything, and a time for every affair under the heavens.

—Ecclesiastes 3:1

My Story

A mother's efforts in the area of time management need to be flexible, because ultimately in serving our families and our God, things may not always go according to our to-do list or personal agenda. I can remember my early days as a mom, when accomplishing something as simple as taking a shower felt like a major effort. Nowadays, in my work out of my home office, I still juggle meetings, writing assignments, and interviews around the top priority in my life: my family.

Ironically, it sometimes feels as though my most thoroughly planned days are the ones that end up reworked to fit in an emergency orthodontist run or a trip to school to drop off a forgotten lunch. I have learned to be accepting of God's place in my plans and the need to listen to the quiet rumblings of his desires for my days. I have learned that sometimes simplification is in order and that self-imposed deadlines can be shifted within reason. Most importantly, I have learned that the most critical part of managing my time is creating the space I need every day to spend time in prayer and in the service of my family. Ultimately, if those two agenda items have been met with a happy heart, the rest is bound to fall into place in God's good time.

Why Our "First Fruits"?

Just as laborers in biblical times were called upon to tithe the first and best offerings of their harvests, we as Catholics are called to pay tribute to God in our lives each day by offering our efforts for his glory. I believe the most important reason to be concerned with the spending of our time is that it enables us to ensure that we spend time every day in prayer and service. In his wonderful book *Time Management for Catholics*, productivity expert Dave Durand delineates the clear differences between secular time management tactics and what he refers to as "Catholic Time Management." Among the many important distinctions are the following characteristics of the Catholic variety.

* It helps you accomplish God's will.

* It maximizes our potential for God's glory.

* Good time management is ordered toward eternal life.

Our most important goal in life as Catholic moms is to have a relationship with God that will lead us and our families toward an eternity spent with him. With planning and effort, we can order our days in such a way that we are able to commune with God in prayer, even if that prayer is sprinkled throughout the course of our daily work.

I have learned in my own life that it's not good enough to leave finding time for prayer up to chance. I may have the best intentions for finding quiet meditative time and somehow an entire week can slip by without a moment ever spent in fruitful conversation with God. I also know that God certainly doesn't intend that we moms neglect our families in order to spend hours on our knees in a chapel every day.

> Oh, how precious time is! Blessed are those who know how to make good use of it. Oh, if only all could understand how precious time is, undoubtedly everyone would do his best to spend it in a praiseworthy manner!
>
> —St. Padre Pio

My good friend Marlene often uses the phrase, "She's so heavenly-minded that she's no earthly good" to describe those "church ladies" we all know who spend so much time in committees and at church that they neglect their own homes and families. Yes, God wants us to be at work in spreading his good news. He placed us in our homes and work environments to do his work here on earth and to spread our love for him through the love we share with our families, friends, and co-workers. When we give him and those we love the best of ourselves, we offer our own unique first fruits.

Take a Time Inventory

Before we launch into the work of systematically organizing our time, it is good to take stock of our current status to determine where we succeed and fall short in making the most of the gift of time.

I have a tendency to be a "yes" person. I take on more and more tasks, because of the challenge and opportunity they provide, without stopping to look at what will give to make room for new duties. I did this last year to the point where I ultimately had to call a halt for a week and take my own "time inventory." At the beginning of that week, I cleared my calendar of all but my basic familial and work-related responsibilities. Notebook in hand, I went through the week documenting the way in which my days were spent, noting even minute time expenditures. At the end of the week, I was shocked by the results—even during the most basic of weeks my days had been packed to the gills. I'd let things go undone, I felt exhausted and overwhelmed, and my spiritual life had been largely neglected.

Following the inventory week, I spent time reordering some priorities. First and foremost, I looked at how I could build quiet prayer time into each day of the week and put that at the top of my priority list. I've found that when I am the most stressed I tend to neglect a few crucial things—prayer, healthful eating, and exercise. Perhaps you face a similar irony in your own life. These self-care activities may seem on the surface to be selfish uses of our time, so we neglect them hoping to fully devote ourselves to family and work. I know in my head that these factors unite to leave me feeling at my best, but when times are busy these tend to be the things I let go of first. Try making the effort to conduct your own time inventory. It can help you obtain a better picture of your own productivity.

A Mom's Brand of Personal Productivity

These days, the phrase "personal productivity" functions like one of those hated buzzwords associated with corporate America. But I'd contend that today's moms are among the most productive individuals in our country. We feed, shelter, educate, nurse, comfort, challenge, and entertain this country's future leaders. We manage budgets, transport the masses, eradicate germs, and keep track of countless other duties. My children tease me about the number of times each day I say the words, "Have you brushed your teeth?" I tell them that some day they will thank me—that will be about the time I'm happily only worrying about my own teeth!

Your own brand of personal productivity will vary depending upon your unique set of life circumstances. I ask you to work your way through the following questions, taking time to truly reflect upon what it means to you to be a productive steward of the time God has given you each day:

1. When, during the course of your day, do you spend time talking with God in prayer or in other spiritual matters?

2. What are your own goals for how you want and need to spend your time each day?

3. What are your priorities in life today and long term?

4. Do you feel a balance in your life between your work, your service to your family, your other relationships, your care of your physical body, and your spiritual life?

5. Do you have the ability to simplify your load, freeing up any responsibilities you have taken on to make more time for existing priorities?

Tools of the Trade

If you take a trip to any bookstore or discount store, you will find aisles overflowing with tools to help you organize your time and your home. Recently, I was watching a morning show and heard an author discussing her latest, greatest book for dealing with home clutter. I was at my keyboard within minutes flat, preparing to "buy now" when the irony struck me—the worst clutter in my home can be found in my home office, where stacks of books sent to me for review line the floor, waiting their turn for consideration. Was buying another book really going to help me deal with my organizational issues? No book was purchased and I spent a few moments perusing the author's website and then followed her suggested advice and spent some time looking around my home for items, including books, that could be donated to a local nonprofit.

I share this story to warn you that no single calendar, book, or piece of software is going to be the perfect system for every mom. Hopefully by now you have spent time inventorying your own situation and know what type of system best works for you. In some situations, a combination of a few of the following may be just what the doctor ordered.

Paper Calendars: We find them deeply discounted every year, just days after the New Year begins, but many of us still favor the use of paper calendars. A month-at-a-glance calendar, prominently displayed in a common area of your home, can keep your family abreast of upcoming events, appointments, and holidays. My favorite paper calendar every year is the Catholic liturgical calendar provided by a local Catholic mortuary—it lists daily feasts and other important Catholic dates and events and helps me more fully live out the liturgical year.

To do Lists: Whether your to do list is on a piece of paper or on a computer, the key to productive use of your time is consistency. Devise a system of documenting the tasks that need your attention, crossing off completed tasks and updating your list as new tasks arise. Rather than having a variety of lists, adopt a to-do list tool that is constantly with you. When you find yourself with the gift of a few moments of spare time, pull out your list and attend to an item that can be done quickly, such as a phone call or returning an e-mail. Divide your list into short-term projects that can be completed quickly and long-term projects that may involve multiple steps to complete. Many time-management experts recommend breaking long-term projects into multiple short-term action items. Chipping away at the individual steps toward a goal may feel less overwhelming and will likely assist you in not procrastinating on big-ticket projects.

> *Time given to Christ is never time lost, but is rather time gained, so that our relationships and indeed our whole life may become more profoundly human.*
> —Pope John Paul II

Planners: Many companies have evolved the art of the planner, leaving lots of options from day-at-a-glance, week-at-a-glance, or month-at-a-glance views to planners specifically created for mothers. Consider purchasing a planner and customizing it to meet your own needs. The goal of any planner should be that it captures all of the information you will need in one place so that you do not need any additional resources to stay organized. Include a spiritual reference/journal section in your planner to prioritize spending time each day for prayer and devotion.

PDAs and Smartphones: Being a geek, I have learned that my most effective productivity tool is my telephone, which is in fact a computer as well. Personal digital assistants (PDAs) and today's cellular phones contain features from integrated calendars to advanced task-management tools. However, prior to spending a great deal of money on a digital device or an expensive data plan for your telephone, assess your own likeliness to use one of these to its fullest capacity.

St. Alphonsus Liguori once said, "There's no peace outside of God's will." Despite many attempts at effective time management, nothing worked for me until I decided the important factor was God's intent for me, not what I wanted to accomplish. My true productivity has been found in discerning the responsibilities of my vocational call, and acting in fidelity. By doing so, God gives me the strength to get up in the morning with joy, the grace to fulfill my busy family schedule with stream-lined consistency, and grants peace to my day. He ensures that I don't work too hard, nor play too much, but have a proper balance of prayer, personal, husband, and family time in a basically tidy home. In our task-oriented society, it's important to keep a humane view of personal productivity. We are not called to perfectionism or schedule overload. We are called to account for all of our human and personal needs, from daily quiet prayer times where we refresh, to the bubble bath getaway, to the couch-cuddle with hubby, to the bedtime story with the children. These are the heart of a mother's productive time management, because the heart of our call is love.

Holly Pierlot is the author of *A Mother's Rule of Life: How to Bring Order to Your Home and Peace to Your Soul.* Visit her online at www .mothersruleoflife.com.

Don't spend the money if this is going to become just another unused gadget around your home.

Online Calendars and Task Management Software: I use a free online calendar program (Google Calendar) that works together with my cell phone to keep me on top of my agenda and to-do list. I have my calendar set to send me e-mail reminders of upcoming events. I use task-management software that enables me to record a voice note and direct it to either my calendar, my to-do list, or a colleague as an e-mail.

Getting Your Family on Board

We moms are team members, along with our husbands and children. So in this discussion of time management, once we've made our own personal commitment to change, we need to obtain buy-in from the rest of our team. First of all, we need to communicate our goals to our families. If we want them to accept that we are serious about change and growth, we must first convince ourselves that we are ready to take these steps. Kids and husbands can be our best friends or our worst enemies in making substantive change in our lives.

When we involve our children in our own time-management and productivity efforts, we teach them tools that will last them a lifetime. I am often very bad about delegating household chores, since sometimes it feels easier to just do things myself around the house. But I have learned that my teenage sons love to cook. Involving them in meal planning and even allowing them to walk to our local market to purchase items for dinner has made my afternoons much more enjoyable. I'm not certain how a mother who hates cooking has raised two budding gourmet chefs, but I'm happy to delegate one or two weekly dinners to their culinary expertise! How can you involve your children in your success?

* Look at the list of household tasks that you developed in your time inventory. Divide tasks into a schedule and involve children in taking on one or two daily tasks that are age appropriate.

* Post a family calendar in a common area of your home such as the kitchen and encourage your children to make regular updates to the calendar and to check it regularly as well.

* Help your children look at their own tasks in terms of long- and short-term goals. How many items on your to-do list relate to children's homework or activities? Help teach them time-management skills by encouraging them to break large assignments into individual tasks—for example, break "Science Fair Project" into manageable segments and assign intermediary time goals.

Patron Saints of Productivity?

When I struggle with areas of difficulty in my life, it helps me to turn to the intercession of specific members of the communion of saints for their help and guidance. However, when it comes to time management, I've yet to find a definitive answer to the question, "Who is the patron saint of productivity?"

A recent informal polling of my online friends left me with a few contenders for this coveted role. St. Eligius and St. Peter received nods for their roles as patron saints of clockmakers, which left me pondering the importance of good scheduling and the virtue of timeliness. St. Padre Pio was mentioned in jest by a few friends who perhaps coveted his ability to bi-locate—yes, that would certainly be a handy trait for Catholic moms needing to be in several places at one time! St. Augustine was suggested for his work ethic and his ability to multitask by dictating to three secretaries at one time.

My personal favorite for the title "Patron Saint of Productivity" was nominated by many of the Catholic mom respondents to my poll. St. Gianna Beretta Molla was a wife and mother of three, as well as a pediatrician. The Vatican website says of St. Gianna, "With simplicity and equilibrium she harmonized the demands of mother, wife, doctor, and her passion for life." When I am feeling overwhelmed by life's demands and am concerned that my best is never good enough, it helps me to invoke the example of St. Gianna, who once said, "The secret of happiness is to live moment by moment and to thank God for all that he, in his goodness, sends to us day after day." I ask for the intercession of this selfless saint in helping me to serve my family and those around me each day with a loving heart.

With time-management systems in place, my to-do list always at the ready, and short- and long-term goals for each day, I wake up every morning happy and looking forward to spending the gift of time God gives me each day to do his will and to walk a few babysteps closer to him in the process.

Mom's Homework

- ✓ Take a week to conduct your own time inventory, documenting the way you spend your days. Be honest and spend time afterward analyzing and learning from your results.

- ✓ Adopt a time-management master plan. Determine which type of system, calendar, and task-management tools work best for you. Invest in your system, tweaking it to meet your own needs.

- ✓ Carry your calendar and to-do list with you at all times. Look for opportunities to accomplish small tasks with free moments. Build chunks of time into your weekly schedule to plan and carry out tasks toward accomplishing long-term goals.

- ✓ Meet with your family to discuss family time management. Create a family calendar and post it in a common area. Use this tool as a family and update it regularly with your children.

✓ Look for tasks to delegate to your children and communicate with them about their own time-management goals and objectives. Capitalize upon your children's unique gifts and abilities to make your home run more productively and happily.

Web Resources

The Daily Saint: http://thedailysaint.com
The Daily Saint Productivity Blog looks at time-management issues and spirituality at work

A Mother's Rule of Life: www.mothersruleoflife.com
Bring order into your home and peace to your soul

Dave Durand: http://davedurand.com
Catholic time-management consultant and productivity coach

CHAPTER TEN

The Family banker

Family Finances, Financial Planning, Identity-Theft Protection, and Stewardship

Do not store up for yourselves treasures on earth, where moth and decay destroy, and thieves break in and steal. But store up treasures in heaven, where neither moth nor decay destroys, nor thieves break in and steal. For where your treasure is, there also will your heart be.

—Matthew 6:19-21

My Story

In September of 1991, with my promotion to the job title of "mom," I also took on the duties of chief financial officer (CFO) for our little family. Prior to this date, I will admit that my checkbook register was largely the domain of either my father or my husband. But when we decided to cut our income in half so that I could stay at home with Eric, I felt the compulsion to have a better sense of how and where we were spending our money. To be completely honest, the CFO is a role I don't enjoy. At best, it is tedious and at worst it can be treacherous.

In the early days, when our finances were relatively simple, our monthly list of expenditures could be counted on ten fingers. I still have a budget Greg and I wrote out together when we were newlyweds—it is written on the back of a business card! In those early days, we survived contentedly on my sub-$6 per hour salary and were deliriously happy. As our family grew and my husband moved from medical school to residency and then a "real job," our income steadily rose as we were blessed abundantly. I've always found it disconcerting that as our income grew, our expenditures did as well. In our home, the division of labor has evolved so that Greg now handles long-term financial issues such as mortgages, investments, and the dreaded annual taxes. It's still my job to pay the bills and to ensure that we are saving and acting as good stewards of the gifts God has showered upon us, along with teaching our children to handle money responsibly. Someday, I hope to retire my CFO position, but for now I embrace this responsibility as yet another way to love and serve my family.

Family Finances

Most of the moms I've surveyed share my CFO title as the primary bill payers in their homes. If you are not responsible for paying monthly bills, you still have a role to play in the responsible handling of your family's finances. If you have not already done so, meet with your spouse soon to discuss an equitable and efficient division of labor when it comes to the handling of family finances. If you take on the role of paying bills, be sure to give yourself fully to this weighty responsibility. Just as you wouldn't risk your children's physical safety, you will want to safeguard them emotionally and financially by being a good steward of your family's resources.

With your partner, determine who will handle each of the following financial duties:

* day-to-day bill paying
* creation and monitoring of a family budget
* banking and account reconciliation
* retirement investments
* mortgages
* taxes
* college savings
* insurance issues
* credit report issues
* creating and maintaining a will

Having a solid system for organizing your family finances will be critical to your success. Create a "bill paying center" in your home and keep it fully stocked with all of the supplies you will need, including file folders, envelopes, return address labels, and postage stamps. Create and maintain a filing system to organize finance-related papers. Many moms have found that online banking can streamline and greatly increase the efficiency of bill paying. If you are not already banking online, speak with your bank about online services and determine if this system will work for your family. I love online banking for the decrease of paper clutter, the ability to schedule and track payments, and the ease and accuracy of nearly instantaneous updating of my accounts. If you bank online, read carefully about your financial institution's security system and about the safeguarding of your personal and financial data.

> Let us more and more insist on raising funds of love, of kindness, of understanding, of peace. Money will come if we seek first the Kingdom of God—the rest will be given.
>
> —Blessed Mother Teresa

Your job as family finance manager is not a once-per-month responsibility. Throughout the course of every month, you can help your family to prosper financially by taking a proactive approach to your family's economic situation. Moms can and should take a few simple steps each month to keep on top of things. Keep a master calendar of your payment cycles for basic bills. Look to group bills together and periodically reassess the services for which you are paying. For example, can you save money on car insurance by grouping it with your homeowners' insurance provider?

It is also part of our mom "job description" to help create and carefully monitor our families' budgets and expenditures. Consider how you can economize on recurring expenses such as food and clothing. Carefully and continually assess your expenditures with an eye toward maximizing your budget. If the newspaper is sitting on the counter unread most days of the week, suspend your subscription and read the news online. Carefully plan your meal planning and grocery shopping around what is on sale, in season, or available in less-expensive bulk quantities. Look for other simple ways to be fiscally prudent.

Many moms fall into the dangerous trap of consumerism. We justify our overly materialistic ways by stating that we simply want the best for our families. Do our children really need every new toy or brand-new clothes for every season? Many couples benefit from having an agreed-upon spending limit and not exceeding that limit without first consulting with one another. If you find yourself in a pattern of overspending, limit your elective shopping trips. Do not shop without a prewritten list and stick to only purchasing items on your list.

Prior to making impulse purchases, ask yourself what item you are replacing with your purchase—if you are purchasing something merely to have "more" or "better" put the item back on the shelf and wait one week prior to buying it. I have made a rule for myself that I do not buy new clothing without removing something from my closet and donating it to charity. When I think I want a new shirt, for example, I must stop and ask myself, "What shirt am I going to donate in place of this new one?" More often than not, I stop myself from spending needlessly and adding to the existing pile of clutter in my closet. Consider learning to live within your means one of your greatest priorities and work every day to make it a reality in your life.

There are many tools available to help you in your day-to-day financial responsibilities. Books, financial seminars, radio programs, and websites related to personal finance topics are plentiful. My favorite resource for considering money management from a Catholic perspective is the book *7 Steps to Becoming Financially Free: A Catholic*

A Letter to Mothers

Mom. Think about it for a moment. That one word conveys so many images: heart, homemaker, healer, cook, teacher, banker, patience, dependable, taxi driver, glue-that-holds-things-together, and of course love. Those are just a few of the thoughts that come to mind about my mom, as well as my wife Chelsey, the mother of our seven children.

To be a good mom—the mom God wants you to be—you'll have to stretch yourself. You'll be asked to develop and use talents—some of which you didn't even know you had. One of those talents is managing the resources the Lord has entrusted to you so that you can fulfill your family responsibilities well.

But you're not alone. Did you know that there are hundreds of references to money and possessions in the Bible, and that the Lord used money and possessions in about half of his parables? These references paint a mosaic for what our attitude toward money should be and how we can manage it effectively.

Godly principles include generosity, temperance, industriousness, planning, a cautious attitude toward debt, saving, unity within marriage, and developing priorities for the long run.

Many fail to apply these principles in their lives, with the result being financial chaos and tension in the home. But it need not be that way. I encourage you to take the time to learn, reflect on, and apply God's principles for managing money in your home. By doing so, you'll be on the road to *true* financial freedom and reach the peace that comes with it. God love you!

Phil Lenahan is the author of 7 Steps to Becoming Financially Free: A Catholic Guide to Managing Your Money. *Visit him at www.veritasfinancial ministries.com.*

Guide to Managing Your Money by Phil Lenahan. Phil's system and his accompanying workbook can help you and your spouse develop a fiscal plan that is both financially sound and in line with God's ultimate plan for your life. Many parishes and dioceses around the country offer small group ministries for Catholic families working through Phil Lenahan's program.

If you are struggling in your responsibilities as family CFO, speak honestly with your husband about your anxieties and get some help. Your local Catholic Charities organization may be able to assist in times of financial crisis. They may also offer programs devised to help individuals with the management of their monthly financial resources. In an age of spiraling debt and out-of-control spending, maintaining control of your family's finances can be a critical component of your mental and spiritual well-being.

Long-term Financial Planning

I am by no means a financial expert, so I would never presume to give you advice on the topic. But I do know that we moms sometimes neglect to pay attention to critical long-term financial planning measures. In conversation with your spouse and in partnership with trusted advisors, please ensure that you have accounted for the following long-term components of your family financial plan:

* Last Will and Testament
* Insurance: Life, health, disability, automobile, homeowners/renters
* Retirement planning
* College savings
* Emergency funds

Regardless of your family's income level, these are basic items that should be addressed from the very earliest years of your marriage. We assume that we will always be young and healthy, but disaster, health considerations, or disability can strike when we least expect them. If you are uncertain how to proceed in tackling these long-term financial planning measures, consider purchasing Phil Lenahan's system or inquire at your parish about other financially related family ministry opportunities in your diocese.

Identity Theft

In May 2007, I fell victim to identity theft, a crime that is plaguing our country as we move more of our economy onto the Internet. As surely as if he had walked into a home and stolen our family's valuables, the thief who preyed upon me took away my personal security along with my property. An estimated ten million Americans per year fall victim to identity theft, with less than half of all victims discovering the theft in less than three months after it has occurred.

In my case, the criminal who victimized me somehow obtained my social security number and enough other personal information to open multiple credit cards in my name. One day, I received a suspicious telephone message from a creditor I did not recognize, asking me to contact them. Ignoring this red flag as a "wrong number," I did not return the call. Approximately two weeks later, I received a credit card bill in the mail from a major retailer stating that I owed several thousand dollars on a new account. When I called the customer service number to dispute the bill, it was determined that my identity had likely been compromised. Within hours, I learned that several other credit cards had also been opened in my name and that tens of thousands of dollars had been spent on these cards. I spent the next two months untangling the mess, filing police reports, contacting creditors, and repairing my good credit.

In the process, I learned some very important lessons that I vowed to share with other mothers to perhaps help you avoid heartache, stress, and financial impact. The first lesson I learned and the one I most want to share with you is that I could have saved myself a lot of pain and suffering by carefully monitoring my credit. I assumed that since I was not the breadwinner of my family and since I carefully guarded my personal information, I was not at risk. The fact of the matter is that we are all at risk for this crime, including our children. Even if your wallet or purse is not stolen, your identity can be prey to fraud and you are at risk.

To protect yourself and your family:

✳ Educate yourself on the topic of identity theft immediately.

✳ Check your credit reports from the three major bureaus at least once per year. Obtain one free credit report annually at 877-322-8228 or www.annualcreditreport.com.

✳ Consider purchasing a credit monitoring service through one of the three major credit bureaus, your bank, or other private providers.

✳ Use a locked mailbox, shred all documents prior to disposing of them, and send all mail from indoor U.S. Postal Service mailboxes whenever possible.

* Use only secure and encrypted websites for online purchases.

* Limit the number of credit cards you carry and never carry your Social Security card with you.

* Document every credit card and piece of personal identification you use, including account numbers and contact numbers to report loss or theft.

If you are victimized by identity theft, you need to act immediately to protect yourself and your family. You should immediately contact your local police and file a police report, since this will be essential to recovering or preventing any financial damages. Next, contact the three major credit bureaus:

* Equifax: 800-525-6285

* Experian: 888-397-3742

* TransUnion: 800-680-7289

Christians long for the entire human family to call upon God as "Our Father!" In union with the only begotten Son, may all people learn to pray to the Father and to ask him, in the words that Jesus himself taught us, for the grace to glorify him by living according to his will, to receive the daily bread that we need, to be understanding and generous towards our debtors, not to be tempted beyond our limits, and to be delivered from evil.

—Pope Benedict XVI

Additional and immediate calls should be made to your bank, each of your existing creditors, the Social Security Administration, the U.S. Postal Service, the Internal Revenue Service, and the Federal Trade Commission. Methodically document each and every telephone call you make to these agencies and to the creditors in the event of unauthorized charges in your name. Learn your rights and protections under the law, as well as the limits for which you can be held personally responsible.

Stewardship—Passing It On

Moving from a slightly negative topic to a much more positive one, let us talk about how our role as our families' CFOs can bring us and our families closer to God. Along with providing for our shelter and needs, our income enables us to act as stewards of the gifts God has given us. As Catholics, we must always be cognizant of Christ's call to love one another and to care for those in need. If we carefully manage our own finances, we will be better able to respond to that call.

The United States Conference of Catholic Bishops has stated in *Stewardship and Young Adults* that Catholic stewardship comprises four elements:

> Receiving the gifts of God with gratitude
> Cultivating them responsibly
> Sharing them lovingly in justice with others
> Standing before the Lord in a spirit of accountability

As Catholics, we are not necessarily called to "tithe" a fixed percent of our income, but rather to give according to our means. You and your spouse need to be in control of your family finances, therefore, to make responsible decisions about stewardship and charitable gifts. Our gifts of time, talent, and treasure should contribute to the building up of our Church and to assisting in the corporal works of mercy:

1. Feed the hungry
2. Give drink to the thirsty
3. Clothe the naked
4. Shelter the homeless
5. Visit the sick
6. Visit those in prison
7. Bury the dead

It is also our duty as moms to pass along to our children the true joy of stewardship and service to others. Challenge your children from an early age to look at their gifts from God and to handle them responsibly. Financially, you may want to assist your child in establishing a plan for saving and setting up a bank account. Talk as a family about spending, saving, and stewardship. Even from a very young age, we can help our children understand that helping others is a blessing.

Many parishes and schools offer opportunities for giving. Your child can purchase a can of soup to be donated to a local food shelter. She will enjoy donating gently used clothing and toys to those less fortunate. Speak with her about ways to give of her time as well, either in your parish or your community, and be on the lookout for stewardship opportunities for your entire family.

Mom's Homework

✓ Take the next month to draft a family budget, tracking income and expenditures and projecting the next twelve months in your household.

✓ Meet with your spouse to begin discussing your long-term financial plans.

✓ Inquire about the existence of a *7 Steps to Becoming Financially Free* small group study in your parish. If none exists, consider undergoing leadership training and starting this ministry in your community.

✓ Check your annual credit report and take the steps necessary to ensure that your identity is protected.

✓ Help your children identify and commit to a local stewardship project. Choose a family charity and establish a plan for giving time, talent, and treasure to help the organization you select.

Web Resources

Veritas Financial Ministries: www.veritasfinancialministries.com/index.asp
Small group financial freedom studies by Phil Lenahan

Federal Trade Commission Fighting Back Against Identity Theft: www.ftc.gov/bcp/edu/microsites/idtheft
Learn more about protecting yourself from identity theft or what to do if your information has been stolen

Catholic Charities USA: www.catholiccharitiesusa.org
Get help or get involved in your local community

CHAPTER ELEVEN

Weaving Your Way through the web

Using Today's Internet Technology in an Emotionally Healthy Fashion

Beloved, do not trust every spirit but test the spirits to see whether they belong to God, because many false prophets have gone out into the world. This is how you can know the Spirit of God: every spirit that acknowledges Jesus Christ come in the flesh belongs to God, and every spirit that does not acknowledge Jesus does not belong to God.

—1 John 4:1-3

My Story

The note in the principal's weekly school newsletter in the autumn of 1999 held a simple request "Parent needed to coordinate new school website. Training provided. Flexible way to earn your required parent volunteer hours."

At that point in my life, the totality of my computer skill was the ability to check my e-mail on AOL, word processing, and the design of an occasional birthday card. I'm not sure what I was thinking when I marched into the principal's office the next day and volunteered my services. Inspired by the opportunity to learn something new and to contribute in a unique way to our school community, I walked blindly into a volunteer gig that would eventually come to define my life and greatly impact my spirituality.

With Eric in third grade and Adam starting morning kindergarten, I felt my life at a turning point. For the past nine years, I'd had a child in the home with me for most of the day and thoughts of employment had been on the back burner. But with Adam's entry into school, I began to think about ways in which my newfound spare time might be used to serve others. By taking on the school website, I acquired a new skill set.

A few months and several "dummies" books later, I had a brainstorm. Since at that time Greg had not yet joined the Catholic Church, I felt a great responsibility as a mother to pass along my Catholic faith to my sons. I saw the Internet as a wonderful forum to connect with and learn from other mothers who faced the same challenges I was feeling. In November 1999, with little knowledge and a lot of prayer, I registered the domain name CatholicMom.com and took the plunge into the World Wide Web.

Brave New World

Since it became readily available to the public in the early 1990s, the Internet has changed our world. In today's parenting environment, "to Google" is a verb and "mommy blogger" is an in-vogue occupation.

When my children were young, I met other mothers on the playground and exchanged phone numbers on pages torn from coloring books in hopes of setting up playdates. Today's moms can visit websites that connect them instantaneously with like-minded families in their own communities both virtually and in person. The end goal is the same—to connect them with others in hopes of learning the ropes of parenting. Those hours I spent talking about (or sometimes even crying about) breastfeeding, potty training, and "sharing" while pushing my babies in a swing at the park are now replicated by today's young moms all over the Internet.

I see the tremendous value in the nurturing role of the Internet for today's moms. At our fingertips, we have a power-packed toolbox that is part encyclopedia, part scrapbook, and part playgroup. However, just as learning to use power tools requires training and safety measures, a mom's use of the Web requires forethought and precautions.

Mom's Encyclopedia

The power of the Internet as an information source is unparalleled. I'm a huge fan of libraries, making weekly trips with my sons. But when I really need to find information quickly, I turn to the Web. A world of information is at our disposal, making finding anything from childhood symptoms to tips for teen driving easy and accessible. Along with searching traditional websites, today's new "Web 2.0" technology gives moms greater creative power. Simply defined, Web 2.0 means using the Internet not only as a consumer of information, but also as a part of a community of users who actually interact with and enhance the flow of information. Wikipedia describes it this way:

> Web 2.0 is a term describing the trend in the use of World Wide Web technology and Web design that aims to enhance creativity, information sharing, and, most notably, collaboration among users. These concepts have led to the development and evolution of Web-based communities and hosted services, such as social-networking sites, wikis, blogs, and folksonomies.

Here are some of my favorite Web 2.0 applications for moms.

Blogs: Moving beyond static webpages, blogs allow moms to not only garner needed information, but also to engage in follow-up conversations and to have additional questions answered. A quick Google search for the term "mom blog" yielded over eight million results. Now certainly not every one of these blogs will contain useful and relevant information, but the chances of finding one that does are relatively high. When I find a blog I love, I always subscribe to its "RSS Feed." This is a free subscription service that enables me to be notified every time the blog owner updates her site. Using the free Google Reader application (www.google.com/reader), all of my blog subscriptions are delivered to me in one place. I can read them at my own convenience and make a follow-up visit directly to the blog if I care to comment or request additional information on the topic being discussed.

Wikis: A "wiki" is a collection of Web pages that allows end users to contribute easily to a growing font of information. Wiki articles tend to be concise, easy to read and interactive, containing numerous links to relevant information. The most famous wiki is undoubtedly Wikipedia.com, a massive conglomeration of facts and fiction. Discerning moms know to exercise caution when using wiki information, which is not always accurate but can be a great jumping-off point for research.

It is clear, then, that while the Internet can never replace that profound experience of God which only the living, liturgical and sacramental life of the Church can offer, it can certainly provide a unique supplement and support in both preparing for the encounter with Christ in community, and sustaining the new believer in the journey of faith which then begins.

—Pope John Paul II

Podcasts: The term "podcast," coined in 2004, refers to digital files—either audio or video—that are available on demand via the Internet and can be subscribed to freely. Think "talk radio" but with a twist. Most podcasters are people like you and me who have a passion for something and want to speak about it with others. The thing that makes podcasts so wonderful for moms is that we can listen to or view them at our own convenience. An MP3 player is not required, but certainly makes listening even more pleasurable. I am a notoriously bad housekeeper, but with my iPod and a stock of good Catholic podcasts, I'm happy to spend a few hours cleaning boys' bathrooms and folding laundry. While I toil, I can listen to parenting shows, reflections on the upcoming Sunday's readings, tour Rome with a Dutch priest, or even learn a new language. I love podcasting so much that I've picked up my own microphone and joined the fray with my own weekly Catholic faith and family talk show. Check it out at www.catholicmoments.com.

We all need to find a silent moment, a place to center ourselves, a time to rejuvenate and renew our spirits. I have been actively listening for God's word in my life and find myself called to support other moms as they seek out the face of Christ and the presence of God in their children, spouses, and everyday lives.

Through the extraordinary knowledge and support of my brother I now have an active blog. Faithfilledmom.com has given me a voice to share my message with all moms: in the chaos, stress, and imbalance of our lives God remains with us. We are not alone; there is support, friendship, and inspiration if we seek it. Within my soul a fire burns to write the words that can draw the world closer to God. In this modern world the Internet is the tool through which I can reach so many moms who are searching.

The journey of becoming a blogger has deepened my faith. It is my outlet, my peace of mind, and my remedy for the stress of the everyday grind. I click on my website, choose one of my pictures, and set my fingers free—to open my soul, to speak my faith, and to give my love to the people who visit my site. I connect with them through the vast venue of the Internet, and through a simple website and daily blog. But I am still merely one mom—two hands, ten fingers—spreading God's love upon the screen and into the hearts of those who visit and choose to start the search.

Lori Hadorn-Disselkamp is a stay-at-home mom of four and a blissfully married writer who blogs at www.faithfilledmom.com.

Video Sharing: The mother of all video-sharing websites, YouTube, was created in February 2005. Video-sharing sites allow users to freely upload, share, download, and comment upon user-created videos. Much of what is found on sites like YouTube is a complete waste of time, but there are also incredible riches to be mined through these services. Many traditional media outlets are observing the public's consumption patterns and making their content available on video-sharing sites and through their own sites on an on-demand basis. Catholic moms will find a wealth of faith and family resources online, including shows for themselves and their children. Family-friendly and Catholic video-sharing sites such as Catholic-tube.com offer safe, pre-screened video selections.

Mom's Scrapbook

When my children were younger, I went through a big scrapbooking phase. For two years, I gathered with friends in quilting-bee-type fashion, creating lovely pages that highlighted my family's events and vacations. However, I'm not a very crafty person and I soon grew overwhelmed by the task. I found myself taking pictures with an eye toward where they would fit on a scrapbook page rather than treasuring the memory they captured. I quit scrapbooking and turned to digital photography, which more nearly suits my geeky ways.

The Internet offers countless ways to capture and chronicle their family's history and high jinks. My scrapbook of choice is now my blog at CatholicMom.com. Since mid-2005, I have written about our travels, the boys' activities, and my own personal reactions to family life. At times, my blog is very personal, recounting the trials and tribulations of life as a Catholic mom. At other times, I aim for more of an information-flow-type approach. The beauty of the blog is that I'm author, editor, and consumer of my own work. Sometimes I look back on past entries and am overcome with the power of precious memories. Free blog editing and hosting sites enable you to become a mom blogger overnight. You choose how much you want to write and what you want to disclose to your audience. You can choose to write only for family and friends by choosing a password-protected blogging service or show off your family blog to the world.

The Internet provides other great tools for the family historian. Digital-photo-sharing sites such as Flickr and Picassa offer free storage for your family photos and the ability to share them either with trusted family and friends or on a worldwide basis—you decide. By using tags and keywords and creating albums, you can readily organize and easily access photographs. With a Flickr account, your own blog, and a camera phone, you can take a photo on the fly and instantly post it to your blog or photostream to capture that special moment. Imagine watching your toddler take her first steps at the playground and posting the image to your blog within sixty seconds for Dad and proud grandparents to enjoy immediately.

With video-sharing sites, you can satisfy your inner movie producer by creating and sharing family videos. I remember as a child being fascinated by our old family movies and slides—we would drag out pillows and blankets and plop down on the living room floor. My mom and dad would screen their 8mm film of us hunting Easter eggs

Science and technology are precious resources when placed at the service of man and promote his integral development for the benefit of all. By themselves however they cannot disclose the meaning of existence and of human progress. Science and technology are ordered to man, from whom they take their origin and development; hence they find in the person and in his moral values both evidence of their purpose and awareness of their limits.

—Catechism of the Catholic Church, 2293

or learning to water ski and we'd all laugh at those silent depictions of ourselves and beg to watch them over and over. I remember this when I capture my own sons playing music on video. They may express a certain hesitancy at being filmed, but they love watching themselves on YouTube and reading family comments about their performances. Numerous free video-sharing sites are available, each with different features and built-in security measures.

Mom's Social Circle

I've recently been reading *The Story of a Family: The Home of St. Thérèse of Lisieux*, a book regarding the family of my favorite Doctor of the Church, and particularly about her wonderful parents. What strikes me about the book is the number of letters exchanged between Thérèse's mother, Zélie-Marie Guérin Martin, and her siblings. Through letters detailing the day-to-day routines of the Martin home, we come to a more complete understanding of the upbringing of this remarkable saint. I regret that our current society no longer values the exchange of handwritten correspondence and that my own children will not find a trail of letters exchanged between their aunts and me when I am gone.

In many ways, however, I am in much closer contact with my family than was Mme. Martin. I speak with my parents and siblings several times per week using a very affordable Voice over Internet Protocol (VoIP) broadband phone connection. We swap e-mails and instant messages to share important thoughts throughout the day. Families can videoconference over the computer, allowing users on either end to connect visually. Free VoIP technology such as Skype has come in handy for parents deployed overseas, who can even read bed time stories to their children over the Internet.

Moms today can nurture themselves and one another through responsible use of "social networking" sites. Through sites such as Facebook or the Catholic site 4Marks.com, moms can befriend women of like-minded interests, swap ideas, share prayer requests, and be of loving support to one another. At Twitter.com, a vibrant Catholic community shares their daily faith journeys with a word limit of 140 characters per post. Using these small blurbs, they make prayer requests, recommend books or websites, share stories, and grow as a faith community. It's not unusual for me to pray three or four times a day with my Twitter friends and followers for requested intentions. I find these types of social networking sites to be a modern-day equivalent of the work the early Christians undertook in spreading the Gospel to the masses. Used responsibly, faithfully, and with compassion, social networking sites offer us the opportunity to respond to Jesus' great commission that each of us work to spread his teachings to all the nations of the world. Moms like me have the potential to connect worldwide and to share and nurture our beliefs beyond the four walls of our homes.

Avoid Getting Tangled in the Web

Many moms, especially those who may not work outside the home, view some of these new Internet technologies with caution and trepidation. They may feel overwhelmed by the jargon or are skeptical because they've heard of social networking gone awry. Such concerns are valid, and certainly these types of Internet tools are not for everyone. For those with limited computer access or experience, most public libraries and many community colleges offer technology instruction free of charge. Each of the resources I recommend is free and can be used from any computer with Internet access.

When using this technology, I strongly recommend the following guidelines for making the most of the Internet in an emotionally and physically healthy fashion.

Personal Security: Before becoming active online, learn how to protect yourself and your family. Above all, use common sense and an extreme dose of caution when venturing online. Do not give out personal or identifying information. Check out www.WiredSafety.org for specific recommendations.

Filters and Antivirus Software: Any computer you use must have Internet filtering and antivirus software that is regularly monitored and updated. Just as you wouldn't live in a home without a smoke detector or put your child onto a boat without a life vest, you should never use the Internet without these safety provisions.

Time Limits: Many people, moms included, fall into abuse of the Internet. When life is full of mundane tasks and your most regular companions can't speak in complete sentences, the lure of an adult conversation online can be intoxicating. If you are going to be online, set time limits for yourself and abide by them. You wouldn't spend all day talking on the phone and neglecting your children or your duties at work. Don't assume that just because you're chatting online it's not as egregious a waste of time and neglect of your responsibilities.

Don't Trust Everything: Especially when using the Internet as an information source, do not trust everything you read online. Seek trusted second opinions, multiple sources, and your own gut instincts. Wikipedia may contain a lot of information about the Bible, but it's not the Bible itself!

Respect Family Boundaries: I blog regularly about my family life, but I would never write about anything that my children or my husband would not want shared outside of our family. For safety reasons, but also simply out of respect for their privacy, I never write anything about a family member that would be embarrassing, hurtful, or endangering to that person.

Connecting vs. Stalking: My friend M. regularly uses the Internet to connect with people from around the world. She recently shared with me the simple statement that, "It's emotionally healthy to keep in touch with people, but not so healthy to stalk people from the past." I had a recent online correspondence with a former co-worker that started off with a simple e-mail he sent to check in on me. We exchanged pleasantries and updates on spouses and children. Beyond that, I limited my e-mails with him, taking into consideration how I would feel if my husband suddenly began a regular correspondence with someone from his past.

Real vs. Virtual: Always remember that online relationships should never take the place of real relationships in your life. Keep virtual "friends" in their proper perspective and never let them stand in the way of your marital covenant or your precious time with your children.

Don't Be "That Mom". You know—the one who is always online and who irritates everyone. "That mom" is the one who over-shares, who spends all her time online night and day, who has an opinion about everything, and who thinks she's always right. Internet communities form around people who share common interests and passions. For example, my friend Zina frequents an Attachment Parenting support group. Zina's wise counsel is to treat people online as you would IRL ("in real life"). Many times, moms will abuse the anonymity of online forums to say spiteful and hurtful things they might never utter to a fellow mom face to face. Think before you speak online and ask yourself if the comments you choose to share are edifying and uplifting for others. If not, walk away from the keyboard and play Legos for a while. In turn, don't allow yourself to be cyber-bullied, and don't frequent communities that don't inspire or nurture you.

Mom's Homework

✓ Sign up for Google Reader and subscribe to a few blogs you enjoy.

✓ Consider starting your own free blog at Blogger.com or Word press.com.

✓ Learn how to post and share your photos and videos online.

✓ Check to see that your computers are protected by filtering and antivirus software.

Web Resources

Wired Safety: www.wiredsafety.org
All-inclusive, free resource focusing on Internet safety, help, and education for Internet users of all ages

WordPress: http://wordpress.org
Free blogging tool and publishing platform

Google Reader: http://reader.google.com
Use Google's web-based feed reader to keep up with blogs and news

CHAPTER TWELVE

Cultivating creativity

Discovering Your Inner Artist

Finally, brothers, whatever is true, whatever is honorable, whatever is just, whatever is pure, whatever is lovely, whatever is gracious, if there is any excellence and if there is anything worthy of praise, think about these things.

–Philippians 4:8

My Story

I hesitate to call myself an "artist," since the extent of my ability is limited to drawing stick figures, but these days I am coming to embrace some of the creative forces God has placed within me. Rather than limit myself to endeavors at which I'm "good," I have found great joy in opening up my heart and my hands to new ways of glorifying God in art.

My husband handed me the "keys" to this new kingdom with the gift of a violin one Christmas. I had long professed my love for the instrument and my desire to learn to scratch out a few tunes "someday." Greg knew that "someday" would likely never come if I waited until I had sufficient time to explore this interest, so he dove in and purchased an inexpensive student model, encouraging me to take lessons.

Let me just say that a forty-year-old woman has *no business* trying to learn to play the violin. As my lessons began and I embraced my daily practice schedule, I noted that my playing had the ability to quickly clear the house—the boys seemed to suddenly head outdoors to play and Greg spent extra time on yard work to escape my "music." A badly played violin can emit horrific sounds, but I was oblivious. Along with my simple exercise pieces, I learned to play some of my favorite church songs, humming along with my haltingly slow versions of "How Great Thou Art" or "Ode to Joy" with renditions that surely had their composers rolling over in their graves!

The point is, taking a few moments each day with my violin opened up a piece of my heart that had long been dormant. My family lovingly supported my efforts with their share of good-natured teasing. I will never be a concert violinist, but my time spent on learning to pursue one of my passions has made me a better, happier mom.

Blessings and Balance

God has given each and every one of us a unique set of gifts and talents with which to pay him homage. As moms, however, we may focus exclusively on the talents that enable us to serve our families—those domestic skills that seem to take precedence over all else in the day-to-day running of a home. We have so many physical and emotional demands on our time that we set aside what may seem to be trivial pursuits.

"Michele" is a mother of two special needs children and a classically trained singer who set aside her training and work to commit herself full time to her family. Michele contemplates her talents and gifts:

> Now, ten years later with two young special needs children and no realistic way to sing on a regular basis, I always wonder if the gifts

I was given were used as God wanted them used. I'm toying with the idea of taking lessons again and I'm also very interested in writing. But I'm fearful of taking something away from my family. I mean, it's always so busy already and such a struggle to keep the house going and give everyone the loving attention they need.

Michele's story so eloquently represents many of the daily compromises we make as moms. We want to give our very best to our families in every way. We set aside interests and hobbies because we deem time spent on them to be selfish or just simply can't seem to find the time to enjoy them in the midst of diapers to be changed, dinners to be cooked, and endless messes around us.

The truth is, taking time to let ourselves enjoy creative efforts may ultimately make us even better wives and mothers. As with so many other mothering issues, the key here is *balance*. Just as we care for ourselves emotionally through our relationships, and physically through fitness and proper nutrition, God desires that we care for ourselves mentally through the development of the gifts he has showered upon us. In Michele's case, I doubt God would want her to walk away from her family full time to seek the bright lights of Broadway. But the Source of her talents would likely love to see her glorify him in song, nurturing her skills with a weekly one-hour voice lesson.

When we take time to tap into our creative abilities, we acknowledge the God who placed them within us and who crafted us, just so, knowing every aspect of us and loving every hair on our head. Look at the rhythm of your life and the flow of your week. Are there small periods of time each week that you could devote to pursuing a creative endeavor?

These days, as full as my life is, I block off time every Wednesday morning for one of my favorite hobbies, knitting. The truth is, I'm not a great knitter and I'm very slow. As I write this, I have been working for the past fourteen months on one pair of socks. My fellow knitters bear with me patiently as I join them weekly for friendship and bonding around a common love of yarn. I rarely knit outside of that particular Wednesday morning time period, but look forward each week to the challenge of completing a project on my own and spending time in fellowship with wonderful friends. When my friend and knitting teacher Cindy taught me to love her favorite hobby, she gifted me not only with a skill, but more importantly with another facet of myself I had never known before.

With and For Our Children

Taking time to explore our interests sends our children the message that they should do the same. I would never in a million years think to tell my son Adam, "You're not very good at the violin, so why don't you just give it up?" Why should I say that to myself? When we open our hearts and minds to exploring new treasures within ourselves and around our world, we set an example for our families that each day is a treasure from God and that we want to live it to its fullest in ways that bring him honor, glory, and pleasure.

cannot teach or preach or govern me. I can but use my gift of painting for the glory of God.

—Blessed Fra Angelico
(Patron Saint of Artists)

I was not a creative person before I had my children. Immersed in the world of work, the most creative thing I did was decorating the file folders in my office with color-coordinated labels. But when Eric came along, my heart began to view the world in new and wonderful ways. One of the wonderful things about having kids is that they remind us of some of life's little pleasures—things like a fresh box of crayons, homemade play dough, or the fun of finger-painting. For moms with young ones, your creative time will likely be spent in the company of your precious little ones. But guess what—that counts too!

When you have "three under five," it's unlikely that you'll find time for voice lessons or oil painting. What you will find, though, are companions for your creative journey. Rather than plopping the toddler into the playpen in front of a video, spread a blanket in the backyard and spend time making leaf rubbings or collecting sticks for a collage. Capture the sunset in a watercolor or collaborate with your four-year-old on a story, taking turns coming up with plot twists and turns.

When my children were little, we used to play a game in the car as we drove, called the "What do you hear?" game. I would play a selection of classical music and ask the boys, "What do you hear?" The tales they wove, of pirate ships or twinkling stars, of battles or bulldogs, clued me in to the vivid imaginations of my two budding writers. But rather than just listening to their accounts, I joined in.

Sometimes I would have to force my tired, dulled mind to hear something more than just the notes of the tunes. It's hard to feel creative when you are exhausted and when the highlight of your day is that you had a five-minute shower! But one of the many blessings of being around children is their vantage point for viewing the world. If you are blessed enough to share your days in the company of young souls, embrace the opportunities that present themselves to you each day to see the world through their eyes. Play with, imagine, color, taste, and feel God's beauty with the outlook of your children, and be cognizant of your own inner artist in the process.

Creative Outlets

If you don't consider yourself a creative person, maybe your definition of "creative" needs a little examination and refinement. When I recently surveyed a group of Catholic moms and asked them how they nurture themselves creatively, I was thrilled and amazed by some of their responses.

For many moms, capturing and documenting our families' lore and memories can be a perfect creative outlet. We are often the family photographers and photo historians. Consider your camera as a tool for creativity. Along with the normal, posed photos of your children in front of monuments or at school events, capture their world—and yours—on a typical weekday. Spend a few moments at your toddler's vantage point and take a snapshot or two of his favorite hangout or toys from that level. Photograph your home in all its "dinnertime" glory, mess and all. Truthfully, when I look at old family photos from my parents, my eyes go to the tiny details that bring back the days of my childhood—a '70s-style oil painting on the wall or a favorite afghan slung across the couch. Let your photographs be an outlet to capture the entirety of your family's story, not just the part that happened on good hair days or under perfect lighting conditions.

Scrapbooking has also become an art form these days, both in traditional crop-and-place albums and in the world of digital photography. Remember that the photos you leave behind will tell only a part of your story—along with decorating your albums, be sure to document the small accounts behind them. As we discussed in the last chapter, today's Internet tools enable any mom to become an author and artist as we document our family histories.

There's no doubt that being a mother is an incredible journey unto itself. But our life journey, and our legacy, can't just rest within the walls of motherhood. We can't just teach our kids how to live by example; we have to BE the example for them. We can't just direct them on the right path unless we ourselves have traveled many paths. We can't just tell them to reach for their dreams if we don't reach for our own. We can't just teach them to live by faith if we don't stand up and share our own faith testimony. We can't just live in the light; we have to BE the light. Many of us search for our sole purpose in life by seeking things that give us fulfillment. Is it motherhood? Is it a comprehensive education? Is it a rewarding career? Is it a creative avenue? For some of us, it's one of these things. For others, it's ALL of these things. But the excavation of this purpose is ultimately the treasure that is really found. Open your eyes, open your heart, open your life . . . and BE found!

Sharmane Adams is a singer/songwriter/speaker and "spiritual champion for faith and family." Visit Sharmane at www.sharmane.com.

Nurturing our creativity is such an important part of what it means to be human. God is the ultimate creator and we were all made in his image, so we all have that creative bent within us. Your creativity may show itself in some traditional artistic outlet such as performing music or dance or painting or sculpture. On the other hand, your creativity might shine in an area you never really considered to be creative, such as cooking or gardening or computer programming. Regardless of where your talent and passion lies, it is important to continue to nurture that side of yourself even after the children come. Yes, it is hard. There may seem like there is never enough time or money to spend on yourself in such a frivolous pursuit. After all, the to-do list goes on for pages and the bank account is woefully low. I understand! But we all need time for recreation, literally to re-create ourselves. Moms give so much of our lives to our children, it is necessary to spend time with something that is just for us. It is also possible to use your creative talents to make gifts for others, thereby giving an added purpose to your efforts and lessening the guilt factor.

In my own life, I set aside Saturday evenings to work on some creative project—usually scrapbooking or quilting. My husband and I watch a video from the library and I get to work. It's not a lot of time—only a couple hours a week, a hundred hours a year. But I look forward to that time so much, and in the process I keep my children's scrapbooks up-to-date and usually complete one quilt a year. It fills my creative need and gives me a sense of accomplishment. I wish the same for each of you!

Patrice Fagnant-MacArthur is a homeschooling mother of two young sons. She has a master of arts in applied theology and blogs at http://spiritual womanthoughts.blogspot.com.

These days, traditional needle arts are enjoying a resurgence as chunky knit scarves or cool crocheted capes hit the runways. If you don't know how to knit, crochet, or sew, investigate local community groups that will likely offer free lessons to help you get started.

If music is your passion, look for opportunities in your home, parish, and community to share your gifts and hone your skills. These days, it's easy to find lessons online via YouTube or other services that can help you learn to play just about any instrument, and there are even video games to help nurture your inner diva!

Many of the mom respondents to my creativity query shared their passions for a host of creative outlets: cake decorating, sewing, writing, style and makeup, and even "dancing to imaginary music while folding laundry" are great ways to tap into the talents God has given us. Lisa, a knitter, wisely called creativity "a way to approach problems—really, making anything is just a way to solve a problem and its little attendant problems." She shared that her creativity has even been turned into an opportunity for service as she shares her talents by donating knitted projects she has completed. What a wonderful way to nurture yourself and help others in the process! We can encourage our children to develop a giving attitude with their own creative talents by helping them to draw cards or pictures for homebound parishioners or perform their singing or dancing at a local nursing home.

A Window on the World

There are many ways to foster your creativity and to pass a love of the arts along to your children. In your own community, look for opportunities to see and explore creative endeavors. Along with museums and art galleries, you can explore and be inspired by new ideas in craft fairs, art schools, and even outdoor markets. Take a weekend morning to wander an art exhibit or finger the fabric or fiber in a local craft store. Commit to a small project and see it through to completion, even if it seems to take forever! When you feel like giving up, think of my pair of socks that took two years to complete and remind yourself that patience is a virtue.

Travel, whether to great distances or even locally, can be a wonderful way to stir your creative soul. When I travel, I have a special hobby that fuels me creatively and spiritually. I love to visit new churches in every town to which I travel. When I enter a new church, along with saying private prayers, I visit the Mary statue of the parish and, if appropriate, take a few photos of the representation of the Blessed Mother in that church. Over the years, these photos of Mary statues have become some of my most favorite treasures from our travels.

When you travel, look for opportunities to be open to creativity. Along with visiting all of the highlights in the area you are touring, be sure to look for hidden treasures and opportunities to interact with local residents, who can give you a true feel for the spot you are seeing. My teenage sons love to play Irish music. When we travel, we choose destinations that offer "jam sessions" where area musicians come together in a pub or family restaurant to play traditional tunes. Over the past few years, Eric and Adam have met and introduced Greg and me to so many wonderful local musicians in the areas where we have visited. A common love of music serves as a way to meet and interact with folks who give us a greatly enhanced perspective on their hometowns. When you travel, if you have a creative passion, consider looking for opportunities in the area you are visiting to meet up with others who enjoy your form of art. You will be amazed at the hospitality you will encounter and at the impact it will have upon your own creativity level.

If you are unable to travel physically to the places you dream of, you can still travel virtually and explore many great things through the Internet. Why not spend thirty minutes visiting the Vatican's chapels or the masterpieces of the Louvre? You will be amazed at the way in which today's technology enables us to quickly and easily access sights and sounds from every corner of the world. Along with visiting the official websites of your desired destinations, look for online videos shared by fellow travelers or podcasts that capture the local feel as you are led on "sound seeing tours" of many of the worlds' greatest cities. Traveling, even if it's just a quick local trip or a virtual visit, can help open your heart and your mind to new, fresh ideas about the world in which we live.

When we model a love for creativity and share it with our children, we develop the next generation of artists. We teach them—and ourselves—to respond to each and every one of God's calls in our lives, even the call to beautify our world in our own unique and special ways.

Mom's Homework

✓ Take a month to truly ponder your creative interests. Journal about your curiosities, limitations, frustrations, and joys. Try out one new creative endeavor this month.

✓ Visit an area museum or art gallery or attend a concert or play in your hometown.

✓ Seek out a group in your parish or community that is pursuing a hobby you enjoy or might like to try.

✓ Visit the library this week and check out books and DVDs with instructional concepts or inspirational ideas to help you pursue your creative efforts.

✓ Pull out one "UFO" (unfinished object)—a project that has been languishing in a drawer or closet. Commit to completing it or donating it to a local organization for completion.

God therefore called man into existence, committing to him the craftsman's task. Through his "artistic creativity" man appears more than ever "in the image of God", and he accomplishes this task above all in shaping the wondrous "material" of his own humanity and then exercising creative dominion over the universe which surrounds him. With loving regard, the divine Artist passes on to the human artist a spark of his own surpassing wisdom, calling him to share in his creative power.

—Pope John Paul II

Web Resources

CatholicArtists.org: www.catholicartists.org
Prayers, papal addresses, documents, and articles of relevance for Catholic artists

Vatican Museums: http://mv.vatican.va/StartNew_EN.html
View the collections online, take virtual tours, zoom in on details of artworks

PART III: Body

LEARNING TO LOVE,
CARE FOR, AND CHALLENGE
OUR PHYSICAL BODIES

Fitness focus

Cultivating and Maintaining a Physically Active Lifestyle

He gives strength to the fainting; for the weak he makes vigor abound. Though young men faint and grow weary, and youths stagger and fall, they that hope in the LORD will renew their strength, they will soar as with eagles' wings; they will run and not grow weary, walk and not grow faint.

—Isaiah 40:29-31

My Story

As I crossed the finish line of the Los Angeles Marathon, clutching the hand of my dad who was running with me to celebrate his fifty-fifth birthday, the theme song to *Chariots of Fire* rang in my head, and I felt sobs of happiness welling up within me. I thought back to the first grade teacher who had once told me, "You run more slowly than a turtle." Those words had stuck with me throughout my childhood, convincing me that I would never be an athlete. But life is funny, and while I still wouldn't call myself an athlete, I had just achieved a life-long goal by completing my very first marathon.

I came to my love for fitness late in life, giving myself a gym membership on my birthday the year Eric was a baby. In truth, I was desperate for a bit of time to myself and to regain some semblance of my pre-baby body. For the first few months, I spent my time at the gym savoring forty-five minutes of freedom, slowly walking on a treadmill, and mostly looked forward to taking a shower without having to worry about my baby. But one day, I turned the treadmill up a bit too quickly and loped into a bit of a jog. I thought to myself, "Let's see how long I can go!" That first day, I jogged for less than two minutes, recalling that teacher's prophetic words and vowing not to repeat the experience.

But something nagged within me, and the next day—and those that ensued—found me adding, "One more minute, one more tenth of a mile." I don't want you to get the false impression that I am, by any means, a real runner. I'm still dreadfully slow, but I persist. Over the years, my fitness goals progressed to 5Ks, long bike rides, and hikes in the foothills with Eric in a backpack. In the years since Eric was born, I have completed three marathons, zip-lined in Costa Rica, snorkeled in Hawaii, and hiked to the bottom of the Grand Canyon and back.

I have learned to look at this body God gave me and to accept its limitations, but to gently challenge them as well. I have learned to say "yes" to opportunities to see the beauty of God's creation by being out in it walking, jogging, swimming, or biking. I will never break world records, but I have broken many of my own and have learned to love God and myself more with every step of every walk.

Why Bother?

Many of you may find yourselves wanting to skip this particular chapter, deeming me crazy for thinking that a busy wife and mother, especially one on a tight budget, can ever hope to find the time and the motivation to make physical fitness a priority in life. But just as it is important to care for ourselves emotionally and spiritually if we are to give our best to our families, we absolutely must care for ourselves physically as well. St. Paul frequently used sports analogies in his epistles, for example when he challenged the Corinthians to train themselves spiritually with the exhortation:

> Do you not know that the runners in the stadium all run in the race, but only one wins the prize? Run so as to win. Every athlete exercises discipline in every way. They do it to win a perishable crown, but we an imperishable one. Thus I do not run aimlessly; I do not fight as if I were shadowboxing. No, I drive my body and train it, for fear that, after having preached to others, I myself should be disqualified.

—1 Corinthians 9:24-27

Pope John Paul II was a wonderful example of someone with a lifelong commitment to physical fitness. I like to believe that the hours he spent hiking or skiing equipped him physically, emotionally, and spiritually to deal with the demands of his papacy.

But neither St. Paul nor John Paul II were moms, so they likely didn't deal with such issues as juggling laundry, babies, and often frenzied dinner hours. Why should we bother with frivolities such as working out? Fitting into pre-pregnancy jeans should never be the main motivator for exercise. Rather, having a regular fitness regimen is absolutely essential to a woman's overall physical health.

The Physical Activities Guidelines for Adults released by the U.S. Department of Health and Human Services recommend that every adult woman between the ages of eighteen and sixty-four should be doing an equivalent of at least 150 minutes of moderate-intensity aerobic physical activity each week. Additionally, the guidelines recommend women do additional overall strength training activities that focus on all of the major muscle groups at least twice per week. Devotion to regular physical activity directly relates to substantial health benefits, and these numbers are simply the baseline for leading a healthy lifestyle.

It is a fitting occasion to give thanks to God for the gift of sport, in which the human person exercises his body, intellect and will, recognizing these abilities as so many gifts of his Creator.

—Pope John Paul II

Equally as important as the health benefits we achieve through regular exercise are the emotional and spiritual blessings that come our way as well. Most moms prioritize everyone else before themselves. By giving yourself the time each week to exercise and strengthen your body, you arm yourself for all of the demands of motherhood.

Do you remember the famous Proverbs 31 mom? It was said of this model of femininity, "She is girt about with strength, and sturdy are her arms." For this worthy wife, valued beyond pearls, physical strength gave her the tools she needed to be extolled by her husband and respected by her children. A mother's days are filled with physical, backbreaking demands. Training ourselves physically can help us to meet those challenges with joy rather than dreading the pain they induce.

As moms, we take time for such health preserving activities as buckling up our seat belts and looking both ways before crossing the street. We want to ensure our safety, so that we can continue to care for and enjoy the love of our families. With the knowledge that engaging in physical fitness activities will make us healthier, let's look at some ways of making "working out" into less of a drudgery and more of a lifelong pleasure.

Making Time

Now that we're motivated to get healthy and include fitness as a regular part of our lives, let's look at the cold, hard reality many of us face—how to find time to get it done! I absolutely love exercising. But I admit that when I'm having a busy week it's one of the very first parts of my self-care regimen that I let slip. I want to let you know up front that I struggle with this topic, too, despite my best intentions. Ironically, I find that when I skip workouts because I'm stressed and overworked, I only intensify my stress level. I've learned that even a fifteen-minute stroll around the school parking lot "counts" and can help put things back in perspective.

So let's look at a few creative ways to make time for fitness in your busy schedule.

Calendar It: If you find "fitting in fitness" to be a challenge, commit this month to adding a regular workout to your schedule three days per week. Hopefully by starting with even a small amount of exercise on a regular schedule, you will find time to expand upon your efforts. Sit down with your calendar and take a look at the course of your

When I exercise, I feel good about life.

While exercise shouldn't take the place of a healthy prayer life or a good relationship with my husband, it is an important part of keeping a healthy, happy outlook on whatever my day might bring. There is something about getting my heart pumping and that rush of endorphins that makes life wonderful. I need exercise.

Some seasons it's hard to find the time to exercise—and I notice that I suffer. So I work hard to figure out how to make exercise happen. Sometimes I have the energy and grace to get up early and hit the gym, or do an exercise video at home. Sometimes I can squeeze in a run in my neighborhood, or even just a brisk walk with a friend. And during really tight seasons, I have been known to run up and down my stairs or around my house! Whatever my schedule can best handle, that's what I'll do.

God created us to know, love, and serve him—and to drink in the beauty that surrounds us. When I take time to focus on fitness, this effort has a positive impact on everything I do. (I think my husband and boys appreciate the difference, too!)

Rachel Balducci is a wife and mother of five boys. She is a writer and a weekly columnist for the newspaper of the Diocese of Savannah. Visit her at http://testosterhome.net.

week. Carve out a minimum of three thirty-minute blocks of time this week for exercise. Wake up fifteen minutes earlier, take an after-dinner walk, or better yet, get the whole family involved by playing in the backyard on the weekend. But don't leave your fitness schedule to chance—make an appointment with yourself to keep your fitness commitments each week, and then look for those extra opportunities that arise on the spur of the moment.

Buddy Up: I have found that arranging to meet my best friend Mara for a workout two or three days per week is my most effective strategy for getting myself to the gym or to the park for a walk. Find a friend who shares your goal of getting healthy. Plan to meet on a regular schedule, and keep your commitment to each another. Your "buddy" could be a girlfriend, a sister, your thirteen-year-old, your spouse, or even your dog!

Just Kidding: Many of us moms use our children as our built-in exercise excuse. We don't want to leave our precious little ones or cannot afford to hire a sitter. The answer is simple—work out *with* them! Push a baby in a stroller, play tag with a toddler, jog next to a kindergartner's bike, or dance with your teenager. Look for opportunities during the course of your day to get out and play like your children. Some of my happiest workout memories came with Eric and Adam in the child seat on the back of my bicycle or snuggled into a frame backpack as we hiked along nature trails with other moms and tots. Use your children as your role model and your motivation, not your excuse!

When it comes to finding time for "fitting in fitness," I feel your pain. I am not a wonder woman who wakes up at 5:00 a.m. to rush off to an aerobics class, donning the cutest in coordinated workout attire. I'm a mom who has walked in circles around fields while my sons practice and who sees unloading groceries as an opportunity for a strength workout. I fit in pushups between blog posts and park in the remote areas of the lot to add steps to my pedometer. If you look at your life, you will find small windows of time to be physically active presenting themselves to you.

Full-time Fitness

With so many moms employed in full-time positions outside the home, we need to give some special encouragement to those who spend forty-plus hours per week at work and face the strains of commuting, often spending time away from their children to help in the financial survival of their families. For those of you in this situation, working fitness into your schedule may feel overwhelming and impossible. It's likely that your precious time at home is best spent enjoying the company of your family and dealing with cooking, cleaning, homework help, and rest. Let's look at a few suggestions that will enable you to "fit in fitness" during the course of your workday.

Create a Team: It's likely that many of your co-workers face the same time restraints and pressures you do when it comes to making time for regular exercise. Look around your place of employment for a few friends or co-workers who might like to join you two to three times per week for a lunch or break time walk. Agree on a schedule and start scouting locations for your route. Start simply, walking fifteen to twenty minutes at a brisk pace. In fair weather, the employee parking lot can serve as your "track." In inclement weather, create a "route" inside your place of employment, incorporating stairs if possible. Bring a pair of comfortable shoes and some toiletries to freshen up after your walk. Walking at a moderate pace will help you get your heart pumping and burn calories. But more importantly, making time to exercise with co-workers a few days per week will likely have a positive impact upon your stress level and build camaraderie that may also impact upon your overall performance and job satisfaction.

Employee Wellness Programs: Many employers provide "Employee Wellness" programs as a part of their corporate or health benefits. Such programs typically support employees with everything from nutritional counseling to smoking cessation programs and immunizations. Some wellness programs may also include access to corporate or community exercise facilities. Contact your company's human resources department and inquire about available wellness programs provided by your employer. If your employer offers health insurance as part of your compensation package, your insurer may also offer healthy living programs and discounted rates for health related services.

Sedentary Solutions: Many of us have sedentary jobs that keep us sitting at a desk or behind a counter for several hours a day. As a writer, I find myself often suffering from back, neck, and shoulder strain and try to remember to stand up and take a brief break at least once per hour to stretch. If you work at a desk, a quick Google search for the phrase "office exercises" will yield over fifteen million results for everything from quick stretching moves to strength building techniques to flexibility and isometric exercises that can be done sitting or standing at your desk. On your morning or afternoon break a few times a week, begin implementing some of these simple moves into your schedule.

Make Every Move Count: For those of us facing fitness time restraints, look at the everyday tasks that make up your workday. Are there ways in which you can make more deliberate efforts to expend greater energy in these tasks? Park in the far corner of the lot, take the stairs rather than the elevator, or deliver a message to a co-worker in person rather than by telephone or email. If you work in a standing position, such as in retail, as a nurse, or out of doors, wear a pedometer and note how many steps you take in a day's work. You may be surprised to find that you are walking a few miles each day as you go about doing your job.

Frugal Fitness

We don't need fancy gym memberships, expensive workout cloth-ing, or complicated equipment to make regular exercise a part of our well-being regimen. Look around you for fun, creative ways to break a sweat. Walking or jogging in your neighborhood or even in place inside your home is a quick and simple form of exercise that costs nothing more than a sturdy pair of workout shoes. Check out exercise videos and DVDs from your local library, experimenting with differ-ent types of workouts you may not have tried before. YouTube.com is also packed with exercise videos of varying duration. Scour Craigslist.com for used exercise equipment that can often be found for drastically reduced prices. But don't think you need fancy equipment or weights to get into shape. For less than ten dollars, a simple jump rope and some inexpensive hand weights can provide a terrific work-out and be shared with your children too! And speaking of children, an energetic game of freeze tag or hide and go seek can be a fun, free way for the whole family to get into the groove.

Baby on Board

Prior to beginning any physical fitness routine, it's important that you speak with your physician, physician's assistant, or nurse practi-tioner about your overall health and readiness to begin exercising. This is especially important for pregnant women and those who have recently given birth, as well as anyone with special health considera-tions. Make your medical care professional a partner in planning your fitness routine. Obtain his or her advice and clearance and listen to your body as you begin a pregnancy or post-delivery plan for exercise.

These days, there are terrific resources for pregnant, new, and nursing mothers, including specially designed fitness routines that take into account your overall health and the health of your baby. Speak with your local hospital about exercise classes in your area that cater to expectant or new moms. Gather with other mothers in "stroller brigades" and take to the streets or a local mall. When my boys were little, during winter months, I walked the mall with friends a few times a week. When our toddlers grew tired of being pushed in concentric circles, we would take turns with a mom or two watching the kids at the shopping center's indoor play space while the others continued to walk.

Sport, properly directed, develops character, makes a man courageous, a generous loser, and a gracious victor; it refines the senses, gives intellectual penetration, and steels the will to endurance. It is not merely a physical development then. Sport, rightly understood, is an occupation of the whole man, and while perfecting the body as an instrument of the mind, it also makes the mind itself a more refined instrument for the search and communication of truth and helps man to achieve that end to which all others must be subservient, the service and praise of his Creator.

—Pope Pius XII

You will find that the best part of your time spent exercising in the company of other moms is the opportunity you have to share stories, ask questions, and sometimes complain to someone who understands the ups and downs of new motherhood. You may even find that you begin to look forward to exercising with friends and the companionship that accompanies the physical benefits you derive from physical activity.

Make It Fun

There's something about the phrase "working out" that implies difficulty, drudgery, and perhaps even pain. I'd love to know at what point in my life activities such as running, riding my bike, or going for a swim went from being part of my play to something I learned to dread. Our kids have the right idea—they head outdoors as frequently as possible, run everywhere, bounce, burn energy we can't imagine, and just plain *play* as long as we'll let them.

We should learn to emulate them and look for opportunities in our own lives to incorporate everyday play back into our days. Start thinking about physical fitness as your opportunity to play, to embrace the body God gave you and to use it to its fullest potential. In a famous line from one of my family's favorite movies, *Chariots of Fire*, Olympic runner and Christian missionary Eric Liddell tries to explain his love of running to a loved one who feels it is a superfluous use of his time and talent. "I believe God made me for a purpose, but he also made me fast. And when I run I feel his pleasure." You and I may never earn accolades for our athletic exploits, but we too can feel that same pleasure when we allow ourselves to make the most of the physical gifts with which God has gifted us.

I've learned to love long, solitary walks as my primary form of exercise. An hour can seemingly pass by in moments in the company of a good friend or a compelling audio book that I've borrowed from the local library. Try different types of exercise and vary your routine frequently. Challenge your assumptions about your abilities and explore new fitness environments, or work out at a different time of day or night. Keep a fitness journal or log to track your progress. Be patient with yourself if you are new to exercising. Do not expect to see overnight results—remember that this will be a lifelong process, a commitment to your long-term emotional and physical well-being.

Sick of your usual workout and want to try a few new exercise options? Here are a few suggested activities enjoyed by Catholic moms like you:

✳ Erin lives in Chicago where it is cold and windy. Before beginning her workday as a lawyer, she uses a video to go for a two-mile "walk" and do a light weight routine in her basement.

✳ Lynn just took up jogging. To motivate her and help her remain committed, she registered for an upcoming fun run that will raise funds for a nonprofit organization in her neighborhood.

✳ Martha meets friends three mornings per week for a circuit-training workout at a ladies' gym in her neighborhood. Her workout is done before her kids even wake up in the morning.

✳ Jennifer can frequently be seen walking, or even being "walked by," her three large dogs.

✳ Barbara loves to ride her bicycle and cycles with her children or friends a few times per week.

✳ Nancy is learning to Irish step dance at the local community center. Her class is so enjoyable that she hardly notices the great workout she's getting.

✳ Kelly is a master gardener who donates some of her produce to the local food pantry on a regular basis.

* Kathy and her youngest child enjoy "Mommy and Me" swim lessons twice each week.

* Michelle does strength training with resistance bands three times per week and has added "wall" pushups and light weights to her workout.

* Dee takes regular hikes on the nature trails around her desert home with her husband or friends from church.

* Monica enjoys Pilates and stretching classes at her city park's department recreation center.

* Kay has begun taking karate classes at the studio where her children take their lessons.

* Karen rides horses once per week.

* Theresa plays an active lifestyle video game with her children four to five times per week.

* Jayne meets friends for tennis at a local high school and also plays with her daughter and husband regularly.

* Lisa looks for new workout ideas on the Internet and keeps different playlists on her iPod to match her mood and boost her energy level.

If you find that you are resistant to exercise, begin with "baby steps" this week and commit to fifteen minutes of physical activity today. Give yourself permission to take the time you need to ensure your health and emotional well-being.

The Church looks at sport with great sympathy, since it considers the human body as the masterpiece of creation.

> God the Creator gave new life to the body, thus making it the instrument of an immortal soul. . . . When sport is practiced in a healthy way, it exalts the dignity of the human body without risking idolatry. The Church sees sport as a mighty element of moral and social education.
>
> —Pope John Paul II

Answer Pope John Paul II's call to use your body, your "masterpiece of creation" in a way that will bring a big smile to your own heart, and to the heart of the loving God who created you.

Mom's Homework

✓ Sit down today and block off three periods of time on your calendar this week to commit to physical activity, even if it's only fifteen minutes at a time. As you begin to have a more regular commitment to exercise, aim to reach or exceed the U.S. Department of Health and Human Services recommended 150 minutes of aerobic exercise and two strength training sessions per week.

✓ Investigate recreation and fitness opportunities in your community, at your local library, or at area community colleges.

✓ Find a "workout buddy" in your area or a friend online with whom you can share your commitment to getting fit.

✓ Sign up for an upcoming fitness event. Ride in a bicycle race, do a neighborhood fun run, Walk for Life, or even sign up for regular dance classes.

✓ Keep a fitness log or diary to track your progress. Congratulate yourself for your accomplishments and treat yourself to something special like a new article of exercise wear or a bubble bath when you accomplish a fitness-related goal.

Web Resources

Catholic Athletes for Christ: www.catholicathletesforchrist.com/
index.htm
Serves Catholic athletes and shares the gospel of Christ in and through athletics

Physical Activity Guidelines for Americans: www.health.gov/
paguidelines/default.aspx
Recommendations from the U.S. Department of Health and Human Services to achieve health benefits from physical activity

Get Active: www.healthfinder.gov/prevention/ViewTopic
.aspx?topicID=22
Quick guide to healthy living

CHAPTER FOURTEEN

Fuel for the journey

The Importance of
Good Nutrition in Our Lives

I know indeed how to live in humble circumstances; I know also how to live with abundance. In every circumstance and in all things I have learned the secret of being well fed and of going hungry, of living in abundance and of being in need. I have the strength for everything through him who empowers me.

—Philippians 4:12-13

My Story

Of all of the vices in my life, the one with which I most consistently struggle is my inability to do things in moderation. Unlike my husband, who is the most moderate person I've ever met, I seem to be plagued by excesses. In some areas, being an obsessive person can be a merit if the energy is fueled properly toward good action. But in other areas, being immoderate brings pain, self-doubt, and sin.

For most of my adult life, like many women, I have struggled to maintain a healthy weight. I was never a "skinny" child, but have also never been morbidly obese. If you were to look at me today, you might not recognize the internal struggles that go on inside my head when it comes to nutrition. Following the birth of my children and nearing my forties, I recognized the need to address my eating habits and over the course of a year successfully lost fifty pounds through diet and exercise. But in the ensuing years, I continue to struggle with regained pounds. I have come to terms with the fact that I will never be a size four, and am honestly reconciled to that fact. But what continues to plague me is my inability to gain mastery over the appetites that lead me to make unhealthy choices when my mind knows better.

So I write this particular chapter as much for myself as for you, dear moms. All too often, I have justified unhealthy eating habits that are caused by the dueling capital sins of gluttony and sloth. I want you to know that I share your goal of healthful eating, but also the pain you feel when you fall short and make bad choices. Let's look together at how healthful eating and a positive self-image in this regard can come together to benefit our overall sense of well-being.

You Are Worth It

Ironically, my nutritional "come to Jesus" moment happened in a cooking class. I sat next to a friend named Lilly, watching the teacher demonstrate a culinary skill I would likely never master, and noted that my friend was looking particularly healthy. When I remarked on her appearance, she happily informed me that she had joined a well-known weight loss program and was making great progress. Her confidence and happiness attracted me more so than the amount of weight she had lost, and I vowed to myself that my first stop the following Monday morning would be to sign up for the program.

When I signed up for the program the following week, I had to give myself permission to spend not only the money involved in joining, but more importantly to give this project a level of importance in my life. I would be preparing different meals for myself, expending

At all times a constant habitual moderation is better than occasional excessive abstinence, alternated with great indulgence.

—St. Francis de Sales

mental and emotional energy on this struggle, and singling out my needs for the next few months apart from those of my family. "You are worth it," I told myself.

And that is the message I most want to share with you here in this chapter on healthy nutrition. You, your husband's best friend and partner, your child's mother, are worth the effort that it takes to eat healthfully. Moreover, it is your responsibility to your family that you do so, and that you learn and pass along the healthy eating strategies that will keep your family strong and fit. The more you learn to care for yourself, the better able you will be to attend to the needs of your family.

One of my favorite verses in St. Paul's epistle to the Corinthians could be asked of moms like you and me.

> Do you not know that your body is a temple of the holy Spirit within you, whom you have from God, and that you are not your own? For you have been purchased at a price. Therefore, glorify God in your body.
>
> —1 Corinthians 6:19-20

Whether our temple is a size four or fourteen is not what matters most in our journey to salvation. But if we let our appetites and our likely resulting depression or negative self-concept begin to become our "idols," we pollute our temples in a way that does disservice to our relationship with God, with our families, and with ourselves. You are worth the time and effort it will take to eat healthfully not only because you want good physical health, but also because keeping your temple pristine will make you more open to the fruits of the Holy Spirit within you. You, my friend, are worth it!

Planning Makes Perfect

How many times have you stood next to the sink, clearing a toddler's remaining chicken nuggets into your mouth rather than in the compost, and called that dinner? How many times have you bought snacks or treats "for the kids" that ended up being your lunch, or dinner, or the thing you munched on all afternoon that took the place of real meals? How many times have you eaten standing up, on the run, or in your car? How many times have you "driven through" to pick up dinner for your family because you had nothing in the fridge that was appealing or convenient to fix on short notice?

I'm convinced that two factors contribute to my problems with eating perhaps as much as the psychological and spiritual pitfalls that may cause me to overeat:

1. I don't like to cook.
2. I hate to grocery shop.

I look at my best friend Mara, a fit, healthy woman, and get frustrated sometimes by her slender frame. This is not a woman who starves herself, but rather someone who is very fit and who continually fuels herself with good, healthy food. One of our long-standing jokes is that Mara *loves* to shop, and has turned the game of coupon shopping into an art form.

The fact of the matter is that one of our main duties is to provide for the healthful nutrition of our families. And so whether I like it or not, this duty causes me to spend time each week on menu planning, shopping, and cooking. So if we're going to be successful at fueling our bodies for life's challenges in a healthful manner, we need to become adept at the skills of menu planning, shopping, and basic food preparation. Without going into great detail, let's take a look at a few tips for each of these three essential elements:

Menu Planning

* Sit down with your family and develop at least seven basic dinner menus that will appeal to all members of your family. Avoid becoming a "short order" cook and encourage your children to dine with the family, offering healthy alternatives and sides for pickier eaters.

* Assess your menu selections and review your recipes, looking to reduce calories and fat in your family's favorites.

* Consult menu-planning websites, family Web forums, your newspaper, and other resources for new menu ideas. Talk with friends and family about what they serve and remain open to new recipes, ethnic dishes, and healthy seasonal favorites.

As busy moms in this crazy world, there are days when we feel beaten down. The whining, the cooking, the cleaning, the arguing, the laundry piles, and long to-do lists are just a few of the reasons we are often plain *tired*. Don't forget those things we "should" be fitting into our day but can't always pull off: daily devotion time, exercising, reading to our kids, serving healthy meals, volunteering at church and school, helping the needy, and that list goes on as well. There are many demands on us! This is why it's so important to take care of ourselves. Just like you're instructed on an airplane when there's trouble, "put your own oxygen mask on and then help your children," we need to take care of ourselves, so we can take care of our families and enjoy them. Some things are obvious, like getting enough rest and exercise. Other areas are not so simple. Do we believe everything "they" have told us about foods deemed unhealthy, or do we eat naturally, the way God intended? (Think butter vs. margarine . . . ?) Start with gathering knowledge so you'll have the truths you need to nourish your body, and then you'll have the energy it takes to be the mom you want to be.

Kelly has been blogging about "politically incorrect" health and nutrition topics since January 2008. She converted to the Catholic faith in 1993, and lives near Grand Rapids, Michigan, with her husband of twenty-one years and four children. Read her blog at www.KellytheKitchenKop.com.

Shopping

* Never shop without a list or while hungry. Create a master list on your computer that can be printed out, kept in your kitchen, and taken to the store for big shopping trips.

* Avoid falling into the pitfall of shopping in club or warehouse stores exclusively. It's fine to purchase some items in these types of stores, but your family may end up wasting food or making poor eating choices if you are not supplementing bulk staple foods with fresh healthy produce and lean meats.

* Learn to shop around the "outside" of the grocery store where produce and fresh ingredients are found, avoiding the overly processed food in the stores' center aisles.

* Shop locally. Investigate farmers' markets, agriculture co-ops, and local bakers in your neighborhood. When possible, incorporate as

much locally grown food and as little processed food into your family meals as possible.

Cooking

----

* Involve your children. Helping to prepare dishes gives them a sense of pride, openness to trying new things, and important health skills that will help them to make their own healthy choices when they grow up.

* Make it into a pleasant time rather than a dreaded time. As I've said, I don't enjoy cooking, but I do *love* time spent in the company of my children. Cooking dinner, while Adam sits at the table working on homework with music playing in the background, has turned into one of my favorite times of the day.

* Learn to experiment. Share recipes with friends, check out healthy living resources online, and make seasonal produce the centerpiece of your meals.

Dine, Don't Diet

While you may need to work substantially on your own healthy eating skills and sharing these with your children, I urge you to avoid thinking of healthy eating as a "diet." For too many of us, the word "diet" conjures pain, sacrifice, doing without, and also a temporary exercise. If you look at the precepts of most healthy eating programs, including weight loss programs, there are a few consistent strategies amidst the widely varying fads:

* Work on portion control. Carefully examine the portion sizes of the food you eat and avoid eating more than the recommended portion size to control caloric intake.

* Limit foods and drinks high in calories, sugar, salt, fat, and alcohol.

* Keep a food log. If you are actively trying to lose weight, document each and every morsel of food that enters your mouth before you eat it. Licks, nibbles, bites, and club-store samples count as calories (even if they're free) and add up!

* Assess your food log on a weekly basis. Where do you struggle during the course of the day? Do you have "trigger foods" or beverages that cause you to overeat?

* Hydrate properly. According to the Mayo Clinic, healthy women should drink at least nine cups of liquids per day to maintain proper hydration. Pregnant women need at least ten cups of fluids daily, and breastfeeding mothers should drink at least thirteen cups of fluids each day. Special health considerations, exercise levels, and environmental issues may further impact your hydration needs.

While I don't intend here to recommend specific diets or weight loss programs, you may determine, in consultation with your healthcare professional, that you desire to lose weight. I want to emphasize that this decision should be based upon health and well-being considerations, rather than on worldly standards. Reflecting back on our wonderful Proverbs 31 mom, "Charm is deceptive and beauty fleeting; the woman who fears the LORD is to be praised."

If you find, as I did in my life, that an unhealthy nutritional life is leading you to spiritual separation and even potential sin, it is time to actively look at gaining control in this area of your life. Meet with your physician or other healthcare professional to discuss your goals, gain his or her support, and seek recommendations. Talk with those closest to you—your family—about your need to eat more healthfully. You will need their support and encouragement, and your life choices will be a wonderful role model for them. Seek spiritual support by linking your weight loss goals with spiritual disciplines.

Many find that periodic fasting from particular foods, in conjunction with penance and intercessory prayer, can bring the "mastery over our instincts and freedom of heart" noted in the *Catechism of the Catholic Church* (2043). When I talk of "fasting" in this context, I would like to emphasize that you can "fast" from particular items, even non-food items. I always welcome my Lenten fasts as a purification of my body in preparation for the Easter feast, and have begun to incorporate the process of occasional fasts during the remainder of the liturgical calendar for special intentions and to draw me closer to God.

So along with your healthcare professional, consider finding a spiritual director or religious support group such as Celebrate Recovery or other parish-based groups to support you in your healthy eating choices. Looking at the emotional and spiritual issues that cause us to make unhealthy decisions in our lives can help us get to the root of our problems.

If your goal in eating is to fit into a certain size or to look great for an upcoming vacation, it's unlikely that you will find the long-term peace and also the healthy living skills that will enable you to accomplish lasting change in your life. But if you are able to couple increased nutritional knowledge with a pursuit of true spiritual growth, it's likely that you will attain not only your health goals, but more importantly a lasting sense of spiritual and emotional well-being that will help you care for yourself and your family for years to come.

Mom's Homework

✓ At your annual physical, speak honestly and openly with your physician or other healthcare provider about your weight, addressing any concerns you may have and seeking input on good weight loss programs and strategies.

✓ Meet with your family to hold a "what's for dinner" summit. Create a family list of favorite meals and create a meal-planning calendar.

Temperance is the moral virtue that moderates the attraction of pleasures and provides balance in the use of created goods. It ensures the will's mastery over instincts and keeps desires within the limits of what is honorable. The temperate person directs the sensitive appetites toward what is good and maintains a healthy discretion: "Do not follow your inclination and strength, walking according to the desires of your heart." Temperance is often praised in the Old Testament: "Do not follow your base desires, but restrain your appetites." In the New Testament it is called "moderation" or "sobriety." We ought "to live sober, upright, and godly lives in this world."

—*Catechism of the Catholic Church,* 1809

✓ Find out the times and locations of farmers' markets or other local shopping opportunities in your area. Shop locally at least once per month to supplement your staple purchases.

✓ In the next month, try one new recipe with your family. Choose a recipe that is low in fat and involves at least one child in meal preparation efforts. Consider having your children take turns being "mom's helper" in the kitchen or even allow older kids one night per month to plan and prepare a special menu.

✓ If you are seeking spiritual support on your weight loss journey, contact your parish or diocese to learn about resources in your area that combine spiritual healing and the recovery process.

Web Resources

National Institutes of Health Body Mass Index Calculator: www.nhlbisupport.com/bmi
Calculate your healthful body mass index

The Light Weigh: www.lightweigh.com
A Catholic spiritual growth weight loss program

Cooking with CatholicMom.com: http://new.catholicmom.com/family/cooking
Family recipes, meal planning tools, meatless recipes, and more

CHAPTER FIFTEEN

"And Protect Us from All anxiety"

Stress Reduction and
Sleep Hygiene Strategies

Can any of you by worrying add a moment to your lifespan? If even the smallest things are beyond your control, why are you anxious about the rest? . . . Instead, seek his kingdom, and these other things will be given you besides. Do not be afraid any longer, little flock, for your Father is pleased to give you the kingdom.

—Luke 12:25–26, 31–32

My Story

I find that issues of stress and sleep are inherently related and that both are greatly impacted by the state of my spiritual life and my emphasis on healthy living. When I make time for my spiritual disciplines, exercise regularly, and sleep sufficiently, my stress level decreases dramatically. When I let my life spin off its normal axis, the wheels fall off the cart and things begin to go a little crazy in my home. It can be a vicious cycle. If I feel too distracted to take my morning quiet time, too busy to head to the gym, or so overwhelmed with tasks that I cut short my sleep, I only make matters worse.

Ironically, although I know these facts to be true, I continue to repeat the cycle when life is at its most hectic pace. It's easy to tell a friend not to stress out over her toddler's misbehavior or her teen's latest antics—it's another thing entirely to take my own advice to heart.

I have never had a problem with falling asleep at night—if you ask Greg, he will tell you that I'm out like a light before my head hits the pillow. But I have a tendency to mull things over in my sleep and to wake in the pre-dawn hours with a list of worries and concerns, most typically revolving around the lives of my sons. I have learned to turn to Our Lady in these moments, to take up my maternal grandmother's rosary and ask Mary to help me take these concerns to her beloved Son. Some days, with her divine intercession, sleep overtakes me again prior to praying my way through the mysteries of Jesus' life. Other days, this is the practice that starts my day and helps me to lay my concerns at his feet as I rise and seek his perfect will for whatever is troubling me.

Prayer and Partners

Any responsible discussion of stress-related issues should begin with the caveat that if you suffer unduly from anxiety, stress, depression, or other mental health issues, you should actively seek medical attention. Many women are prone to clinical disorders that can and should be treated medically. You should feel no embarrassment or distress in seeking professional help if you note the signs of clinical depression or anxiety disorders in your life. If you suffer from the warning symptoms of depression, please seek immediate medical intervention for your own well-being and for the sake of your family.

That being said, most moms I know have the tendency to be worriers. In one of my favorite Bible scenarios, the evangelist Luke says of Mary that she, "kept all these things, reflecting on them in her heart." I love to imagine our Blessed Mother throughout the events of her pregnancy, the Nativity, Jesus' childhood, the commencement of his public ministry, and his ultimate sacrifice and resurrection. It inspires me that she—who likely carried with her the most stressful situations any mother could possibly face—continually responded to God's challenges in her life with a quiet "yes." In times of stress and anxiety, I attempt to follow her lead and to turn to her for prayerful intercession.

In the next section of this book, we will look at the spiritual tools God has given us to nurture our families and ourselves. In this discussion on stress, I want to point to a few specific spiritual tactics that may provide relief. At every Mass, during the Liturgy of the Eucharist, the priest speaks some of my favorite words near the conclusion of the Our Father:

> Deliver us, Lord, from every evil, and grant us peace in our day. In your mercy, keep us free from sin and protect us from all anxiety as we wait in joyful hope for the coming of our Savior, Jesus Christ.

I have learned in my own life that staying close to the sacraments and frequently receiving the Eucharist helps me to decrease the anxiety I feel in my life. Seeking spiritual reconciliation with God and those I may have harmed through the sacrament of penance brings peace and a sense of healing

Many Catholic moms find that daily prayer helps them battle anxiety. Chris prioritizes her time with Jesus in perpetual adoration of the Eucharist every week. Tricia keeps a "gratitude journal," dwelling at the close of each day on the many blessings—large and small—that fill her life. Paula's devotion to the rosary and the Chaplet of Divine Mercy help her keep things in perspective. In my own life, on days when I'm unable to attend daily Mass, I try to make a quick visit with Jesus in the chapel at my parish to share my day with him and to seek a few moments of quiet in the midst of frenzied days. If you find that anxiety and stress are causing you spiritual distress, seek immediate spiritual direction from your pastor or other professional pastoral minister.

Along with our spiritual resources, God has provided each of us with a support system that can help us deal with life's many stresses. Rather than carrying the load yourself and becoming bitter in the process, learn to share your concerns and difficulties with those around you. Your husband, your life partner, is likely not a mind reader. With his own set of distractions, he may not automatically clue into the cause of your distress or even notice that your stress level is off the radar. But he can likely be one of your best resources when it comes to sorting things out and gaining control. Open up to him in a positive, loving way and seek his help and support in dealing with issues large and small that are stressing you out.

Mothers, sisters, and girl-friends are special gifts from God—they are his ears that listen to our daily woes and empathize, his arms that offer hugs or help us get our heads on straight, and his mind that helps us to determine the best course of action. Cultivate productive female relation-ships in your life. If you do not have close women family members or friends in your life, look for spiritual support groups or begin a moms' group in your parish that can help to meet this need in your life.

Linda recently began a mother's rosary group in her home and welcomes mothers of young children once a week to pray for their families

God is there in these moments of rest and can give us in a single instant exactly what we need. Then the rest of the day can take its course, under the same effort and strain, perhaps, but in peace. And when night comes, and you look back over the day and see how fragmentary every-thing has been, and how much you planned that has gone undone, and all the reasons you have to be embarrassed and ashamed: just take everything exactly as it is, put it in God's hands and leave it with him. Then you will be able to rest in him—really rest—and start the next day as a new life.

—St. Teresa Benedicta of the Cross

and for one another. Remember that there are others like you who face life's challenges—in being of support to other women, you will be rewarded with relationships that build you up emotionally and spiritually.

As a wife, mom, writer, and total Type A, I have to be careful to not let stress erode my otherwise joyful life. When I start to feel myself becoming as tightly clenched as a fist, here's what helps me to unfurl.

Daily quiet time with God: This is not an indulgence; it's a need. To truly pour ourselves into others, we need to be filled. The best way to do this is to spend time in prayer.

Sleep: I'm often tempted to skimp on sleep to get things done, but when I do, my emotional, physical, and spiritual health suffers. The bottom line is, it's not going to be easy to rest in God if I'm not resting at all.

Saying no graciously: This is a lesson in humility for me, but I'm learning (ever so slowly) that accepting my limitations implies that I'm inviting God into my life.

The sacraments: The Eucharist nourishes my soul. Confession renews it and allows me to let go of past hurts and to move on instead of letting my transgressions build up inside of me. Tank up on Christ through the sacraments, and he'll give you all the graces you need to be the peaceful heart of your home.

When she's not searching for sippy cups gone MIA, wife and mom Kate Wicker writes for a variety of secular and faith-based publications. She shares tales from the trenches of motherhood at www.KateWicker.com.

Survival Strategies

Just as the leader of any organization faces stress in his life, a mom's vocation as the glue that binds a family together will by definition bring moments of stress. Gratefully, there are a few tried and true tactics for minimizing the detrimental effects of stress and managing it from day to day. In Matthew's gospel account of Jesus' Sermon on the Mount, Jesus exhorts the crowds to "be perfect just as your heavenly Father is perfect." But sometimes we moms fall prey to the sin of perfectionism, placing an emphasis on things that won't ultimately benefit the spiritual perfection Jesus had in mind.

Being "perfect" for the average stressed-out mom may actually mean learning to simplify, to let perfectionism go in place of balance and well-being. If you are stressed beyond belief, take an objective look at an average week in your life. Are there ways in which you can simplify your schedule? Do you set unduly high expectations upon yourself or your children? Has financial mismanagement or an attempt to "keep up with the Joneses" caused your family anxiety?

If your answer to these questions is yes, begin the immediate and healing process of peeling away some of the complicated layers of your life. Retire from a committee or volunteer duty. Stop feeling the need to throw lavish dinner parties, dress in the popular trends, or decorate your home in the latest styles. Limit your children's extracurricular activities to one or two commitments at a time. Stop living by other people's standards and start focusing on the things that will increase your spiritual well-being and your family's happiness. Catholic moms around the country chimed in with these stress reduction strategies:

* Linda strives for a consistent daily routine. Her children welcome the comfort of a regular schedule and the consistency helps avoid little "emergencies" that can stress out the entire family.

* Barbara notes that her stress level rises when she varies her daily sleep schedule, so she goes to bed and rises at the same time every day.

* When Kristen is stressed, she finds it helpful to write a list of the things that are causing her anxiety. She looks to come up with a specific action plan for each item, breaking them down into manageable pieces.

* Maria de Lourdes, a writer, tries to maximize her exposure to fresh air and light during the course of her day. If weather permits, she works out of doors. On cold days, she works near the natural sunlight by positioning herself near a window.

* Kristina finds that exercising and getting outside as frequently as possible help her attitude. She ends her day by writing a to-do list and asks God to help her sort her priorities. This enables her to let go and begin each day with a fresh perspective.

By following some of these strategies and employing the time-management and productivity strategies detailed in chapter 9, you may find that your simpler life leads you to greater happiness and allows you more time for prayer and quiet reflection time in the midst of a mom's chaotic day. While our days as moms will always be action packed, the attitude with which we greet the many demands upon us can determine whether we live our lives filled with joy or plagued by stress and fatigue.

Sleep and Stress

Many Catholic moms find that physical exhaustion can intensify the negative effects of stress and anxiety. For moms, sleep problems can come in a variety of shapes and sizes. Young moms with infants and toddlers can fall into the dizzying cycle of being perpetually sleep deprived. As moms age, they may find themselves falling into patterns of insomnia or nighttime waking.

If you are a new mom, you may doubt that you will ever again get a good night's sleep. Both of my boys were horrific sleepers, rising for middle-of-the-night visits with mom well into their second years of life. I remember as a young, nursing mom being overjoyed by the prospect of three uninterrupted hours of sleep. If you find yourself in this position, I hope you will take steps to ensure your physical health by getting sufficient rest. Learn to lay down to sleep as soon as you put your baby down, even if you are tempted to use this time to tackle items on your to-do list. When you rise to breastfeed, avoid turning on the television or computer and do not snack. Nap when your baby does. If possible, seek the support of your husband a few nights per week to help you get caught up on needed rest.

Catholic moms around the world emphasize getting a good night's sleep and having good sleep hygiene as important elements in their overall happiness and their service to their families:

* Pamela has removed the television from her bedroom.

* Linda avoids alcohol and certain foods that keep her from getting a good night's rest.

* Paula finds that regular exercise and a hot shower prior to bedtime help her to fall asleep quickly.

* Natalie uses her bed only for sleeping, never reading in bed or watching television. She is able to fall asleep within minutes of going to bed.

* Maria shares that making time for quiet, centering prayer prior to bed helps her to drift off to sleep more peacefully.

If you find yourself unable to regularly get restorative sleep, you may need to consult your physician for medical intervention. Insomnia, sleep disorders, and sleep apnea issues are prevalent and can be medically managed. Studies recommend that the average woman needs seven to eight hours of sleep per night to maintain good physical and emotional health. Getting sufficient sleep will help you to have the energy and positive attitude you need to be your best as a wife and mom.

Deliver us, Lord, we beseech you, from every evil and grant us peace in our day, so that aided by your mercy we might be ever free from sin and protected from all anxiety, as we await the blessed hope and the coming of our Savior, Jesus Christ.

—The Order of Mass

Mom's Homework

✓ Document and assess your daily schedules and weekly routines for a four-week period.

✓ Identify support systems that can help you simplify your life: carpool to practices, limit kids to one activity per season, or speak with your supervisor at work about required overtime or unreasonable professional expectations.

✓ "Retire" gracefully from at least one volunteer commitment this month.

✓ Keep a gratitude journal, documenting each night at least three blessings, large or small, that occurred during that day.

✓ Hold a "meeting" with your family to discuss stress reduction strategies by pitching in as a team to minimize mom's load and make life function more smoothly for everyone.

✓ Strategize with your husband to get sufficient sleep.

Web Resources

SacredSpace: www.sacredspace.ie
  *Irish Jesuit site that enables you to spend ten minutes praying at your
  computer, with the help of on-screen guidance and scripture chosen specially every day*

National Sleep Foundation: www.sleepfoundation.org
  Sleep facts, information, strategies, and referrals

Doctor's orders

An Overview of Recommended Medical and Dental Routines and Screening Protocols for Women

Not only that, but we even boast of our afflictions, knowing that affliction produces endurance, and endurance, proven character, and proven character, hope, and hope does not disappoint, because the love of God has been poured out into our hearts through the holy Spirit that has been given to us.

—Romans 5:3–5

My Story

As I stood in the radiologist's office staring at a giant blowup of the mammogram of my right breast, the recurrent thought in my mind was, "It will be your own fault if something is really wrong."

You see, despite my good intentions it had been close to three years since I'd been to the doctor for a checkup. Having put on weight since my last gynecological appointment, I kept telling myself, "I'll head to the doctor as soon as I lose these ten pounds." A year became two years and then almost a third. As a favor to a friend in the pharmaceutical industry, one day last fall I attended a brief health screening his company was sponsoring. When my blood pressure was higher than normal and a trace of blood was detected in my urine, I decided it was finally time to pay the piper. I headed into my gynecologist's office and emerged with a referral for the mammogram I'd skipped for the past few years.

At no point in the process was I nervous, convinced that I was still relatively young and in good shape physically. A month later, when I was diagnosed with ductal carcinoma in situ, I actually counted my blessings. This most common form of non-invasive breast cancer was caught early in my case and treated with a lumpectomy and radiation treatments. Ironically, during the three months between my diagnosis and the end of my daily radiation treatments, I more than made up for my three-year break between doctors' visits.

I also became a major nag to my family and friends. "Have you been to the doctor? Have you had your mammogram this year?" I asked nearly everyone I knew. In my case, an early diagnosis enabled me to avoid chemotherapy and taught me about the fragility of our health. I pondered how I could feel fine and yet have a condition that, if left unchecked, might eventually lead me to an early grave.

Not every woman is as lucky as I have been. A friend's recent diagnosis with stage-four cancer has left me reeling emotionally as I pray for her healing. Despite her attention to her health and regular checkups, she is in for the battle of her lifetime. Surrounded by prayer warriors, she has accepted her cross with grace.

Spending almost seven weeks as a daily visitor to the Cancer Center has taught me to never again take for granted the value of preventative healthcare. Just as I fervently want to share my faith with others, I want to encourage the women in my life to care for themselves physically as well. From the practitioners at the Cancer Center, I learned the importance of reaching out to the sick and infirm with compassion and dignity. From my fellow patients, I learned strength and conviction of faith I never knew I had. I am now convinced that God authored this chapter of my life to teach me a few lessons, and encourage me to share them with those I love. These lessons have a little to do with seeking regular healthcare, and a lot to do with seeking his perfect will in our lives, regardless of the hand we are dealt.

No medicine is more valuable, none more efficacious, none better suited to the cure of all our temporal ills than a friend to whom we may turn for consolation in time of trouble, and with whom we may share our happiness in time of joy.

—St. Aelred of Rievaulx

What's the Prescription?

Catholic mom and soccer player Michelle Giannetta awoke one night with crushing heart pain, suffering a nearly fatal heart attack. She was a twenty-eight-year-old mother of two who fit none of the stereotypes. Young, athletic, and in peak physical condition, she spent hours each week coaching her sons' soccer teams and playing competitively with adults. A subsequent triple bypass and years of follow-up care from some of the nation's top specialists saved her life. Michelle, who had every reason to pack up her coach's whistle and take to a rocking chair, instead became a leading advocate for women's health. Her mission became informing women of every age that heart disease is the leading cause of death among both men and women. Today, in the decade since her heart attack and near-death experience, Michelle is a principal spokeswoman for the American Heart Association and an active volunteer in the campaign for women's health issues.

What Michelle shares, and what you and I need to embrace, is that we each have a role to play in our own healthcare legacy. According to the Centers for Disease Control and Prevention, women can reduce our risk of heart disease and other ailments by:

* preventing and controlling high cholesterol, high blood pressure, and diabetes
* avoiding smoking
* limiting alcohol
* keeping a healthy weight
* being active
* eating healthy
* getting check-ups

The early detection and diagnosis of many diseases and today's advances in healthcare make the prognosis for overall women's health better today than it has ever been. The U.S. Preventive Services Task Force recommends the following screenings. Always consult with your physician for the most up-to-date information.

* **Obesity:** Have your body mass index (BMI) calculated to screen for obesity. (BMI is a measure of body fat based on height and weight.) You can also find your own BMI with the BMI calculator from the National Heart, Lung, and Blood Institute at www.nhlbisupport.com/bmi.

* **Breast Cancer:** Have a mammogram every one to two years starting at age fifty.

* **Cervical Cancer:** Have a Pap smear every one to three years if you have ever been sexually active or are between the ages of twenty-one and sixty-five.

* **High Cholesterol:** Have your cholesterol checked regularly starting at age forty-five. If you are younger than forty-five, talk to your doctor about whether to have your cholesterol checked if you have diabetes, high blood pressure, smoke, or heart disease runs in your family.

* **High Blood Pressure:** Have your blood pressure checked at least every two years. High blood pressure is 140/90 or higher.

* **Colorectal Cancer:** Have a test for colorectal cancer starting at age fifty. Your doctor can help you decide which test is right for you. If you have a family history of colorectal cancer, you may need to be screened earlier.

* **Diabetes:** Have a test for diabetes if you have high blood pressure or high cholesterol.

* **Depression:** Your emotional health is as important as your physical health. If you have felt down, sad, or hopeless over the last two weeks or have felt little interest or pleasure in doing things, you may be depressed. Talk to your doctor about being screened for depression.

* **Osteoporosis (thinning of the bones):** Have a bone density test beginning at age sixty-five to screen for osteoporosis. If you are between the ages of sixty and sixty-four and weigh 154 lbs. or less, talk to your doctor about being tested.

❋ **Chlamydia and Other Sexually Transmitted Infections:** Have a test for Chlamydia if you are twenty-five or younger and sexually active. If you are older, talk to your doctor about being tested. Also ask whether you should be tested for other sexually transmitted diseases.

❋ **HIV:** According to the U.S. Department of Health and Human Services, you should have a test to screen for HIV infection if you:

- have had unprotected sex with multiple partners.

- are pregnant.

- have used or now use injection drugs.

- exchange sex for money or drugs or have sex partners who do.

- have past or present sex partners who are HIV-infected, are bisexual, or use injection drugs.

- are being treated for sexually transmitted diseases.

- had a blood transfusion between 1978 and 1985.

To avoid my bad habit of healthcare procrastination, tie your scheduling of your annual healthcare checkups to a significant event in your life so that you will remember to schedule and keep your appointments. Make a commitment with your mother, sister, or a special girlfriend to be healthcare partners and to schedule coinciding appointments, reporting back to one another after your appointments. Additionally, do not disregard warning signs that may be the symptoms of disease thinking that "it will go away." Along with the above-mentioned screenings, women should visit the dentist twice per year for checkups and cleaning, and should have eye examinations at least once per decade prior to the age of forty and every two to four years thereafter.

Cost Considerations

Sadly, many women neglect their own healthcare because they are one of the nearly twenty percent of Americans under the age of sixty-five not covered by insurance. That number continues to increase. If you find yourself without healthcare insurance for any reason, inquire in your community about healthcare assistance programs and resources. If you fall outside the eligibility requirements for Medicaid,

The human body is the most precious gift given to us by God. Only through the senses of the body are we able to relate to God's beautiful world. Through our bodies we are able to give and receive love, work in service to and for others, recreate in countless ways, and reach for our highest potential—reflecting God's glory.

Reflecting God's glory within, to our families, neighbors, and the world, is a long-term commitment. As St. Paul so eloquently says, "I have run the good race," and what is it we have been given to run the race with? It is not someone else's body, but our own.

So why is it that we find far too many excuses to neglect such a gift?

Do we put off, excuse ourselves, from following a reasonable course of taking care of ourselves? Do we not consider the gift of our bodies to be a precious resource that needs protection?

As wives and mothers, our role is a forever role. It is a role that means being committed to the goal we are charged to seek—to give to others in such a way that we model what giving truly is.

Only by giving to ourselves first—not in self-centered or selfish ways, but in ways that reflect self-discipline through an appreciation for life—will we understand what it means to be called a follower of Christ. Did Jesus not weep and ask, "Father, let this cup pass me by?" With these few words, he demonstrated the ultimate appreciation and love for his body and for his life. It was in this "giving over" of his body in love for others that he became the glory of God.

Taking care of ourselves is ultimately a responsibility entrusted to us through our birth as children of God. It is our "pre-commandment," a first responsibility because it is only through our bodies that we are able to bring the life and love of Jesus to our world.

Best-selling award-winning Catholic author Sue Stanton writes from her family's home in Iowa.

you may still be able to seek preventative screenings, immunizations, and medical care through local clinics and subsidized programs. Additionally, speak with your parish, your diocese, and your local Catholic Charities agency to obtain assistance referrals within your community.

Illness can lead to anguish, self-absorption, sometimes even despair and revolt against God. It can also make a person more mature, helping him discern in his life what is not essential so that he can turn toward that which is. Very often illness provokes a search for God and a return to him.

—Catechism of the Catholic Church, 1501

If you have healthcare insurance, weaving your way through the minefield of insurance regulations and paperwork may be nearly as stressful as dealing with a difficult diagnosis. While you are healthy, learn about your healthcare coverage, benefits, filing for reimbursement, and any special requirements of your policy. If you are part of a health maintenance organization (HMO) or other entity that requires referrals, establish a relationship with your designated primary healthcare physician. This will be helpful to you in the future if you need a referral to a specialist. Many HMOs will only reimburse for procedures authorized through a primary care referral. Save yourself anxiety, heartache, and financial distress by becoming acquainted with the proper procedures for your healthcare insurance when you are healthy and well.

Care for Catholics

Many Catholic moms avoid healthcare screenings because of a sense of discouragement or lack of understanding from their healthcare providers. As Catholic women, we are called by our faith to openness to life in the sacrament of marriage. As a result, many Catholic moms practice Natural Family Planning (NFP) or are willing to welcome large families. I have had Catholic moms tell me that they are frequently harassed or belittled by healthcare professionals who do not accept or concur with their Catholic healthcare choices.

For your relationship with your primary care physician to function effectively, there must exist a relationship of trust, open communication, and mutual respect. If you find that, as a Catholic mom, your needs and values are not taken into consideration in your healthcare, you should seek another physician who can deliver care that will conform to your ethics, values, and needs. While my personal physician is not Catholic, she has been respectful of our family's stance against birth control and has worked with me to seek healthcare options that conform to my Catholic faith. This trusting relationship has been nurtured over years of conversations and has functioned efficiently because I am open and communicative about my beliefs.

For many Catholic moms, our obstetrician/gynecologist frequently acts as the "gatekeeper" for many of our healthcare services. Finding a family practice or OB/GYN physician whose practice openly embraces Natural Family Planning can be difficult in many areas of the country, but is not always impossible. To locate physician referrals in your area, visit the website of One More Soul (www.omsoul.com/nfp-only.php), which runs a directory of NFP-only healthcare providers and pharmacies. Additionally, on the site you can locate referrals to teachers and centers that instruct on the methodology of Natural Family Planning.

Beyond fertility issues, other stages of life and disease will bring moments when you may want to seek the advice of a priest or Catholic chaplain relating to healthcare decisions. If you find yourself ill or facing a serious healthcare diagnosis, inquire at your parish about the sacrament of the anointing of the sick. Today, the graces of this sacrament are no longer reserved as "last rites" for the dying. The sacrament may be received in times of grave illness or prior to a surgical procedure, and may be repeated if necessary. If you or a member of your family is hospitalized, inquire during the registration process about the availability of a priest who can celebrate this sacrament and minister to your family. Today, many parishes around the country offer healing Masses and anointing of the sick on a regularly scheduled basis.

If you become ill or face a serious medical procedure or diagnosis, remember to turn to both your immediate family and to your parish faith family for their prayers, as well as their emotional and physical support. Very frequently, we moms want to "do it all" ourselves, refusing to admit that we need help. In the face of illness, embrace support and spiritual counseling as it is offered to you. In my own journey through the trials of breast cancer, I have found great wisdom in the words of the *Catechism*, which states that illness "can also make a person more mature, helping him discern in his life what is not essential so that he can turn toward that which is" (*CCC*, 1501). The essentials in my life are my faith, my family, and my friends. Dealing with visits to physicians' offices and medical procedures helped me to look inward for the fruits of the Holy Spirit in my life and to offer intercessory prayer for all facing illness.

Mom's Homework

✓ Today, schedule an appointment with your physician for an annual checkup.

✓ Create a "calendar of care" for your family. Schedule routine screenings, immunizations, and dental appointments for each member of your family—including your husband if he is not doing so himself.

✓ If your current healthcare provider does not respect and uphold your Catholic values, find a new provider and schedule an appointment to establish care.

✓ Review the provisions and requirements of your healthcare policy.

✓ Take a Natural Family Planning refresher course, read a book on NFP, or visit www.catholicmom.com/nfp.htm for archived NFP columns and resources.

Web Resources

One More Soul: www.omsoul.com/nfp-only.php
   Referral of NFP-only healthcare providers

Catholic Medical Association: www.cathmed.org
   Upholds the principles of the Catholic faith in the science and practice of medicine and assists the Church in the work of communicating Catholic medical ethics to the medical profession and society at large

Catholic Health Association of the United States: www.chausa.org
   The nation's largest group of not-for-profit healthcare sponsors, systems, and facilities

PART IV: Soul

THE BEAUTIFUL RITUALS
AND TRADITIONS OF OUR
CATHOLIC FAITH

CHAPTER SEVENTEEN

Prioritizing prayer

Incorporating Prayer Rituals into Our Daily Lives

Have no anxiety at all, but in everything, by prayer and petition, with thanksgiving, make your requests known to God. Then the peace of God that surpasses all understanding will guard your hearts and minds in Christ Jesus.

—Philippians 4:6-7

My Story

In the opening moments of one of my favorite musicals, *Fiddler on the Roof*, we find the lead character Tevya plaintively conversing with God in an almost playful fashion. Perhaps I enjoy this scene so much because it mimics the ebb and flow of my own prayer life. Try as I might to incorporate more structured prayer disciplines into the course of my days, I almost reflexively convert back to my daylong chats with the God I'm convinced hears and knows every prayer of my heart.

From the moment my eyes open in the morning, I greet God and offer him my day's prayers, works, joys, and sufferings. As I slip from the bed, which typically still contains the slumbering body of my beloved Greg, I pray for my husband's health and the well-being of the patients he will see throughout his workday in the ER. Passing the bedrooms of my boys, I plead for their happiness and their safety—the first of many times I'll offer this intention throughout the day.

By the time I've made it downstairs to the coffee pot, I wonder whether or not God is already sick of my petitions and of me in general. As I down three separate prescription medications, a silent intention accompanies each. With a steaming cup of decaf in hand, I make my way to my favorite oversized chair in the library and spend time meditating upon the day's Gospel passage.

So begins the day of one Catholic mom, storming the heavens on behalf of her little tribe. My prayers will continue throughout the course of the day—a rosary fit in during a walk or while driving, more prayers for the boys as I fold their laundry or clean their rooms, and silent prayers for the intentions of friends and colleagues show that I'm following St. Paul's counsel to "pray constantly."

And yet, somehow I am left with the nagging sensation that my prayer life is never good enough. A small part of me envies the rhythm of the life of cloistered nuns, whose days are marked by prayer first and all else afterward. With the exception of my morning quiet time, which never seems to happen every day of the week, my prayers often feel reactive and self-centered. I know a day is coming soon when I will have time to linger in our lovely Eucharistic adoration chapel at church or to spend an hour each day in silent scripture study. In the meantime, my version of "pray constantly" will continue to occur in the laundry room, the shower, behind the wheel of my car, and wherever else a small patch of silence can be found in a busy Catholic mom's life.

What's the Problem?

When I raise the topic of prayer with Catholic moms, I am sometimes saddened by the honesty with which so many of us admit that our personal prayer lives are strained nearly to the breaking point. But I cannot say that I am surprised. Even spiritual giants such as Blessed

We need to find God, and God cannot be found in noise and restlessness. God is the friend of silence. See how nature—trees and flowers and grass—grow in silence. See the stars, the moon, and the sun, how they move in silence. The more we receive in silent prayer, the more we can give in our active life.

—Blessed Mother Teresa

Mother Teresa, St. Thérèse of Lisieux, and St. John of the Cross confessed to knowing the "dark night of the soul." If these and other holy men and women can know moments of doubt, spiritual dryness, and feelings of abandonment, then you and I surely belong to a communion of saints for whom prayer has not always come easily.

A Christian's life is all about serving others. As moms we are so constantly assaulted by the physical and emotional needs of those around us that we often neglect ourselves and our relationships with God in the process. Moments of silence are few and far between during days spent feeding, shuttling, educating, cleaning, working, and dropping into bed exhausted. One mother recently shared with me her frustration over finding quiet time for prayer:

> I have to admit that I am one of the ones whose prayer life had died out over the years. It was much easier a few years back to take the time to go off and pray. Lately though, I find it very difficult. There is not really anywhere that is very quiet in our home, with the exception of the bathroom, and at times that is not a quiet place either. I do try each night when I go to bed to pray, but often find my mind wanders because I am so tired.

This is a refrain that's being sung by Catholic moms all over the country. Indeed, the issue is so pervasive that the *Catechism of the Catholic Church* devotes a section entitled "The Battle of Prayer" to the issues of difficulties in prayer, dealing with distraction, and spiritual dryness (see #2725). The demands of our motherly vocation, coupled with an ever-increasing societal "noise" level and the busyness of the schedules we keep, leave our spiritual reserves running on empty. In this chapter, we look at different types of prayer and how busy moms have succeeded in prioritizing prayer in their lives.

A Place and a Time

Most Catholic moms agree that if you leave finding time for prayer to chance, it's likely that you may not feel truly fulfilled in your prayer life. We moms may do well to emulate the example of those in monastic life. Their "rule" of life contains prescribed times of common prayer throughout the day and night, around which all other activity is planned. While you and I may not be able to regulate our days with such exacting standards, we can and should aim to have periods of relative quiet throughout the day for prayer and introspection. That being said, it's also important that we find ways to pray along with our families, since the best of our waking hours are usually spent in their company.

You, more than anyone, know the flow of your day. Begin to take baby steps to incorporate a few protected moments during your day to turn to God in silent or verbal prayer. In my home, predawn mornings have always been the time when I could find a few moments of silence and stillness. These days, as my children have grown, it is much easier to incorporate other periods of prayer into my days. But if you have small children in the home, you may need to accept humble beginnings and settle on one five- to ten-minute prayer time per day. Speak honestly with your husband and children about your needs, and listen to theirs as well. Many families find that praying together is a wonderful practice. Other couples may find that providing some solitude for each individual is better suited to their particular spirituality.

Create a "sacred space" in your home that can become "mom's prayer corner." This doesn't need to be anything more grandiose than a simple, comfortable chair that is somewhat out of the center of most activity in your home. In our house, we recognized that the formal dining room went largely unused and subsequently transformed it into our "library." Surrounded by my favorite books in one corner of the room is a green oversized chair. The small, adjacent table holds my bible, whatever spiritual book I am currently reading, a rosary, a candle, and some inspirational holy cards. In five minutes, I can have a private "retreat" from the hustle and bustle of the day. If you have very small children, your prayer corner will need to be a child-friendly environment where a small blanket nearby might contain a few quiet toys for little ones to play quietly while Mom spends a few moments in prayer. Just as we treasure our church buildings as havens of solace, let's create a prayer haven within our home where we can go at any time of the day or night seeking God.

What Works

I want to offer you the following examples of "prayer in action" in the homes of Catholic families around the world. With these models, you can see a lovely cross-section of moms making prayer a priority in their lives.

Beginning and ending the day in prayer: Cynthia and her husband begin and end their days with scripture study.

> My husband and I have tried to do Bible devotions morning and evening for the four years we've been married. My devotional and bible are on the kitchen table where (six days out of seven) we eat breakfast. The odd day sometimes does get missed. His devotional and the family bible are on a table in our foyer within eyeshot of the living room, and we try to do his devotion before we go to bed if we don't fall asleep on the couch!

Liturgy of the Hours: Debra shares, "I like to start the day with the Office of Readings and can usually tell the difference when I don't!" In the Thomas home, Roger and Ellen found that praying the Hours together as a family brought discipline and structure to their prayer time and drew their children closer to scripture.

Prayers of the Faithful: The *General Instruction of the Roman Missal* calls each of us, as Church, to remember one another and the needs of our world in our prayers during Mass.

> In the Prayer of the Faithful, the people respond in a certain way to the word of God which they have welcomed in faith and, exercising the office of their baptismal priesthood, offer prayers to God for the salvation of all.

> *—General Instruction of the Roman Missal, 69*

As mothers, we can and should keep these same prayers in our hearts and minds during the course of the week. As a priestly people, we pray for the needs of our Church, for those in public authority, for those burdened by any type of difficulty, and for the needs of our local communities. Once again, uniting our prayers with others around the world, we Catholic moms can be a part of lasting civic, social, and

Prayer began for me in my heart when I was young. Even though I knew the Our Father, Hail Mary, and Glory Be, the prayers I most remember sprung spontaneously from inside of me and often after I had received the Holy Communion.

I am old enough to remember the Latin Mass and I'd always pepper my father with questions each time we'd go. I didn't understand any of the words, but somehow, I knew what the Eucharist was. The prayer in my heart spoke volumes, with images like that of a child's picture book: a rose bush growing in my heart, a house with shiny floors after being swept clean. Only later as an adult did I realize that those pictures reflected Jesus' Blessed Mother in the rose, and the state of my soul, cleansed after receiving Christ in the Eucharist.

These days when I receive the Eucharist, it's not so much pictures I see as it is an overwhelming sense of love, awe, and gratitude that Jesus would humble himself to the point of becoming a common piece of bread so that I could commune with him in the most intimate of ways. There are still no real words to explain what the Eucharist is to me. I just know in my heart that I believe. No words are needed.

Susan Bailey uses her abilities as a singer/songwriter, recording artist, and blogger to encourage the faithful as an expression of her Catholic faith. Visit her at www.SusanBailey.net.

economic change and amelioration. Catholic mom Eileen shares, "I start most every day scanning the headlines so that I remain engaged in the political, social, and cultural issues of our time, beginning with holding those issues in prayer."

Let's follow the tremendous role model provided to us by those in monastic communities who spend their lives ministering to the needs of the world community through their prayers. By holding those in need in our own communities and in far-flung corners of the world in our intentions, we can remain positively engaged in the larger issues of society.

Praying for others: Devotion to intercessory prayer seems to be a common theme among Catholic women. Catholic author Meredith Gould writes out her prayers for others, confiding that the commitment of keeping a list of intentions keeps her accountable to those for whom she has offered to pray. Kelly Murphy has a few "triggers" that are constant prayer reminders during her day. "I see a bird fly and I pray to forgive my enemies," Kelly explains. "I drop my children off at school and pray for the school. I have certain people I pray for when I brush my teeth and do other activities throughout my day. I see the sunset and thank God for the day." Mom and swim coach Kim offers prayers during the course of her routine work around her home, offering sometimes mundane tasks such as folding clothes for the intentions of her children. I have found that keeping a prayer journal helps me to focus my thoughts during moments of distraction that may discourage me from praying.

Praying as a family: Throughout the course of our days, we can find moments to incorporate family prayer rituals. Many families take extra time for prayer prior to family meals, recalling intercessions and celebrating the liturgical seasons during the dinner hour. Celia and her husband have the wonderful habit of singing Vespers together with their children each night at bedtime. In our family, the morning drive time has always been a time of family prayer as we begin our day by offering it to the Lord. Now that I no longer drive my boys to school, I ask them frequently about their prayer intentions and pray for and with them prior to their departure.

Kelly Lynch, founder of the nonprofit organization Mychal's Message, does not take her family's prayer life nor her personal blessings for granted:

> I pray as I breathe. Being *aware* helps me to pray more. If my children are sick and I'm bringing them lunch trays, I pray, "Thank you God that I am a stay-at-home mom and can do this." If my hands are numb due to MS symptoms, "Thank you God that I have hands." If my pantry door won't close, "Thank you God that we have a stocked pantry." Since my children were little, our evening prayers went like this:
>
> Today, God, I am thankful for . . . (they each share something they're thankful for that day).
>
> Today, God, I am sorry for . . . (again, they each share). We then pray an Act of Contrition.
>
> Today, God, I want to pray for . . . (they share the name of someone who is alive and then the soul of someone who has died).

And today, God, this is what kind thing I did for someone else (we never share that one out loud but instead say, "Got mine!" The kindness stays between each of us and God). We end in an Our Father, Hail Mary, and Glory Be

Eucharistic adoration: For those fortunate enough to live in a parish with an adoration chapel where the Blessed Sacrament is exposed in a monstrance, Eucharistic adoration is a beloved form of devotional prayer. Moms can either schedule an hour for a regular prayer time in front of the Blessed Sacrament or "drop in" for a visit as their schedule permits. Even very young children can be taught reverence for the Eucharist and may accompany mom on her visit. Catholic mom Chris treasures her weekly middle of the night visits with Jesus in the Eucharist. She brings her rosary, inspirational reading materials, and her bible, but frequently simply spends this time in silent, solitary prayer.

Prayer is the raising of one's mind and heart to God or the requesting of good things from God." But when we pray, do we speak from the height of our pride and will, or "out of the depths" of a humble and contrite heart? He who humbles himself will be exalted; humility is the foundation of prayer. Only when we humbly acknowledge that "we do not know how to pray as we ought," are we ready to receive freely the gift of prayer. "Man is a beggar before God."

—Catechism of the Catholic Church, 2559

Using sacramentals and non-traditional prayer tools: Many families have prayer aids and sacramentals in their homes that remind them to keep prayer a daily priority. Sacramentals such as blessed candles, rosaries, statues, scapulars, and holy water remind us to lead lives of devotion to God. In today's Church, new prayer aids emerge every year. Debi and Caroline use their iPods and cell phones as important components of their prayer lives. On Debi's iPod, special software helps her to pray the rosary every day. Caroline's cell phone alarm rings daily at noon, calling her to pray the Angelus and again at 6:00 p.m. when she prays Evening Prayer with the aid of a podcast and an application on her phone. Around the globe, Catholics gather online in communities each day to pray communally for the intentions of our Church and for each other's private intercessory needs.

Making Prayer a Top Priority

Paula Rutherford and her husband Ian are the owners of Aquinas and More Catholic Goods. As a homeschooling mom of eight, Paula shares that her prayer time takes top priority in her life.

> Prayer is THE priority. I try not to "fit it in" wherever I have extra time—I actually schedule prayer into the day first, and then fit the rest around that. Use natural lulls in the day (kids' nap time, before they get up in the morning, after they go to bed, etc.) to schedule in prayer. I pray my rosary in the morning before the kids get up, sometimes while I nurse the baby. Liturgy of the Hours is a good way to pray: it is already scheduled! All you need to do is open it up at the right times of the day for the various parts. We do night prayer, but haven't yet added any other hours. Ian calls me from work at noon and we pray the Angelus on the phone. I also am in constant contact with our family's guardian angels. With eight kids, I rely on their help every day. We ask for the intercession of the kids' oldest sibling, who is in heaven now praying for us. Whenever I see or use something someone has given me, I pray for that person. And I look to the Blessed Virgin Mary as my model.

Mary, a mother of four children ranging in age from teens to toddlers, sums up the feelings of many Catholic moms on the topic of prayer.

> I do morning prayers with the children before we start school and I do raise my mind and heart to God whenever I think about it many times during the day. I feel as though I have learned to make my life a prayer amidst the "noise" that is forever present. It's not perfect but I am trying to work with what God has given me . . . an active healthy family who all look to me to nourish their bodies and souls in the many ways that a mother needs to care for her family.

Mom's Homework

✓ Create a schedule for daily prayer in your life. Write your appointment with God on your daily calendar and inform your family of your intentions to reserve quiet moments of prayer during the course of your day. Seek their input and their participation.

✓ Create a "sacred space" in your home—a simple prayer chair or corner where you and your children can go to quietly pray and read.

✓ Investigate prayer groups and women's groups in your parish or join a prayer community online.

✓ Begin a prayer journal or a simple list of intercessory prayer intentions.

✓ Does your parish or a nearby church offer Eucharistic adoration? Take your children for a brief visit to the Blessed Sacrament or simply pay a mid-week visit to your parish for a few quiet moments with Jesus.

Web Resources

Universalis: www.universalis.com
   The Liturgy of the Hours online

Pray Station Portable: http://psp.libsyn.com
   Daily morning and evening prayers in audio format

Verbum Domini: http://sqpn.com/2008/03/10/verbum-domini
   Daily Scripture Readings of the Roman Catholic Liturgical Calendar in audio format

Mass matters

Preparing Ourselves
for the Celebration of Sunday Eucharist

Then he took a cup, gave thanks, and said, "Take this and share it among yourselves; for I tell you (that) from this time on I shall not drink of the fruit of the vine until the kingdom of God comes." Then he took the bread, said the blessing, broke it, and gave it to them, saying, "This is my body, which will be given for you; do this in memory of me." And likewise the cup after they had eaten, saying, "This cup is the new covenant in my blood, which will be shed for you."

–Luke 22:17-20

My Story

My love for and appreciation of the Mass has taken years to evolve to where I find myself today. Growing up as a child, attendance at Mass was always a focal point of our family Sunday. Invariably, we attended together as a family and hung out socializing for at least thirty minutes after Mass. As I grew older, I learned to play guitar and frequently attended Mass two or three times a weekend, in the hey-day of '70s folk Masses. I loved the feeling of service and participation that came with playing for Mass and the tight bond our parish community shared. Our Irish pastor, Msgr. Michael Collins, remains to this day one of my favorite homilists—his words never ceased to inspire me for the week ahead. In typical childish fashion, I didn't realize how truly blessed I was or how much I took our parish, St. Barbara's, for granted.

When I graduated from high school, I set off for college at the University of Notre Dame. My love affair with the Mass continued and blossomed. On the Notre Dame campus, it seemed that Mass was being celebrated at almost any hour of the day. I became a daily communicant. Campus Masses were intimate and liturgically beautiful. I was always keenly aware of the presence of the Holy Spirit moving among my friends and me and inspiring us to live lives rooted in faith.

When I graduated from Notre Dame, I was unprepared for the spiritual "real world." After Greg and I, newly engaged, landed in Nashville, Tennessee, I found myself for the first time surrounded by non-Catholics. Greg, who had not yet joined the Church, was always tremendously supportive of my faith life and frequently accompanied me to Mass at our parish, the lovely Cathedral of the Incarnation. But I soon came to realize that what I'd taken for granted basically since birth, the celebration of Mass in a loving, closely connected community, was no longer a part of my life. At the Cathedral, we knew no one and never felt closely bonded to the priests of the parish. My heart ached for those liturgies celebrated in the company of my family and friends. I fulfilled my Sunday obligations with a heavy heart and found sadly that going to Mass often left me homesick, lonely, and depressed.

As our marriage took us home to southern California, we spent some time "church shopping" and settled on a parish in Los Angeles. Our fellow parishioners lived in the upscale homes that surrounded our little apartment. Greg attended with me as often as he could, but his hectic schedule as a first-year ER Resident frequently kept him busy on Sundays. I fell into the trap of leaving Mass thinking, "I didn't get anything out of that!" When little Eric came along, I dragged him to Mass every Sunday, fulfilling my obligation as though I were punching a time card. Even though I wasn't working, I never took advantage of the opportunity to attend daily Mass sadly, at that time, attending playgroup felt like more of a priority and I didn't relish the thought of keeping a toddler quiet in church.

Hear Mass daily; it will prosper the whole day. All your duties will be performed the better for it, and your soul will be stronger to bear its daily cross. The Mass is the most holy act of religion; you can do nothing that can give greater glory to God or be more profitable for your soul than to hear Mass both frequently and devoutly. It is the favorite devotion of the saints.

—St. Peter Julian Eymard

At the conclusion of Greg's residency program, we made our home in Fresno and again found ourselves looking for a parish home. We eventually landed at our current parish, St. Anthony of Padua, when Eric was three years old and Adam a newborn. I began to fall into a dangerous habit of attending Mass without Greg. If he worked on a Saturday evening, the boys and I would attend Mass then so that we could have time with him on Sunday morning at home. If I attended Sunday morning Mass, I frequently dropped Eric off at the preschool and took baby Adam to the babysitting room so that I could "get something out of" the Mass. But then I'd find myself alone in Mass, surrounded by families who seemed so perfect. The Sunday blues continued.

A turning point came for me when Eric was four years old and a friend from playgroup invited me to become her RCIA sponsor. I think we lifelong Catholics often take the blessings of our faith for granted. Since we've received communion since childhood, we don't experience the deep longing for the Eucharist that many RCIA catechumens and candidates feel. As April's sponsor, my eyes were opened to the miracle of Christ's true presence in the Eucharist. I began to see, for the very first time, the centrality of the Eucharist as the source and summit of our Catholic faith. I began to realize how deeply separated I'd been from Christ in the Eucharist for so many years. Even though I was a "cradle Catholic" it was as though I viewed the Mass with new eyes for the very first time. I realized the error of my outlook in wanting to "get something out of Mass" rather than looking at the absolutely precious gift of Christ in the Eucharist that was present at every Mass, regardless of the priest, the music, or the families surrounding me.

I had fallen into the trap that many Catholics face—if we don't like what the homilist has to say, or we don't enjoy the music, or we don't have a relationship with other families in your parish, we feel wronged. We may stop attending Mass, or even worse, find ourselves headed to nondenominational churches with uplifting choirs, pastors who seem to live in the "real world," and fancy day care centers. Now when I attend a non-Catholic worship service or wedding, I find myself walking away feeling empty for want of what is truly at the heart of our Catholic liturgies—the Eucharist.

Ironically, it took worshipping in the presence of a group of people who were working and praying diligently to be initiated into our Church to open my eyes to a blessing that had been given to me in childhood by my parents, the true fullness of my Catholic faith.

The Heart of Our Faith

The *Catechism of the Catholic Church* expresses in beautiful terms the nurturing element of the Eucharist:

> What material food produces in our bodily life, Holy Communion wonderfully achieves in our spiritual life. Communion with the flesh of the risen Christ, a flesh "given life and giving life through the Holy Spirit," preserves, increases, and renews the life of grace received at Baptism. This growth in Christian life needs the nourishment of Eucharistic Communion, the bread for our pilgrimage until the moment of death, when it will be given to us as viaticum.
>
> —*Catechism of the Catholic Church,* 1392

Along with solidifying our union with Christ, the *Catechism* reminds us, the Eucharist separates us from sin, unites us as a Church, and commits us to the poor.

I want to share with you that I still struggle to keep my mind focused on what is truly the greatest gift of attending Mass with my family each week—the Eucharist. I so often fall short in my worthiness to receive Christ in the Eucharist. I process in the communion line feeling the gulf that separates me from all that God wants me to be in my life, but I know that true union with Christ in Holy Communion is my only hope and a true joy. With this understanding, I am now frequently moved to tears of happiness on Sunday mornings.

Ironically, I find myself once again alone in the pew. But this is because Greg, Eric, and Adam are part of our parish music ministry, frequently playing for two Masses each week. Our bodies are not physically together as we celebrate Mass on Sundays, but our hearts are united in the Eucharist. For me, there is no greater joy than this and I never cease to praise God for the turns my journey to him has taken and for the gift of the Eucharist as the greatest source of strength in my life.

Preparing for Mass

One Mass is enough to make us the greatest saint, yet, most of us have attended thousands of Masses and leave as we came. What can we do to open ourselves to God's graces at Mass? Our preparation begins long before we enter the doors of the church and continues long after. Prayer is the foundation. Without a daily prayer life, our hearts will not be open at Mass. A prayerful reading of the scriptures of the day will ready us to hear more attentively during the liturgy. Arriving early enough to spend a bit of quality time will quiet our hearts and our heads as we enter into the prayer of Christ to the Father. I always say, "You can't go to Mass dry, you have to be wet with the Holy Spirit." We get wet in prayer! Listen attentively to every prayer and reading and pray them from your heart. After receiving holy communion, use the time as a time of communion. We often receive Jesus and forget he is within—enter into your heart with him, and experience his love and peace. After the closing hymn, don't rush off. Take a few moments to thank him and carry that thanksgiving throughout your day.

Fr. Jay A. Finelli was ordained a priest for the Roman Catholic Diocese of Providence on June 13, 1992, and is currently pastor of Holy Ghost Church in Tiverton, Rhode Island. He is also the host of the iPadre Podcast at www.iPadre.net.

Pope St. Pius X once said, "Holy Communion is the safest and shortest way to heaven." As moms, we should want nothing more for our families and ourselves than to have eternal salvation with God in heaven. Unfortunately, we may also find ourselves viewing Mass as more of a stressful situation than a pathway to the Almighty. I almost hesitated to write this chapter of the book myself, because I have fallen so short of what I hope for you, my fellow moms. Now that my boys are teens, I'd love to call for a "do over" and retake the days of their early childhood when I dropped them off in the childcare room so that I could have a little peace and quiet in Mass. Sadly, their absence, and Greg's as well, brought me anything but serenity. Nothing makes me happier now than to sit near a big family in church and to try to share a few words of encouragement with moms who seem to struggle under the burden of keeping little ones from distracting others.

I see you in the pew, moms, and you're my heroes. You're the one with the five children who's brave enough to come by yourself while your husband sits home watching professional football. You're the grandma who brings your granddaughter to Mass every Sunday—I don't know where her own mom and dad are, but she's lucky to have you in her life. You're the one whose toddler always needs to go potty during Mass and who races back to join her husband in the communion line. You're the widow whose husband left us much too soon and whose four boys are frequently dressed in matching Sunday suits. You're the one whose son is serving in Iraq, and I share your prayers for his safety as you quietly finger your rosary after communion. You're the one whose son is preparing for first communion and who quietly whispers words of instruction into his ears to help him understand what's going on. You're the one who missed most of the homily as you quietly nursed your baby in the vestibule. You're the one with sulky teens in tow—don't worry, someday they'll thank you. You are my heroes, you are raising the future priests, sisters, and lay leaders of our Church, and you inspire me.

Preparing Ourselves for Mass

As I've stated before, attending Mass as a mom can feel like anything but a spiritual experience, but there are a few steps we can take that will help us in preparing for Sunday's liturgy. They are simple suggestions and may enhance our participation in Mass.

Follow the liturgical calendar: I find great symmetry in our Catholic calendar. The passing of the liturgical seasons often has greater meaning for me than does the change of traditional seasons. I love the anticipatory nature of Advent and the penitential quality of Lent. I love celebrating the saints' feast days and our parish processions for major liturgical occasions. If you don't have a liturgical calendar in your home, you can find an inexpensive one at a local church supply store. By becoming more aware of our journey through the liturgical year, you will begin to appreciate the unfolding of the Sunday liturgies.

Read the readings in advance: This is one of the best bits of advice I've been given and one that continues to enhance my appreciation of Sunday's Liturgy of the Word. Mass readings are available online at www.usccb.org/nab/index.shtml for both Sunday and daily Masses. Many parishes have groups that gather together during the week to read and study the Sunday readings. I also listen to some wonderful podcasts that read and reflect upon the readings. I find that when I've studied the readings in advance, I am more tuned into the homily. For moms with young children, you can study the Mass readings with your children and you may find that all of you will end up benefiting. At CatholicMom.com we offer free, downloadable activities to help you and your children prepare for Sunday. Visit CatholicMom.com for age-appropriate coloring pages, games, and worksheets, as well as religious education lesson plans for every Sunday of the school year.

Keeping Sunday Holy

With our crazy schedules and today's society that looks at Sunday as just another day, it may be difficult to truly take Sunday as a day of rest. But we should definitely try to settle our souls and place Mass attendance as the focal point of our family time on the weekend. I try to keep these priorities in mind every weekend.

Attend Mass as a family: I wish I had done a better job of this when my children were little. I wish someone would have turned to me and said, "It's OK if your boys wiggle or make noise—they too are part of our Church," rather than politely reminding me of the parish babysitting schedule. How can our children learn to sit through and ultimately grow up to love Mass if they never attend? Also, once children age and their schedules begin to be filled with activities, it's very easy to fall into the trap of everyone going to separate masses. Whenever possible, try to celebrate Mass as a family, even if this means altering your normal attendance schedule. I know that sometimes this is impossible, but we should always do our very best to make Mass attendance our greatest family priority.

Dress appropriately: This is a very controversial topic, and I'll agree that it's better to go to Mass dressed casually than not to go at all. But there is something truly wonderful about dressing up for Sunday Mass. It may be the one occasion during the week when we don a skirt and feel truly lovely. Sunday clothes don't need to be fancy or expensive, simply tasteful and respectful. In my parish, there is a family with nine (and soon to be ten) young children who come to Mass every Sunday impeccably dressed. I wonder how early their mother gets up to ensure that all of those outfits are ready. Simple, appropriate attire can come from a thrift store or consignment boutique. My boys each have one pair of "Sunday shoes," which they regularly wear on Sundays. Dressing for our celebration of the Eucharist is yet another signal of the priority it should play in our lives.

Arrive early: This is a tough one for moms. We always seem to need to head into the house just one more time after a forgotten bottle or jacket. But it's important, so establish a Sunday routine that enables you to park at church and be seated at least five minutes before Mass. This will alleviate your stress and help to settle your children before Mass begins.

Sit close to the front: Some of my worst Mass experiences when Eric was a baby and toddler came when I tried to sit with him in the "cry room." Who invented the "cry room" and for goodness sake, why did they ever call it the "cry room"? If we deposit our children in babysitting or sit in the back of the church, they frequently have no concept of what is going on in Mass because they can't see or hear what is happening on the altar. Of course, as moms, we need to exercise respect for those around us. Sit somewhere with an "escape route" that will allow you to quietly and respectfully attend to potty training emergencies or unhappy toddlers.

Take the Word of God with You as You Go

One of my favorite recessional hymns underscores the challenge I feel each Sunday as I depart our sanctuary:

> Take the word of God with you as you go.
> Take the seeds of God's word and make them grow.
> Go in peace to serve the world, in peace to serve the world.
> Take the love of God, the love of God with you as you go.

—Christopher Walker and James Harrison
"Take the Word of God with You"

I find it very helpful after attending Mass with my family on Sunday to spend some time after Mass contemplating the week ahead. I may try to reread the gospel or the psalm and reflect upon its relevance to my own life. Every Sunday, I also listen to a few podcasts that review the Sunday Liturgy of the Word. One of my favorites is the "Techno Priest" (www.technopriest.org), where Fr. Bill Kessler shares his Sunday homilies online. I also love to listen to Fr. Jay Finelli's "iPadre show" (www.ipadre.net), which follows the liturgical calendar and explains "all things Catholic and then some." In my home, I frequently spend Sunday afternoons folding and putting away laundry in anticipation of the school week. These two priests help me to digest the week's scripture message as I serve my family. I also enjoy taking notes during the Sunday homily and journaling my reflections after Mass. Granted, this is very difficult to do when your children are small, but even the busiest mom can spare a few moments most Sundays to write about her feelings and prayers following the Sunday Eucharist.

> If from the beginning Christians have celebrated the Eucharist and in a form whose substance has not changed despite the great diversity of times and liturgies, it is because we know ourselves to be bound by the command the Lord gave on the eve of his Passion: "Do this in remembrance of me."
>
> —Catechism of the Catholic Church, 1356

In sharing my thoughts and feelings with you on the Mass, I hope that you can avoid my painful trap of looking to "get something out of" the Mass. I hope that you will find joy, peace, and ultimately salvation in the frequent reception of the Eucharist. I hope you can persevere though the days of cranky toddlers and brooding teens, or of spouses who might be physically or emotionally absent. If you find yourself worshiping without the company of your spouse or children as I did, I hope you will find solace in Christ's true presence in the Eucharist and a knowledge that when we rest in him, we are truly never alone.

Mom's Homework

- ✓ If you are not already doing so, find a way to attend Mass as a family this weekend. Plan for it as you would an important appointment.
- ✓ Read the Sunday readings in advance at www.usccb.org/nab/index.shtm.
- ✓ Start a small "Sunday journal" to reflect on your feelings and prayers after Mass on Sunday.

✓ Stop looking to "get something out of" Mass and start looking at ways to serve your parish community. If the age of your children prohibits you from taking on a liturgical ministry role, simply pray for your priest and your fellow parishioners during the week. This is likely one of the most important roles a mom can play in the Body of Christ.

Web Resources

United States Conference of Catholic Bishops New American Bible:
www.usccb.org/nab
The daily Mass readings and psalms, as well as daily video reflections on the readings

iPadre: www.ipadre.net
iPadre Catholic podcasting—all things Catholic, and then some! Online ministry of Fr. Jay Finelli

Technopriest: www.technopriest.org
Online ministry of Fr. Bill Kessler, including Sunday homily podcasts

A Mother's mother

Our Relationship with the Blessed Virgin Mary

Standing by the cross of Jesus were his mother and his mother's sister, Mary the wife of Clopas, and Mary of Magdala. When Jesus saw his mother and the disciple there whom he loved, he said to his mother, "Woman, behold, your son." Then he said to the disciple, "Behold, your mother."

—John 19:25-27

My Story

Before I became a mother, I cannot say that I truly appreciated my relationship with Mary in the same way I now know her in my life. In an almost immature way, I saw her as that sweet holy card image from my childhood or the recipient of my special intention prayers that needed a prompt reply—I knew she had a "direct line" to Jesus, but never truly thought about why that was so. A tribe of my mother's Catholic friends who descended upon our home once a week to pray the rosary together formed some of my earliest youthful impressions of Mary. Amidst the smell of strong coffee and sweet donuts, I watched these devout women turn to Our Lady with their most heartfelt prayers, fervently believing that Mary would hear their pleas and deliver them to her son Jesus.

Three people taught me to know Mary in the way I know her today, as a friend, a mother, and the one who ultimately draws me closest to her son Jesus. The first is my childhood pastor, Monsignor Michael Collins, who for the past ninety-one years and counting has been asking Mary every day to intercede for him through his daily devotion to the rosary. Fr. Collins' commitment to Our Lady is infectious. As I watch him enter his twilight years and see him anticipate the glory of salvation that lies ahead, I want to emulate his relationship with our Blessed Mother in my own life, to have that same sense of confidence that in flying to her with my prayers, she will remember me not only at the hour of my own death, but also in my waking hours when I so desperately need her guidance, companionship, and assistance.

Along with Fr. Collins, my two sons teach me every day to know and love our Blessed Mother Mary in new and special ways. By introducing me to the gift of motherhood, Eric and Adam opened my heart to know Mary in her motherly vocation. I recall hours spent pacing with crying babies in the middle of the night, asking for her grace and strength as I prayed decades of the rosary aloud, hoping to lull them back to sleep and to keep myself awake. Now, as I watch my boys grow into young men, I turn to Mary so frequently and ask how she was able to cope with watching Jesus grow and begin his public ministry, and ultimately to stand with him witnessing the moment of his death on the cross. I wonder if she ever wished, as I do almost every day, that she could simply freeze time and keep Jesus home with her forever. Instead, at the time of Jesus' first miracle at Cana, it was she who encouraged the servers—as well as you and I—to "Do whatever he tells you." As a mother, pondering the moments of my sons' lives in my heart, I turn to Mary daily as a role model of strength, courage, humility, and true faith.

A Mother's "Yes"

As Catholics, we embrace the Blessed Virgin Mary as *Theotokos*, "God-Bearer," mother of our savior, Jesus Christ. In the opening

Mary is the fruitful Virgin, and in all the souls in which she comes to dwell she causes to flourish purity of heart and body, rightness of intention and abundance of good works. Do not imagine that Mary, the most fruitful of creatures who gave birth to a God, remains barren in a faithful soul. It will be she who makes the soul live incessantly for Jesus Christ, and will make Jesus live in the soul.

—St. Louis de Montfort

chapter of the Gospel of Luke, we hear of Mary's affirmative response to the angel who appears before her, bearing the news that she is to be the mother of Jesus. Surely, this young virgin, betrothed to Joseph and still a teen herself, must have been petrified beyond words. But with her response, "Behold, I am the handmaid of the Lord. May it be done to me according to your word," Mary offers every Catholic mom the perfect role model for accepting our own vocation to motherhood. I recall with precision the sheer terror that filled me when I saw with my own eyes the results of a pregnancy test that would turn my life inside out. How must Mary have felt hearing such incredulous news? And yet, she unwaveringly said, "yes" to a life that must have known the greatest of joys and the most piercing of sorrows.

One of my favorite moments in scripture occurs in Luke's gospel when Mary has just received such a welcoming greeting from her elderly, also pregnant, relative Elizabeth. Her words today are commemorated in the lovely prayer known as the Canticle of Mary:

> My soul proclaims your greatness, O my God,
> and my spirit has rejoiced in you my Savior;
> For you have regarded me as your holy handmaid;
> henceforth all generations shall call me blessed;
> For you who are mighty, have done great things for me,
> and Holy is your Name;
> Your mercy is on those who fear you throughout all generations.
> You have showed strength with your arm.
> You have scattered the proud in the conceit of their heart.

You have put down the mighty from their seat,
and have lifted up the powerless.
You have filled the hungry with good things,
and have sent the rich away empty.
Remembering your mercy,
You have helped your people Israel
As you promised Abraham and Sarah.
Mercy to their children forever.

Again, we see Mary embracing the path God has set before her and remarking to her cousin that she is indeed "blessed." How many days in our lives as Catholic moms do you and I forget to count all of the blessings our loving God has showered upon us? I, for one, will plead guilty to too frequently listing my complaints rather than thanking him for the great things he has done for me lately.

Mary's "yes" and her subsequent grace-filled living of a journey that surely was filled with trials, suffering, and pain, is a shining beacon for me in my life as a Catholic mom. From the moment I wake up in the morning until my head hits the pillow at night, do I look for ways to say "yes" to the ways in which God is calling me? Catholic mom Angelique shares this same view of Mary: "She is such a wonderful role model for me as a mother. In her balance of love to God and her raising of her child, in the sacrifices she made, I look to her daily for inspiration."

Along with looking to Mary for her positivism, many Catholic moms turn to Mary as a beacon of strength. Catholic mom Erin calls Mary the ultimate "strong woman," who gave up an easy life—even risking her own death—to say "yes" to God and to stand with her son at the moment of his crucifixion. When we lack the strength of our convictions in our job as mothers, we only need to open and read the gospels and view Mary's role as disciple and apostle to find our motivation.

A Catholic Mom's Intercessor

Some Catholic moms have admitted difficulty relating to Mary, not understanding or fully appreciating her role in our Church and in their lives. One mother even shared with me, "Honestly, I always have trouble relating to Mary. I try. But my relationship with my own mom makes it very difficult." So many of us long for, but have never experienced, a mother's love.

I honestly have no division separating my memories between religious devotions to Mary from the rest of my "real life." Honoring Mary, remembering Mary's example, and asking for the intercession of *la Virgencita* in the everyday aspects of my life was simply a natural part of my growing up as a Cuban immigrant. It somehow just seemed natural to talk to Mary, a mother, when it appeared that no one else could possibly understand how I felt.

At Academia Santa María, a co-ed Catholic school in Ponce, an industrial city on the southern shores of Puerto Rico, I was introduced to devotional prayers in a school setting with peers. Although I remember clearly how hard it was for me as a kindergartner to sit through Mass every week, I was thrilled to become a member of the club *las Bernarditas*, named after St. Bernadette of Lourdes. Since my full name (or as I call it, my real name) is María de Lourdes—in English, Mary of Lourdes—I was especially taken by the importance given to this club by the "big" girls. It was provoking that the older girls also found it important to ask Mary for her protection and intercession on behalf of each of us as "women." I still have, in a keepsake box, the small ribbon and medal of St. Bernadette that I received upon entering the club.

As I grew older, Mary remained an integral part of my life. She was the topic of some of my first poems as a child, the kind of poems written by flashlight in a notebook hidden underneath the sheets. It was to Mary I cried seeking comfort as a new kid in a strange school. Years later, when I became a mother myself, I instinctively and unsurprisingly turned to Mary with my fears, hopes, and dreams for my own children.

These are not theological or philosophical reasons for the religious importance of Mary, but I suspect they are not an unusual starting place for a Christian who tries to understand Jesus and his life through scripture and then makes the connection between that and her own life experience.

María de Lourdes Ruiz Scaperlanda is a wife of twenty-seven years, a mother of four, an award-winning journalist and the author of several books. See www.mymaria.net for more information.

There was nothing ordinary about Mary. She wasn't just another Jewish girl. But when I think about how extraordinary she was, I get intimidated. When I focus on her perfection, I get nervous.

We forget about the holiness in the everyday aspects of our life. In Mary, our Blessed Mother, I have found an example of motherhood that's divinely inspired. She was without sin, and yet she must have changed a dirty diaper and wrestled with a toddler. She was—and is—Mother of God, yet she bore the suffering that came without wavering from her "Yes!"

Mother Mary shares my trials and teaches me to lean on her Son. She shows me the blessing of the humdrum chores and the beauty in the repetition of my days. She reminds me, in her hidden life on earth, that I don't need to get credit or be seen to make a difference and have an impact.

Once I became a mother, my devotion to Mary started growing in new ways, and I gained a new admiration for the many ways she can guide me closer to Jesus.

Sarah Reinhard is a wife, mother, parish employee, and avid reader who is enjoying life in rural Ohio. She writes at www.SnoringScholar.com.

I've been blessed by a life-long relationship with the woman our family calls, "the world's best mom." Because I have known firsthand the tender nurturing of a mother's love, it is natural for me to be able to see and embrace Mary as my own spiritual mother and indeed as the "Mother of the Church" as Pope Paul VI proclaimed her:

> We believe that the Blessed Mother of God, the New Eve, Mother of the Church, continues in heaven her maternal role with regard to Christ's members.
>
> *—The Credo of the People of Faith*

Setting aside your own relationship with your children or even with your own mom, think for a moment about the relationship you would truly desire with your mother. Ponder this topic in your mind for a few moments and stop to list a few of the traits she would possess. Perhaps your "mother wish list" would contain some of the following:

✳ listens to my needs and knows me inside and out

✳ has my best interest at heart, wants to protect me

✳ tries to help me to be my best

✳ is my friend, but holds me accountable

✳ loves me beyond measure

The remarkably good news offered to each and every one of us by our Catholic Church is this: the Blessed Virgin Mary is our mother. Regardless of whether you are blessed as I am to know the love of your mom or whether she was never truly a part of your life, you have a mother in Mary. From the moment of her Immaculate Conception, God set her apart and gave her to the world as the one who would bear his son—he who would ultimately give us the gift of salvation. Through Mary we can come to know Jesus Christ. She, who felt him move in her womb, knew him from the moment the angel appeared to her. If your heart's greatest desire is to know and to love Jesus Christ in your own life, ask his mother Mary to hold your hand along that journey.

Our entire perfection consists in being conformed, united and consecrated to Jesus Christ. Hence the most perfect of all devotions is undoubtedly that which conforms, unites and consecrates us most perfectly to Jesus Christ. Now, since Mary is of all creatures the one most conformed to Jesus Christ, it follows that among all devotions that which most consecrates and conforms a soul to our Lord is devotion to Mary, his Holy Mother, and that the more a soul is consecrated to her the more will it be consecrated to Jesus Christ.

—Pope John Paul II

As Catholics, we pray to Mary, asking her to guide, comfort, and protect us and to intercede for us in our need. We turn to her with the words of praise, sorrow, thanksgiving, and supplication that fill our hearts and ask her to convey them on our behalf.

If you have never had a relationship with the Blessed Virgin Mary, I invite you today to begin to enter into a friendship with her. Speak to her as you would to a mother, knowing her care and concern for you and your family. Share with her those anxieties and emotions you carry around with you all day long—your fears for your children, your own shortcomings as a mom, and your relationship with your husband, as well as your work inside and outside of the home. Ask Mary to help you to carry this load on a daily basis

and to relay your prayers and needs to her son Jesus. Let her know that you want a deeper, more complete relationship with Our Lord and ask for her help in finding that path that will lead you closer to him.

Knowing Jesus through Mary

A good way to come to know Jesus Christ through the intercession of his mother Mary is to pray the rosary. At this suggestion, I know many of you—my Catholic mom friends—are now rolling your eyes at me and suggesting that I am crazy. You want fervently to pray the rosary, but may have great difficulty making a place for this special devotion in your daily life. I hear you!

First, let's take a basic look at the rosary for those who may not be familiar with its structure and inception. While its exact origins are unknown, most credit St. Dominic with receiving a vision from Our Lady and with fostering devotion to the rosary among Catholics. In subsequent apparitions, Our Lady has time and again asked that we meditate upon the mysteries of the rosary, and numerous popes have extolled the virtues of this devotion. The rosary is actually a series of prayers, recited verbally or mentally as one contemplates the "mysteries" of the life, death, and resurrection of our Lord, Jesus Christ.

The following are the "mysteries" of the rosary:

The Five Joyful Mysteries

(Commonly prayed on Mondays and Saturdays)

1. The Annunciation: Humility
2. The Visitation: Charity
3. The Birth of Our Lord
4. The Presentation of Our Lord
5. The Finding of Our Lord in the Temple

The Five Luminous Mysteries

(Commonly prayed on Thursdays)

1. The Baptism in the Jordan

2. The Wedding at Cana

3. The Proclamation of the Kingdom

4. The Transfiguration

5. The Institution of the Eucharist

The Five Sorrowful Mysteries

(Commonly prayed on Tuesdays and Fridays)

1. The Agony in the Garden

2. The Scourging at the Pillar

3. The Crowning with Thorns

4. The Carrying of the Cross

5. The Crucifixion and Death of Our Lord

The Five Glorious Mysteries

(Commonly prayed on Sundays and Wednesdays)

1. The Resurrection

2. The Ascension

3. The Coming of the Holy Ghost

4. The Assumption of our Blessed Mother into Heaven

5. The Coronation of our Blessed Mother

Many Catholic moms would love to pray the rosary every day, but seem to struggle to find the time or mental focus for this special devotion. Catholic moms have shared the following suggestions for making the rosary a part of your life:

* Don't worry or feel embarrassed if you don't know all of the prayers of the rosary—print them out and use your instructions to begin praying it aloud. Over time, with repetition, you will learn the prayers and mysteries.

* Keep several small "rosary rings" or one-decade versions of the rosary in your home or car. If you are unable to say an entire rosary in one sitting, begin the practice of pausing for a few moments throughout your day to say a single decade of the rosary.

* Consider praying along with an audio version of the rosary. I have a few different versions of audio rosaries on my iPod and love to pray the rosary while walking or driving. Also consider a "sung rosary" CD such as the one by Catholic artist Susan Bailey. Singing along with the rosary prayers may help keep your mind from wandering and will help you to learn to recite the prayers.

* Pray the "scriptural rosary," which includes specific scriptural references between the various prayers throughout the rosary. This is a wonderful way of learning even more about the mysteries upon which we meditate.

* Share the rosary with your family. Even very young children can be taught to recite and love the prayers of the rosary, or allow them to color quietly in your presence as you recite the rosary aloud. We even offer free downloadable rosary coloring pictures at CatholicMom.com for this purpose.

* Pray the rosary with others. I remember so fondly my mother's group of friends meeting in our home for prayer and fellowship. In those days, our pastor attended the rosary group once per week, praying with the ladies. Praying the rosary in the company of others may help you strengthen your commitment to this form of prayer.

If you begin to grow weary of your attempts to incorporate the rosary into your daily prayer life, don't give up! Many of us struggle with the desire to pray this devotion and our inability to find time for it in our lives. I am heartened by my friend Fr. Collins' words to me on the place of the rosary in his own life. As you read the following words from Fr. Collins about the rosary, imagine the lilting Irish accent of a priest who has given every day of his life to serving the Trinity and Our Lady.

If you meditate on the life and death of Jesus and Mary every day
you can't go very far wrong; and the Blessed Mother, in her appear-
ances, had that one message for people: say the rosary. Pray the
rosary.

All prayer is mental prayer. If the mind is not in prayer then it's
no prayer. We have been given the rosary. St. Dominic was the one
who is supposed to have gotten it from the Blessed Mother. In its
twenty decades, you have all the incidents in the infancy, the life,
ministry, and death of Jesus and his mother Mary. And I've convinced myself that the Blessed Mother has appeared on earth several times, at Lourdes, Fatima, Knock, Guadalupe, Medjugorje, and
at every one of those has asked the one request: please say the
rosary. I've always been afraid of hell, I don't like hell, but I'm convinced that if I'm true to the rosary, which I have been—I've said
the rosary ever since I was a child, I've never deliberately missed
the rosary and I don't say that as a boast, I say that as kind of an
assurance that if I ask the Blessed Mother fifty times a day to be
with me now and at the hour of my death she'll be around somewhere to take me home.

I say myself that I have not omitted the rosary deliberately
since I was maybe six or seven years old—I hold it, and fifty times
a day I ask our Mother, my Mother, to pray for me now and at the
hour of my death. I am convinced that she will somehow or another be there when I need her. That's my message about the rosary.

I was eating an apple the other day and I was thinking about
what they say, "An apple a day keeps the doctor away." Well, I
made up my own adage, "A rosary a day keeps the devil away!"

–Monsignor Michael Collins
Pastor emeritus, St. Anne Catholic Church, Seal Beach, California

Whether your devotion to Our Blessed Mother, the Virgin Mary,
comes in the form of a daily rosary or through simple, informal conversations throughout the course of your day, please embrace her role
in your life as spiritual mother. She wants to nurture and support you
in your vocation as Catholic mom. Remember that she has "been
there, done that," and that her goal is to draw you into closer union
with her son Jesus Christ. Welcome her into your little corner of the

world, share the burdens and joys of your heart with her, and follow her lead in seeking a path to heaven for yourself and your family.

Mom's Homework

✓ Write a letter to the Blessed Virgin Mary. Share with her your joys, struggles, fears, and blessings as a Catholic mom, sharing those things you may hold deep within your own heart.

✓ Join a rosary group in your parish, or if none exists, consider beginning one in your home.

✓ Create an all-twine knotted rosary and give it away to a friend or someone who could benefit from your prayers and support. Find complete directions at www.RosaryArmy.com.

✓ Learn more about the life of Mary by reading the gospels and the Acts of the Apostles.

✓ Emulate Mary's "yes" in your own life, looking for opportunities to do God's will in your life and sharing His love with those around you.

Web Resources

RosaryArmy.com: http://rosaryarmy.com
Basic information on praying the rosary, making rosaries, and free audio versions of the rosary

Mary Queen of Peace Sung Rosary and Meditation Guide: http://sungrosary.com
Lovely sung rosary and meditation guide by Catholic artist and mom Susan Bailey

Pray.ND.edu: http://pray.nd.edu
Prayer resources from the University of Notre Dame

Saintly solutions

Relevant Intercessors for Today's Catholic Mom

Blessed are the poor in spirit, for theirs is the kingdom of heaven.

Blessed are they who mourn, for they will be comforted.

Blessed are the meek, for they will inherit the land.

Blessed are they who hunger and thirst for righteousness, for they will be satisfied.

Blessed are the merciful, for they will be shown mercy.

Blessed are the clean of heart, for they will see God.

Blessed are the peacemakers, for they will be called children of God.

Blessed are they who are persecuted for the sake of righteousness, for theirs is the kingdom of heaven.

Blessed are you when they insult you and persecute you and utter every kind of evil against you (falsely) because of me.

Rejoice and be glad, for your reward will be great in heaven.

–Matthew 5:3-12

My Story

The earliest saintly "friendship" I can recall was born in the early years of my career as a Catholic schoolgirl. A priest friend of our family, Fr. Bauer, had gifted my mother a third-class relic of St. Thérèse the "Little Flower" following his pilgrimage to Europe in the mid-1970s. The relic was placed on the highest shelf of a glass cabinet containing my mother's most prized treasures, and touching was strictly forbidden. It was around this same age that I began to hear of our family's distant relation to the family of St. Thérèse, through my paternal grandmother's "Martin" family name.

I recall sneaking to the cabinet to steal glances at the relic, daydreaming of my "cousin"—the precious "Little Flower" who had loved the Child Jesus so greatly and been lost to the world at such a tender age. That first instance of "saint love" was more hero worship than anything—much the way young girls today might look up to the latest Disney television star.

The witnesses who have preceded us into the kingdom, especially those whom the Church recognizes as saints, share in the living tradition of prayer by the example of their lives, the transmission of their writings, and their prayer today. They contemplate God, praise him and constantly care for those whom they have left on earth. Their intercession is their most exalted service to God's plan. We can and should ask them to intercede for us and for the whole world.

—*Catechism of the Catholic Church, 2683*

When the time came to be confirmed, I eschewed my friend Thérèse and took the name "St. Julia" more for how lovely I thought her name sounded than for any particular merit or intercessory relationship. It wasn't until I landed at the University of Notre Dame that I began to truly cultivate "real" relationships with saints, whose intercession I sought on a regular basis. I would stroll to the campus grotto, light a candle, and present my laundry list of personal needs to an arsenal of saintly men and women, begging their help on my behalf.

As a mother, I've learned so much about the lives of the saints by sharing these holy men and women with my boys. In teaching them, for the first time I saw the "light" for myself—the true wonder of our Church's communion of saints. Those known to all of us, and those who went to their graves after lives of holy service

We must have a real living determination to reach holiness. I will be a saint means I will despoil myself of all that is not God; I will strip my heart of all created things; I will live in poverty and detachment; I will renounce my will, my inclinations, my whims and fancies, and make myself a willing slave to the will of God.

—Blessed Mother Teresa

and living—never formally canonized but no lesser members of that great "cloud of witnesses" to the true meaning of the word "faith." Women like my grandmothers who led their families, large and small, to lives within the Catholic Church. Evangelists like my friend Matt, who was fearless when it came to inviting friends to Mass and would take on any apologetics argument with gusto and passion. Teachers such as my friend Sheree, whose work in the first grade classroom touched countless lives and led thousands to Jesus by the way she so vibrantly reflected his love to others.

These days, in my quiet moments of prayer, as well as those times throughout the day when I have heaven on "speed dial," I turn to a community of trusted saints and beseech their guidance, their favor, and their intercession in our daily lives. On days when it seems the most significant thing I've accomplished is mopping a floor, St. Thérèse of Lisieux and her "little way" are never far from my mind. As I become a more "mature" mom, St. Elizabeth and her joyful later-in-life pregnancy offer inspiration. As my teens grow in size and worldliness, St. Monica has become a trusted friend. I strive every day to live my own life according the examples set by their lives of great virtue, courage, and faith. Most days, I fall very short, but it's so wonderful to know that I have their help and encouragement along my own path to heaven.

Catholics and Saints

Before we begin to look at the lives of specific saints, it's important to reiterate the true relationship between Catholics and our saints. Non-Catholic friends who haven't been catechized in our faith may look at the statues of Mary that grace our lawns or homes or the holy cards of saints we collect with confusion. They may enter our churches, many named for saints, and view elaborate paintings or stained glass windows depicting their lives and assume that we are "worshipping" the subjects of the artwork or engaging in idolatry.

The truth of the matter is that we Catholics don't pray "to" saints, but rather "with" them. In a moment of crisis, you might turn to a trusted friend and ask her prayers on your behalf. The Catholic Church teaches that since the saints dwell in heaven, they may intercede with God the Father on our behalf. Just as you'd ask your friend for her help, you can and should turn to the "communion of saints" and ask their prayers on your behalf.

In today's Church, the canonization of saints is a formal three-stage process involving years of investigation, study, and approval of evidence. Much in the way that we might hang family portraits in our homes, we Catholics frequently keep images of the saints we love and respect to remind us of the lives they led and to inspire us along our own paths to sainthood.

At the time you were baptized, it is likely that your parents (or you, if you joined the Church as an adult) selected a saint to serve as your "patron." You may have been given a saint's name at birth, or formed a relationship with a trusted saint over the period of many years. "Patron" saints are chosen as special guardians or protectors of particular individuals, groups of people, occupations or causes. Let's look at my own life and some of my patron saints as an example.

* St. Elizabeth: My parents named and baptized me "Lisa Marie," a derivative of the name Elizabeth; Elizabeth is the patroness of pregnant women

* St. Thérèse of Lisieux: The patroness of my home diocese, the Diocese of Fresno

* St. Anthony of Padua: The patron of my parish

* St. Francis de Sales: The patron saint of writers

* St. Michael the Archangel and St. Patrick: The patron saints of my sons, Eric Michael and Adam Patrick

We Catholics are blessed to have such wonderful examples of holy men and women who have gone before us and have lived life of heroic virtue or martyrdom. Embracing intercessory relationships with them can help comfort us in times of spiritual need. We can also work to emulate their traits and virtues in our own lives by studying the way they lived and following their lead. If you haven't already done so, spend some time coming to know more intimately your patron saints and cultivating a prayer relationship with them. By asking our saints to intercede on our behalf, by entrusting our children to their

Why aren't there more saints who were mothers? (And I don't mean Mother Teresa!)

There are two reasons. First, until recently, some Catholics thought that being a priest or member of a religious order was "higher" than the calling to be a parent. Happily, since the Second Vatican Council, more Catholics have realized that everyone's vocation is holy—married or single, lay or ordained. But that legacy means that there are far fewer saints who were parents. The second reason for this imbalance is that the canonization process, the "saint-making" procedure, is complicated. Sometimes it takes decades for the research to be gathered for the Vatican authorities. This means dioceses and religious orders have a natural advantage—they've got plenty of staff who know how to navigate the complicated procedures. Families, on the other hand, are at a disadvantage. No matter how holy your mother or father is, it's unlikely that your family has the time (or financial resources) to organize all the necessary paperwork.

That means fewer saints who are married. And, therefore, very few who were mothers.

But no matter—for the ones we have are spectacular! Lisa Hendey, in this wonderful chapter, has offered some of her favorites. Here are the ones that I hear mothers talking about most frequently . . .

The most popular one is Mary, the mother of Jesus. Millions of mothers feel comfortable asking for Mary's help in prayer. That's called "intercession," asking the saint to pray for us, the same way that we would ask a friend to do so. (This is the "patron" model of sainthood.) Mothers also naturally look to Mary as a model of Christian life. (That's the "companion" model of sainthood.) Miriam of Nazareth was a flesh-and-blood woman: she gave birth, raised a child, and even watched him suffer. All the things that mothers experienced, she did as well.

But Mary isn't the only mother-saint. St. Monica, a strong-willed fourth-century woman, refused to give up on her son, even when it seemed he might never embrace Christianity. She prayed constantly for Augustine (later a saint himself), and is the patron of mothers who worry about their children. Centuries later, St. Elizabeth of Hungary (1207–1231), a patron of the poor, was the mother of three children. And St. Elizabeth Ann Seton (1774–1821), the first American-born saint, raised five children before she became a nun.

These women, however, may seem removed from the lives of modern-day mothers. Mary's life was extraordinary. Monica's was in the far-distant past.

Elizabeth Ann Seton started a religious order. And Elizabeth of Hungary gave up the care of her children in order to lead what was considered at the time a more "religious" life.

So let me propose a modern woman who is on her way to canonization: Dorothy Day, the American-born founder of the Catholic Worker movement (1897–1980). Dorothy's ultimate embrace of Christianity came as a direct result of the birth of her child, Tamar, which awakened in her a natural appreciation for God. At the time, Dorothy was living in a "common-law" marriage with a man who refused to follow the Christian path. So, reluctantly, Dorothy left him to be baptized along with infant child. Despite her tiring work helping poor men and women in "houses of hospitality," running a weekly newspaper, and speaking all over the country, Dorothy cared deeply for her daughter and, later, grandchildren. Reading her recently published journals, called *The Duty of Delight*, is like reading the diary of any contemporary mother and grandmother—delighting over her young daughter, worrying about her daughter's marriage, and enjoying a snowy vacation day with her grandchildren.

Holiness often means doing things that won't make the front pages of the newspapers. Mary, Elizabeth Ann Seton, Elizabeth of Hungary, and Dorothy Day knew that the holiest of acts can be something as simple as changing a diaper. The Church is beginning to realize this, too. For Christian mothers, the remarkable mother-saints are powerful reminders that holiness does not have to mean living in a convent or founding a religious order. It simply means being a loving person in whatever task that is yours—that includes bending over a cradle, cleaning a skinned knee, or kissing your child goodnight.

Fr. James Martin, S.J., is a Jesuit priest and the author of My Life with the Saints.

guidance and protection, and by attempting to live virtuously in our own little corners of the world, we will nurture our families and ourselves as wives and mothers.

A Catholic Mom's Communion of Saints

If we were to look at the lives of the saints, we could likely come up with hundreds of role models for today's Catholic mom. One of my favorite ways to learn about the saints is to follow our Church's liturgical calendar. With Pope John Paul II's reorganization of the canonization process, the Church does not now formally recognize every day of the year as a formal feast day of a saint. But around the world, individuals recognize many of the feast days not formally celebrated by the Church in religious orders, local communities, and homes. Each day, I try to read about the saints whose feasts are linked to that particular day. Reading about the histories of these holy men and women never ceases to amaze and inspire me.

Let's take a quick look at the lives of some saints who might serve as intercessors and meet some Catholic moms who have relationships with these holy men and women.

St. Anne: The grandmother of Jesus, mother of the Virgin Mary, and wife of St. Joachim. Patron of mothers, housewives, pregnant women, women in labor.

> Lately I keep looking at St. Anne and thinking of how instrumental she was in preparing Mary for her role in God's divine plan. This has helped me to keep in mind the impact of our silent roles as mothers to our little ones—in as much as the life we make for them in our home will form and prepare them for the life they will live outside of our homes one day. Indeed we do not know what God has in store for each of them but we do know he has entrusted them to us to form and love. I find myself drawn to St. Anne and her example and also keep talking to my children about Mary as a little girl and her example of obedience.
>
> —Elizabeth

St. Anthony of Padua: Franciscan priest, gifted speaker, and Doctor of the Church. Patron of lost articles, pregnant women, against barrenness.

> God bless Saint Anthony! Where would I be without his faithful help in many times of crisis from lost shoes to misplaced car keys. Truly, he is a wonderful saint!
>
> —Nancy

St. Bernadette of Lourdes: Poor shepherdess who received visions of the Virgin Mary at Lourdes and went on to become a religious sister. Patron of poor people, sick people, against illness.

> The first saint I ever received help from was St. Bernadette, and she holds a special place in my heart. If I'm sick, I go to St. Bernadette for her prayers.
>
> —Kim

St. Brigid of Ireland: Virgin, religious sister, monastery founder, and traveler. Patron of infants and babies, midwives, travelers.

> I have a special love for St. Brigid of Ireland, not only because I have Irish heritage, but because of the story that she was told she could be given land for an abbey, but only as much land as her cloak could cover. The story goes that her cloak stretched into enough land for the abbey through the grace of the Lord. It reminds me that, with the Lord, anything is possible!
>
> —Nicole

St. Elizabeth: Relative of Blessed Virgin Mary and mother of St. John the Baptist. Patron of expectant mothers, pregnant women.

> As an older mother, she holds a special place in my heart.
>
> —HH

St. Gerard Majella: Poor and in ill health, he worked alongside his fellow Redemptorist brothers as a lay man, performing simple tasks in service of others and according to God's will. Patron of pregnant women, the pro-life movement, unborn children.

> I prayed through his intercession when I was pregnant and in labor with my children.
>
> —Julia

St. Gianna Beretta Molla: Catholic wife, mother of three, and physician who refused medical care that would have necessitated the abortion of her child. She died one week after childbirth. Patron against abortion, and of pregnant women.

> St. Gianna is one of my favorites. I identify with her as a mother and wife.
>
> —Julie

St. Jean Baptiste Marie Vianney: Devoted parish priest known for his care for poor parishioners, his work with penitents, and his devotion to time spent in prayer before the Blessed Sacrament. Patron of priests, confessors.

> He was a most humble, modest saint. I often pray to him when I need help with my pride and my judgmental ways. He was not brilliant but he was completely and selflessly devoted to God. If I could only be more like him!
>
> —Michelle

St. Joseph: Spouse of the Blessed Virgin Mary and adoptive father of Jesus Christ, he was known for his willingness to follow God's plan for his life. Patron of workers, families, fathers, unborn children, expectant mothers.

> I am inspired by the lives the saints led, and especially by St. Joseph, who I believe is such a wonderful example of trust and faith in the Lord. That's why I named my son after him!
>
> —Kristen

St. Jude: Relative and follower of Jesus, he became an apostle, authored an epistle, and was martyred for the faith. Patron of desperate situations, impossible causes.

> My devotion to him was passed down to me by my mother. She had a particular devotion to St. Jude and I inherited it. He is an exceptionally powerful patron and I have NEVER been let down.
>
> —Shannon

St. Monica: Wife and mother who prayed for years for the conversion of her husband and her son, St. Augustine of Hippo. Patron of married women, widows, homemakers, disappointing children, difficult marriages.

> Her endless prayers for the conversion of her son, St. Augustine, remind me to always be praying for my children.
>
> —Marie

St. Rita of Cascia: Wife, mother, widow, and nun, she was known for her love of the Eucharist and her peacemaking ways. Patron against infertility, and of parenthood, victims of spousal abuse, widows.

> St. Rita is one of my favorites. My husband is agnostic, but is very open to my faith life and raising our children Catholic, and we had big issues early in our marriage. She's really helped our marriage in so many ways.
>
> —Marian

St. Teresa of Avila: Spanish Carmelite, mystic writer, and Doctor of the Church. Patron against headaches, and of people in need of grace, sick people.

> She has wonderful advice for both being in the world and not a part of it. She also appeals to me because she thinks out of the box.
>
> —Jennifer

St. Thérèse of Lisieux: Carmelite nun, supporter of the missions, Doctor of the Church, and known for her *Little Way* of trusting and serving God with a childlike faith and great love. Patron of loss of parents, and of missionaries, sick people.

> Her "little way" has been an inspiration for me on a daily basis as I offer up what sacrifices I can every day.
>
> —Tina

With literally thousands of saints to choose from, you'll have no trouble finding inspirational patrons to help you walk your faith life as a mother. It's important to remember that these men and women were human, just like you and me, and that they were able to overcome their own personal flaws to devote their lives to knowing, loving, and serving God.

When I have days where I feel anxious about my children, frustrated in my vocation, or distant from the Lord, it helps me to pause for a few moments and hold a silent conversation with one of my trusted saint friends. You and I are called by God to be saints and to lead our husbands and children along the path to sainthood as well. It's so wonderful to know that we have companions—the communion of saints—for this mission, holding our hands and pointing the way to heaven.

Mom's Homework

✓ Research the lives of some of your patron saints: your "name" saint, the patron of your parish or diocese, or the patron of your occupation.

✓ Make note of the feast days for important patron saints in your family. Celebrate dinner as a family on these special dates, remembering the lives of the saints who guide and protect your family.

✓ Obtain a medal, holy card, or small statue for your family's most precious patron saint and display this in a place of honor in your home.

✓ Read a biography or autobiography about one of your favorite saints to learn more about his or her life.

✓ Spend a few moments each day reading about the life of the saint celebrated on that day. Share these stories with your children!

Web Resources

Patron Saint Index: http://saints.sqpn.com

> *A tremendous online resource for learning about the lives of the saints.*
> *Profiles of thousands of saints and beati; browse by name or by topic;*
> *sanctoral calendar, timeline, FAQs, images*

Saint Cast: www.saintcast.org

> *Interviews, sound-seeing tours, news, and information that help bring*
> *the saints alive into your daily life*

The Beauty of the bible

The Joy and Importance
of Scripture Study

All scripture is inspired by God and is useful for teaching, for refutation, for correction, and for training in righteousness, so that one who belongs to God may be competent, equipped for every good work.

–2 Timothy 3:16-17

My Story

Fourteen years ago, Greg and I found ourselves one afternoon at the funeral of the father of our great friend Steve following his untimely and tragic death from lung cancer. Greg and Steve had been best friends in medical school. Coincidentally, years later their respective medical careers brought both of them and their young families to Fresno, and old friendships had been rekindled. Greg, Steve, and his wife Jayne—all physicians—and I had been extremely moved by the testimonial of Steve's father, which Steve had just finished reading at the funeral ceremony. In his final message, Dr. Thaxter, a prominent orthopedic surgeon who fell ill in the prime of his career, had shared his personal conversion story. Imagine a church packed to the gills with physicians, many of whom shared a skeptical outlook at best on the topic of organized religion. With his testimonial, Dr. Thaxter had implored them to come to know Christ through his word, the Bible, as he and his wife Ann had done in the years just prior to his illness and death.

Following the funeral, somehow the four of us—the Catholic mom and the three not overly religious physicians—came up with the brilliant idea that we should begin a Bible study group. For guidance, we turned to an older couple, Marlene and Lyman Ehrlich, who had guided Steven's parents along their faith journey. I suppose we thought we would meet for a month or two, enjoy some time together, and then move on. When it became apparent how little we knew about scripture in those first meetings, we christened ourselves "The Sweathogs" and begged Marlene and Lyman's patience with our endless philosophical and theological questions.

The six of us, three married couples, came from across the gamut of the religious spectrum. As evidence of this diversity, we each studied from our preferred versions of the Bible. Along with my Catholic bible, I always consulted my *Catechism of the Catholic Church* as a resource, turning to it privately when ecumenical differences arose. With three scientists, two Evangelicals, and a Catholic in our group, you can imagine the discussions we've had over the years! Slowly, over time, Marlene and Lyman encouraged each of us to take on the role of "leader" for the biweekly sessions—a job we now rotate each time we meet.

Amazingly, fourteen years after our initial study brought this motley crew together, we continue to break open the bounty of God's word in the Bible. Jayne and Steve have found and become involved in a church home. Greg has joined the Catholic Church, and Marlene and Lyman mentor several other Bible study groups each week while continuing their careers and their commitment to the Sweathogs. Our study of sacred scripture has enriched my life beyond measure and deepened my commitment to and knowledge of my Catholic faith in ways I could never have imagined.

Catholic Moms and the Bible

Some of you may initially balk at my suggestion that in order to nurture ourselves, we should be spending time studying scripture. With little ones underfoot, work to be done, and a schedule that never pauses, you may find your reading time limited each day. Honestly, when my boys were little, it felt as though I would go for months without reading anything more complex than a board book!

But the truth of the matter is, we are *already* reading scripture each and every week. At Mass each Sunday, the Church has arranged for us to receive a full four-course meal of scriptural delicacies in the form of the Sunday Liturgy of the Word. After having gathered, and following the opening rites of the Mass, we pause to take in the beauty of God's message to us. We read from the Old Testament, those Hebrew scriptural passages specifically chosen to complement the week's Gospel message. We pray, preferably in song, the psalm prior to reading from the New Testament. Then, with praise and acclamation, we rise to our feet as the gospel passage—the "climax" of the Liturgy of the Word—is proclaimed by the priest or deacon.

The Church's Lectionary is divided into a three-year cycle, offering us the opportunity to hear a broad cross-section of the Bible over the course of the years:

> Year A—Gospel of Matthew
> Year B—Gospel of Mark
> Year C—Gospel of Luke

During the liturgical seasons of Lent, Holy Week, Easter, Advent, and Christmas, we come to know Christ and the Christian story through the readings of the Gospel of John.

If, as busy Catholic moms, we do nothing more than begin to truly, actively listen to the Liturgy of the Word every Sunday, we will already have begun to build a great basis of biblical knowledge.

But that is a big "if," isn't it? The Liturgy of the Word also seems to be one of the times during Sunday Mass when we mothers have to work the most diligently at ensuring the quiet and respectfulness of our broods. Toddlers who have been temporarily pacified by an opening song and the posture of standing during the Introductory Rites seem to spring into action the moment we take our seats to listen to the Liturgy of the Word. This is often when mom has to move into the mode of keeping kids quiet, reminding them of their "Mass manners."

I can't tell you how many times, attending Mass with Eric and Adam during their "devil days" as preschoolers, I walked out of Mass on Sunday with no earthly idea what the readings were about. I was too busy doing "damage control."

Today's technology makes it easy for a mom to avoid the trap I fell into. Thanks to the website of the United States Council of Catholic Bishops (www.usccb.org), we can now read the complete Liturgy of the Word for every Mass, including daily Masses, and view catechetical messages (think a three-minute "mini-homily") in video format. Even the busiest mom should be able to find five minutes, sometime during the course of the week, to sit and read the scriptures for Sunday, view

> interpret as I should, following the command of Christ: Search the Scriptures, and Seek and you shall find. Christ will not say to me what he said to the Jews: You erred, not knowing the Scriptures and not knowing the power of God. For if, as Paul says, Christ is the power of God and the wisdom of God, and if the man who does not know Scripture does not know the power and wisdom of God, then ignorance of Scripture is ignorance of Christ.
>
> —St. Jerome

one of the video reflections, and contemplate the gospel passage prior to attending weekly Mass. If you do not have access to the Internet at home or find it difficult to find time to log on, consider purchasing a missal (available for less than $5) for the year and using it to pre-read the Mass readings.

Taking time to carefully read, pray through, and study the Sunday readings prior to attending Mass is one of the most important ways we can nurture ourselves as Catholic mothers. Once you have begun to truly *pray* the scriptures, you will see how they begin to come alive in your life. Studying the Liturgy of the Word will also give the rest of the Mass greater meaning for you, as so much of the Eucharistic cele-bration is biblically based.

Once you have given yourself this gift, consider sharing it with the rest of your family. Take a few moments with your children during the week to read and discuss the Sunday Liturgy of the Word. Doing this with young children—explaining the Gospel passage in terms they can understand—may even contribute to better behavior on Sunday morning! At the very least, getting into practice of preparing the readings for Mass on Sunday will ease that "I didn't get anything out of this Mass" feeling that sometimes creeps up on stressed-out mothers. If a breastfeeding baby, a trip with a potty-training toddler, or even illness keeps you from quietly listening on Sunday, you will still have the words of everlasting life in your heart!

Studying the Bible

A friend who invited me to attend such a group with her at her Baptist church first introduced me to the concept of women's Bible studies. Not wanting to hurt her feelings, I tagged along cautiously, not quite sure what to expect. I was informed by one of the elderly, well-intentioned members of the group, *Catholics don't read the Bible, honey!"*

For a long time, that Baptist southern belle was correct in assuming that we Catholics didn't spend much time outside of Mass reading our bibles. But today, Catholic Bible study resources abound, and many parishes have vibrant women's groups gathering to study the word together. If you are new to Bible study, consider joining or beginning a study group in your home or parish. Laurie Watson Manhardt, PhD, coauthor of the Come and See Catholic Bible study series, offers the following words of encouragement for moms considering taking on this challenge:

> All you need is a Catholic Bible and the *Catechism of the Catholic Church*. "For with God nothing will be impossible" (Luke 1:37). Of course it is possible to study alone, but I tend to finish things when others are around to encourage me. This is a wonderful study to do in your home or neighborhood or parish. Find a few other young moms to set aside 60–90 minutes a week to study together. Pray to the Holy Spirit and invite a non-practicing Catholic or unchurched friend or neighbor. God can use Bible Study to bless you and to evangelize and catechize others at the same time.

If you don't feel comfortable at this time committing to a Bible study group, don't let this keep you from beginning to dive into the word. Choose a study resource from a reputable Catholic publisher and be sure to use a Catholic bible. I prefer to use *The New American*

Bible translation for study purposes, since this is the version used during Sunday's Liturgy of the Word. I always keep my paperback copy of the *Catechism of the Catholic Church* at hand, since questions frequently arise while studying. The *Catechism*'s comprehensive index and many scripture references make it the perfect companion for scripture study.

Bible study books tend to be either topical or based on particular books of the Bible. These days, many great topical studies have been written specifically for Catholic women. These studies typically take on a particular theme and look at a variety of relevant scriptural references to reinforce that theme. Another way to study the Bible is book-by-book, or looking at particular "characters" in the Old or New Testaments. I find this a particularly appealing way to study, since one can gain both a semi-historical and archeological perspective along with theological knowledge.

So many wonderful resources exist to complement your study of scripture. Books, websites, CDs, and video companions are being released every day to help Catholics who want to study the Bible. But it's important that we exercise caution when selecting materials to choose items that will support, rather than detract from, our Catholic faith. When in doubt, consult a trusted priest or deacon at your parish who can guide you in selecting study materials.

If you do enter into an ecumenical Bible study environment, clarify to group members up front that you are Catholic and will be using a Catholic bible, which may differ from other members' versions. In my own experience, being part of such a group has helped me to research and learn more about particular questions of faith brought up by members of my group. I've been able to share with them my uniquely Catholic perspective on topics discussed, but have always been extremely careful to "do my homework" on controversial topics that may arise. If you join a group that will not allow you to use your Catholic bible or continually attacks your beliefs, it may be advisable to seek out another study environment.

Catholic artist Melissa Dayton credits Bible study with helping her faith life feel more fully alive. She shares:

> I read the scriptures every morning, even if I only have time to open the bible and read the first thing that jumps out at me. I usually read a psalm and then use a devotional that has daily readings or let the Spirit be my guide. A well-written Bible study is key to being comfortable with the scriptures also. Being in a Bible study

Bible Study to the Rescue!

We had it all . . . a perfect parish, lots of playmates the same ages as our children in a great neighborhood, like-minded "mean" Catholic parents who were forbidding the same crazy things we were (like X-rated movies), wonderful friends and family nearby. Then came the move. Now, I was hundreds of miles away from family and friends, sitting in an empty house. We had arrived, but our furniture had not. So, I had no pots or pans, no favorite coffee mug. Why had God taken us out of the promised land and dropped us in the desert?

But, I had a well-worn bible and I invited a few ladies. Soon others joined us in studying God's Word. Some were older and had weathered life's storms . . . difficult children, financial setbacks, health problems, aging parents. They gave prayer, encouragement, and godly advice. Then, there were young moms just starting out on life's journey. And those of us in the middle years offered our prayer, encouragement, and support.

Soon, I had friends in the new place. The friendships grew deep and strong. And the most important friend of all was the author of the book, who had been there all along. In the good times and in the hard times, God was providing comfort and guidance through his word and his real presence in the Eucharist. God provided bread for the journey. Jesus became my forever friend. The sacred scriptures would never be exhausted.

Laurie Manhardt, wife, mother, and grandmother, coauthors the Come and See Catholic Bible Study series, published by Emmaus Road Publishing.

group is best; the fellowship of a group united in Christ studying the word of God is priceless. I would not be the woman I am without these incredible people in my life. My family would not be what it is without the direction and blessings God has given us from what we have studied. Our Catholic faith would not have opened up to us—especially the sacraments—if the Holy Spirit hadn't shown us the beauty in the scriptures guided by the Catechism. My husband would not have become Catholic if Bible studies were not a part of our life. The Bible, reading it and studying it, is a great gift you give your family. Becoming intimate with God in the living word changes your life!

For moms of very young ones, explore Bible study groups that may support you in your parenting vocation. Many parishes offer studies targeted to moms, providing companion lessons for little ones while moms study nearby. You may find that your child loves going to Bible study just as much as mom does!

If, for some reason, you cannot undertake a formal Bible study or commit to a group at this time in your life, you can still benefit from the richness of scripture in your life. Jackie makes time daily to read God's word in the Bible. "I read it usually by opening it up randomly and asking God to open my heart to what he wants me to hear today through his word," she explains. "If the page does not resonate, I give it another try. I have found that when I approach the Bible with trust and openness that God wants to say something to my heart, I will always hear him. Just as water quenches the thirst and food satisfies the hunger, and the air we breathe gives life, so does the Bible offer nutrition for the life of my soul."

Another wonderful way, indeed perhaps the best of all, to nurture yourself through the scriptures is to share this precious gift with your children and husband. Purchase a "toddlers' bible" for your little ones. These sturdy board-book-style bibles have many bright illustrations and tell classic Bible stories from a child's perspective. Take time every day to share "Bible time" with your little ones. Cuddling up in your home's "sacred space," begin the practice of spending even just a few moments every day exploring God's word together. Before you know it, this will become a beloved routine for both of you.

Give each of your older children his or her own age-appropriate bible and spend time studying together and encouraging them to read the word on their own as well. Spend time together after Mass on Sunday discussing the readings and "breaking them open" by looking for an application in your own family life. When I was growing up, my dad was known for his "quiz questions," which encouraged each of us to carefully listen to the readings. With a possible ice cream cone and Daddy's pride in us on the line, you know we listened very carefully!

Bring up the topic of Bible study with your husband. Being part of a couples' Bible study has been one of the greatest graces in my marriage. In our studies together, topics have arisen that we may never have broached on our own. Share openly with him about your desire to bring God's word into your home, but respect his needs and feelings as well. I would caution you not to be disappointed if his response is less than exuberant. Men are sometimes less comfortable

In Sacred Scripture, the Church constantly finds her nourishment and her strength, for she welcomes it not as a human word, "but as what it really is, the word of God." In the sacred books, the Father who is in heaven comes lovingly to meet his children, and talks with them.

—Catechism of the Catholic Church, 104

with discussing issues in the company of others. If your husband is reluctant to join a formal group or even to study with you at home, give him the gift of a Catholic bible and devotional guide, as well as the gift of a few moments each day to spend studying the word. Hopefully, he will reciprocate your generous offer and spell you for a few moments of quiet meditative time as well.

Following St. Jerome's exhortation that "ignorance of scripture is ignorance of Christ," we are each called to nourish ourselves spiritually by learning about the basis of our faith in the Old Testament, making the songs of the psalms our own, coming to know the early foundations of our Church in the New Testament, and studying Christ's life and teachings in the gospels. Spend five minutes per day coming to know Jesus Christ through the world's perennial best seller, the Bible, and you will come to know him and his love in a more profound way than you could have ever imagined. Let his word be a lamp for your feet and a light for the path you walk every day as a Catholic mom.

Mom's Homework

- ✓ Begin reading the upcoming Sunday gospel each Monday or Tuesday and prayerfully reflecting on it before Mass on Sunday.

- ✓ Take five minutes per day to read the daily Liturgy of the Word.

- ✓ If you do not already own a Catholic bible, purchase one for your family.

- ✓ Investigate women's and couples' Bible study groups in your parish or diocese or consider starting a group in your home or at your church.

- ✓ Find a wonderful children's bible to share with your children. Make time every weekday to share a Bible story as a family.

Web Resources

United States Conference of Catholic Bishops New American Bible:
    www.usccb.org/nab
    Readings and psalms for the month

Come and See Catholic Bible Study: www.catholicbiblestudy.net
    *Instructions and resources for beginning a Catholic Bible study pro-
    gram or studying on your own*

Great Adventure: www.greatadventureonline.com
    Catholic Bible learning system

CHAPTER TWENTY - TWO

Culture of faith

Building Catholic Identity in Our Homes

As for me and my household, we will serve the LORD.

—Joshua 24:15

My Story

I often wish I had a magical window that would allow me to look out into the future and know how things would turn out. This mom's heart would love the security of knowing that she had shepherded her little flock to happy lives—to vocations well lived out, to nurturing personal relationships, and ultimately to a salvation spent in heaven together. It's probably for the best that no such technology currently exists. In its absence, I do my best every day in partnership with my husband and best friend Greg to emulate the role models provided by my own parents.

I grew up in the ultimate Catholic home, knowing that our relationship with our God and our commitment to our faith was at the core of our family. I hope when my children look back on their own childhood, they will have the same sense of certainty. In so many ways, I fall short. For the first several years of our marriage, before Greg joined the Catholic Church, I felt the burden of passing along the treasures of our faith to the boys on my own. How could I ever teach them everything they needed to know? Now that Greg is so active in their faith formation, that weight feels more manageable, but no less daunting.

I will confess that in many ways, I have fallen short of the "ideal mom" leading her domestic church. We don't have a home altar and I'm pretty horrible at any type of decorating, so our walls are not adorned with liturgically correct artwork depicting the seasons of the Church year. I'm a terrible cook, so meals cooked in honor of saints' feast days are few and far between. We don't sit together each night praying a family rosary as I've pictured the perfect Catholic family doing.

My shortcomings far exceed my virtues, which has been part of my motivation in writing this book. I am journeying along with you on the path to being a better, happier, healthier, and holier Catholic mom. Along the journey of putting together these resources, I have been educated and inspired by the countless families who have opened up their hearts and their homes and given me a peek inside their own domestic churches. Like you, I have some "Mom's homework" assignments of my own to complete.

And yet, I hope that when my boys are grown, raising families, and worshipping in parishes of their own, they will look back on their childhood and the place that our Catholic faith played in their lives and want to share all of it with their own children. Most of all, I hope that they will always carry with them the certainty that they are loved unconditionally by God and that they can turn to him anytime in prayer. In the meantime, our family will continue to do our very best to love and serve him and one another, day by precious day.

Living Out the Liturgical Calendar

The Church has given us many wonderful treasures to help us nurture ourselves spiritually, and they can be found every day of the year through the gift of the liturgical calendar. By living our lives according to this yearlong celebration of our faith, we can immerse our families in the mysteries of Christ's life, death, and resurrection and come into closer communion with the saints who serve as our role models in knowing and loving him.

When it comes to living out the intricacies of the liturgical calendar, one of my favorite resources is the book *The Catholic Home: Celebrations and Traditions for Holidays, Feast Days and Every Day* by my good friend Meredith Gould. In her work, Meredith offers practical yet faith-filled ways for home-based celebrations throughout the course of the year. Scott and Ellie Gulbransen, parents of three with one on the way, discovered Meredith's fabulous book and have worked to educate themselves in the faith and to share it with their children. "Now, we celebrate all sorts of liturgical events via family activities, meals, and traditions," shares Scott. "I think many Catholics my age grew up at a time when these things were not explained well, even in Catholic school. Constant discussion of and exposure to these liturgical events make Catholicism part of our family life every day."

Different men have different names, which they owe to their parents or to themselves, that is, to their own pursuits and achievements. But our great pursuit, the great name we wanted, was to be Christians, to be called Christians.

—St. Gregory Nazianzen

Many Catholic families have found that a devotion to praying the Liturgy of the Hours brings them into closer communion with the liturgical calendar. Maria Ruiz Scaperlanda and her husband followed a large poster format of the liturgical calendar with their now-grown children and gathered together every night as a family. "Night Prayer became family prayer," Maria says. "When they were older and with friends (many non-Catholic) over, everyone joined us in the living room for Night Prayer. It was a beautiful thing to share with questioning teens!"

A Time to Celebrate

Along with birthdays and anniversaries, many Catholic moms take time each year to celebrate the special feast days and solemnities that are significant to their family members. Beka suggests taking time every year to mark the dates of children's baptisms. "One tradition idea is on your child's baptism anniversary, you and your child (or your whole family) bring the baptismal candle to the church and light it at the Pascal Candle. Say a blessing for the child. Discuss baptism with the child at an age-appropriate level."

In the Thomas home, the family made a point of celebrating confirmed children every year on the feast day of their confirmation saints. In large families, saintly celebrations could be taking place quite frequently, so sit with your children and spouse and make plans for some special celebrations that may be most meaningful to your family.

Speaking of celebrations, I would be remiss in not mentioning that as Catholic moms, one of the most special ways we can nurture ourselves is to truly observe the Sabbath with our families. In a world of hectic schedules and overly planned events, taking a reprieve together every Sunday can stop some of the madness that seems to have overtaken our society. Make every effort to turn Sunday Mass into the highlight of your family's weekend, not just something you check off the list like another errand or chore to be done. Find a parish Mass with a schedule that meets your family's needs and make a point to attend together as a family as frequently as possible. After Mass, spend time with one another perhaps around a simple family meal or on a family outing together. When we take time on Sunday to cherish the Eucharist, we recall the glory of the Lord's resurrection and place it at the centerpiece of our family lives.

Signs and Symbols

Many Catholic moms do a beautiful job of underscoring the centrality of the faith in their family by keeping signs and symbols of their faith in their homes.

I was blessed to be raised in a grace-filled, faith-filled Catholic family of nine children. Now that I am a parent myself, I look back at my parents' accomplishment of raising all of us in the faith with awe.

How exactly did they do that? The good news is that I think the approach my parents used to raising us as Catholics was not a complicated one at all.

My mom and dad quite simply lived and breathed the Catholic faith themselves. They prayed always and in visible ways. They spoke of God's goodness and providence in everyday matters. They encouraged curiosity and fed our hunger for the truth by filling our home with good books, teachings of the Church, and open discussions of everything from bioethics to Catholic tradition. And, finally, they loved each of us with a fierce kind of love that can only come from God.

With my own children today, I enjoy observing the liturgical year, but even more importantly I aim to ensure that Catholicism is a natural, organic part of our everyday living. More than anything else, I want my children to grow up as I did—secure in the knowledge that they have been given a great gift . . . of Faith, Truth, and Love.

Danielle Bean, an author and mother of eight, is senior editor of Faith and Family magazine and web editor of FaithandFamilyLIVE.com.

In the Buckley home, as in a growing number of Catholic homes, decorations around the home reflect the events of the liturgical calendar more so than what's happening in the secular world. They have Advent decorations prior to Christmas and an "icon station" on the wall with rotating images of seasonal saints whose lives they study together as a family.

The Rutherford family has a family altar in their home, and mom Paula takes special care to create simple liturgically colored altar cloths for this special area.

Shelly has taken special efforts to build Catholic identity in her home. "We have a crucifix over every entrance and exit door as well as every bedroom door. I like to think of it as asking the Lord to bless and protect all who enter our home. The children each have a "baptism shelf" in their room to display the rosaries, bibles, statues, and other special religious gifts that have been given to them. We also have a picture of the Sacred and Immaculate Hearts opposite the front door and next to the door to the garage. In this way, Jesus and our Blessed Mother are the first thing that guests see as they enter our home, and the last thing that we see as we leave."

If you would like to decorate your home according to the prescribed colors of the liturgical season, obtain a simple liturgical calendar for your home that will give the prescribed color for each day of the year. The liturgical colors each have their own special symbolism, meaning, and application.

Liturgical Colors Chart

White: Seasons of Christmas, Easter; feasts of the Lord, Blessed Virgin Mary, the angels and saints who were not martyrs, the apostles; All Saints Day; Nuptial Masses; Masses for the dead, for baptized children who've died before the age of reason

Red: Feasts of the Lord's passion and of the martyrs, Good Friday, Palm Sunday, and Pentecost

Green: Ordinary Time

Violet: Seasons of Advent and Lent

Black: All Souls Day; Masses for the dead (Requiem Masses), except for baptized children who've died before the age of reason

Rose: *Gaudete* Sunday (Third Sunday of Advent) and *Laetare* Sunday (Fourth Sunday of Lent)

Gold or silver may be used on more solemn occasions in the dioceses of the United States.

In addition to using liturgical colors or sacred imagery in your home, you may wish to decorate your home in fun, creative ways that can involve your children in their faith. During the season of Advent, place an Advent wreath at the center of your dinner table and take time prior to family meals to pray together. Another special devotion many families enjoy during Advent is the "Jesse Tree." Your children can create handmade symbols from sacred scripture that are then placed on the simple tree. This retelling of biblical events from the moment of creation to the birth of Christ is a wonderful way to lead into the true Christmas season.

Likewise, explore and experience the season of Lent together by talking as a family about the devotions of fasting, prayer, and almsgiving. Prior to the start of Lent on Ash Wednesday, take time with your children and on your own to contemplate your devotions and to discuss how these practices and disciplines will ultimately lead you closer to Christ and help you celebrate the glory of the Resurrection. During the season of Lent, children over the age of fourteen and adults under the age of sixty are called to abstain from meat on Fridays and to fast by partaking of only one full meal and two small meals on Ash Wednesday and Good Friday. The Barker family and others have chosen to make abstaining from meat on Fridays a year-long practice. Catholic mom Lisa Barker also celebrates First Friday and First Saturday traditions with her husband and children, making time each month to receive the sacrament of reconciliation together as a family.

Catholic Culture

Catholic families have come up with so many creative and wonderful ways to celebrate and express their Catholicity. All over the country, and indeed the world, there are faith-filled Catholics using their God-given talents to live out their convictions and to share them with others. In my years of working with CatholicMom.com, I have met countless authors, artists, and musicians whose creative talents are constantly at work.

If you want to nurture yourself and build Catholic identity in your life that you can share with your children, begin to bring Catholic culture into your home. Read Catholic novels such as those by talented fiction authors Regina Doman and Katherine Valentine or grow in your faith by reading nonfiction classics by Amy Welborn, Danielle Bean, or Donna-Marie Cooper O'Boyle. Purchase the music of Sharmane, Susan Bailey, Sarah Bauer, Lynn Geyer, or other talented Catholic moms and play it loudly on your home stereo or iPod as you work or exercise. Hang the lovely artwork of Melissa Dayton or Celeste Zepponi on the walls of your home. Immerse yourself in the vibrant cultural bounty being created by these and other talented Catholic moms and share it proudly with others.

To ensure the future of our Church with increased vocations, it is also important that we expose our children to healthy, nurturing relationships with Catholic priests, brothers, nuns, and religious sisters. Consider "adopting" a priest or sister by praying for them actively and supporting them emotionally and physically. Many families are blessed to have strong relationships with priests and welcome them frequently into their homes. "Develop a personal relationship with your priest," Catholic mom Beka recommends. "Have him over for dinner often and invite him to family functions." Remember your parish priests and sisters at special times of the year with simple notes of thanksgiving or gifts, and continually keep them in your prayers.

Catholic mom Sharon and her husband Gene did a tremendous job of raising her three children, now adults, to love and cherish their Catholic faith. Her son Brandon, now a minister of liturgical music, says of his childhood: "We were all involved in church ministry at a young age and that definitely builds a Catholic identity. From being altar servers to singing in the children's choir to going to summer Bible camp, we learned to be a part of our parish by actively serving." Actively look for ways that you and your children can serve in ministry in your parish. This will help you to meet and form ties with other families in your community who share your values and perspective, and will help you and your children to feel more bonded to your faith community.

Catholic mom Sassy underscores the importance of always looking at life's developments from a Catholic perspective and sharing this vantage point with our children. In discussing important decisions, she recommends using the following prompting-type questions:

* Have you thought about the long-term impacts of this decision?

* Are you going to be placing yourself in the near occasion of sin if you do this?

* How is this going to affect our family as a whole?

> *All members of the family, each according to his or her own gift, have the grace and responsibility of building, day by day, the communion of persons, making the family "a school of deeper humanity": this happens where there is care and love for the little ones, the sick, the aged; where there is mutual service every day; when there is a sharing of goods, of joys and of sorrows.*
>
> —Pope John Paul II

✳ Will this interfere with your commitments to God?

✳ Have you prayed about this, seeking discernment?

Ultimately, the ways in which you live out your Catholic faith in your home will be your decision and will reflect the unique nature of your family. My home and our devotional practices may vary greatly from yours. In our home, one of my greatest hopes is that my children will always turn to the framework of their Catholic faith for a moral perspective when times of choice arise. I hope Greg and I will provide an environment that enables Eric and Adam to cherish and love their Catholic faith, and in turn to share it with others. I hope that they will always rest assured in the knowledge that they are loved unconditionally by God, that they can turn to him at any moment of sorrow or joy in their lives. By passing along this certainty, the most precious gift I received from my parents, to my children, I will have fulfilled the greatest responsibility of my vocation as a Catholic mom.

Mom's Homework

✓ Simplify and celebrate Sunday with your family. Clear your calendar, attend Mass together, and partake of a family meal or enjoy a family outing together.

✓ Obtain a simple liturgical calendar for your home.

✓ Note and celebrate the important feast days that are of significance to your family.

✓ Decorate your home with a few simple Catholic symbols such as a crucifix, sacred artwork, or a home altar.

✓ Spend time in conversation with your family, discussing life's events from a uniquely Catholic perspective.

Web Resources

United States Conference of Catholic Bishops: www.usccb.org
Provides information, devotions, and practices for living out the liturgical seasons within your home

Catholic Culture: www.catholicculture.org
Family activities, reference articles, recipes, and more for every day of the liturgical year

The Catholic Company: http://catholicmom.catholiccompany.com
Supplies, decorations, and gifts for your Catholic home

Acknowledgments

First and foremost, I give thanks and praise to God, our heavenly Father, who has blessed me and our entire family so abundantly and to Mary, our Blessed Mother, who has walked with me along every step of my mothering journey, guiding and supporting me.

I owe a tremendous debt of gratitude to the many contributors who have made this book such a helpful resource. When I set out to write it, I created a wish list—a dream team of talented, faith-filled role models whose work and character I admired. I am so blessed that each and every one of you said "Yes" to my plea to become a part of this project. Your friendship and loving support throughout the creative process and beyond continues to buoy and uplift me.

I have repeatedly stated that my friends largely wrote this book, with me simply acting as an intermediary. To the members of my online community of friends at Facebook, Twitter, Faith and Family Live, SQPN, and the Catholic Mom Community, thank you for sharing your hearts, your stories, and your encouragement.

To my colleagues at Faith and Family Live and the Star Quest Production Network, I continue to be amazed by the depth and profundity of your talent and your commitment to spreading our faith in new and creative ways.

I am forever indebted to our CatholicMom.com contributors, who have shared their words and talents over the years to create an environment that celebrates the true joy of being a Catholic mom. Words can never express the gift each of you has given, not only to me, but especially to families around the world.

To the professionals at Ave Maria Press, especially Tom Grady, Eileen Ponder, and Amanda Williams, thank you for your confidence in me and your limitless guidance throughout this process. I am honored to be a part of your team.

A special hug goes out to the many friends who grace my little world, my Mahj buddies, the girls from knitting, the Sweathogs, our St. Anthony's family, Martha, and Mara.

To the entire Hendey family, I am blessed to have each of you in my life.

To my first and lifelong friends, my siblings and their spouses and my precious nephews, here's to a lifetime of love and family!

To Daddy, you wrote this book in my heart long before I put it down on paper. To the world's best Catholic mom and nana, you *are* the wind beneath my wings.

To Eric and Adam, thank you for putting up with a geeky mom who spends way too much time on the computer. You are my life's greatest blessings and my best teachers. You make our world a better place through your constant sharing of your gifts and talents. As I watch you grow into young men, my heart shines with love and happiness.

To my best friend in the world, Greg, every day with you is a treasure. Thank you for putting up with my messes, for years of fun and adventure, for being the perfect partner in parenting, for your quiet example of faith and devotion, and for always encouraging me to follow my dreams.

LISA M. HENDEY is the creator of
www.CatholicMom.com and the host
of the weekly *Catholic Moments* podcast
and the *Catholic Mom* television show.
Hendey writes regularly for *Faith &
Family*, and her articles have appeared
in *National Catholic Register* and *Our
Sunday Visitor*. She also gives work-
shops on faith, family, and Catholic
new media topics. Hendey lives in the
Fresno, California, area with her husband of twenty-three years and their
two teenage sons.

Founded in 1865, Ave Maria Press,
a ministry of the Congregation of
Holy Cross, is a Catholic publishing
company that serves the spiritual and
formative needs of the Church and its
schools, institutions, and ministers;
Christian individuals and families; and
others seeking spiritual nourishment.

For a complete listing of titles from

Ave Maria Press

Sorin Books

Forest of Peace

Christian Classics

visit www.avemariapress.com

ave maria press / Notre Dame, IN 46556
A Ministry of the Indiana Province of Holy Cross